ESSAYS IN MODERN ECONOMIC DEVELOPMENT

Uniform with this volume:

Essays in Economic Method: Selected Papers read to Section F of the British Association for the Advancement of Science, 1860–1913. Edited by R. L. Smyth with an Introduction by T. W. Hutchison. *Duckworth*, 1962.

Essays in the Economics of Socialism and Capitalism: Selected Papers read to Section F of the British Association for the Advancement of Science, 1886–1932. Edited by R. L. Smyth with an Introduction by T. Wilson. *Duckworth*, 1964.

Essays in Modern Economic Development

Selected Papers read to Section F of the British Association for the Advancement of Science, 1947–1967

EDITED BY

R. L. SMYTH

WITH AN INTRODUCTION BY

G. L. S. SHACKLE

GERALD DUCKWORTH & CO. LTD.
3 HENRIETTA STREET, LONDON, W.C.2

FIRST PUBLISHED 1969

SBN 7156 0418 x

PRINTED IN GREAT BRITAIN BY
COX & WYMAN LTD., LONDON, FAKENHAM AND READING

CONTENTS

PREFACE

THIS is the third collection of papers presented to the Economics Section (Section F) of the British Association for the Advancement of Science. Volume I contained the Presidential Address to the Section given by Nassau W. Senior in 1860, this volume contains the Presidential Address given 100 years later in 1960 by Professor R. S. Sayers.

The papers in Volume I, *Essays in Economic Method* (1962) were selected from the period 1860–1913, Volume II, *Essays in the Economics of Socialism and Capitalism* (1964) from the period 1886–1939. The theme of the first volume was Scope and Method and the themes of the second were Socialism, Competition and Monopoly, Instability and Unemployment. Fortunately most of the authors of the essays in this volume, which relates to the period 1947–67, are still hard at work; its theme is, therefore, contemporary economics. The problems of growth and planning were not absent from the first two volumes, however they dominate this one to a much greater extent.

The audience at the Section meetings is a mixture of professional economists, scientists from other Sections and members of the general public who expect to understand a large part of what is going on. Ideally non-economists expect the speakers to address themselves to the economists in the audience in English and not in mathematics and to translate jargon into everyday language as they go along. The speakers have a difficult task; they cannot afford to be as boring or obscure as they could be when addressing only members of their own profession, nor can they insult their colleagues by talking-down to non-social scientists and housewives; over-simplification and undue popularization are not encouraged. It is the peculiar circumstances of the British Association meetings and the high calibre of the speakers which have sustained the output of excellent papers over a long period of time. Of course, some Section

F papers have been insipid and dull or unduly popular and others were suitable only for an audience composed exclusively of statisticians and economists; however, many speakers, fortunately, met the challenge and communicated understanding to interested and stimulated audiences. One highly successful paper deserves particular mention. In 1952, in Belfast, Professor H. O. Meredith presented his "last formal utterance on economics". As one of his students I can record that we rarely understood what his lectures were about: how different was his British Association address. It is reproduced in this volume.

The essays are presented under three main headings: Economics, Economic Policy and Economic Growth. The two surveys of developments in economic thought and method by Professors Alexander Gray and H. O. Meredith are good examples of the unique and stimulating testaments which appear when distinguished economists, near the end of their professional careers, are invited to explain how they experienced and reacted to changes in their subject. Their essays continue the tradition established by Sidgwick, Bastable, Bonar, Ashley and Wicksteed which were included in Volume I, *Essays in Economic Method*. The section on Economics also contains a demonstration of the scientific approach in economics by R. G. Lipsey, J. K. Galbraith's highly entertaining account of some of the problems involved in writing for and attempting to read economic journals, an introduction by B. R. Williams to the rapidly expanding and important branch of contemporary economics which is cost-benefit studies and, finally, Professor Shackle's discussion of how businessmen make decisions, a matter which is of crucial importance for economic theory and, of course, applied economics.

The second section is devoted to essays on the vexed problem of economic policy in post-1945 Britain. It contains a number of essays which already must be regarded as classics: essays which deserve to be read again and again. Hubert Henderson's "The Price System" must surely be the best possible introduction to the principles which contribute towards an understanding of Government intervention and planning. It continues a discussion initiated by Henry Sidgwick at Section F meetings in 1886, "Economic Socialism" and continued by H. F. Foxwell in 1888, "The Growth of Monopoly, and its Bearing on the Functions of the State" and Alfred Marshall in 1890, "Some Aspects of Competition". The papers by Sidgwick, Foxwell and Marshall were included in the second volume of Section F papers, *Essays in the Economics of Socialism and Capitalism*. The paper by Professor Austin Robinson is an excellent account of the changing structure of the British economy. Events since the paper was presented in 1954 would appear to strengthen his policy recommendation that the British economy should be rendered less dependent on imports. Professor J. R. Hicks in his paper ably defends the proposition that economic forces are more dominant in wage determination than social forces, and Professor R. S. Sayers provides an essential appraisal of how monetary policy in Britain has changed over a period of 150 years. The problems raised by the earlier papers are further discussed and appraised by Professors Victor Morgan and A. R. Prest in their papers on Inflation and Budgetary Policy. Finally in the Section on Economic Policy there is the Lister Lecture by Professor R. J. Ball on short-term economic forecasting which demonstrates how and why computers are being increasingly used to provide a better understanding of how the economy operates. The third section is devoted to two papers by Mr. C. F. Carter and Professor Tom Wilson on the causes and consequences of economic growth. Although the papers have been presented in three groups the reader will find that almost all of them are concerned with the three interrelated topics of economic method, economic policy and problems of economic growth.

The essays have been selected to provide the reader with a reasonably comprehensive and stimulating account of economic thought being applied to contemporary problems by a group of highly gifted economists. Appendix B is a selected bibliography of published papers that were presented to Section F of the British Association for the Advancement of Science for the period 1947–67. It may be seen that it has not been possible to include many excellent papers by leading economists. This book is a tribute to Section F for continuing to sustain a high standard of economic debate at the annual meetings of the British Association.

It has been an honour and a pleasure to edit three volumes of addresses on behalf of Section F. No economist as obscure as myself could reasonably hope to have his name associated with those of Senior, Jevons, Sidgwick, Bowley and Wicksteed; then G. B. Shaw, Sidney Webb, Foxwell, Marshall, Schumpeter, Beveridge and Keynes and now, Henderson, Hicks, Galbraith and Sayers to mention only a few! I have been particularly fortunate in that Professor T. W. Hutchison followed by Professor Tom Wilson and now Professor G. L. S. Shackle provided thoughtful and illuminating introductions.

A useful by-product of producing this volume is the highly original and controversial introduction contributed by Professor Shackle. He refers to the case for "removing Economics from its status as a barely tolerated Cinderella of the Sciences". It would seem, however, that physical scientists have an unfortunate weakness for writing about economics without the benefit of a proper understanding of the difficulties of the subject. It is, therefore, to be hoped that many of them will read some of these essays and come to appreciate that competent economists are so much better at doing economics. The reader will note, however, that Professor Shackle offers an alternative and more elegant solution to the problem.

The papers by H. D. Henderson, Alexander Gray, E. A. G. Robinson, J. R. Hicks, R. S. Sayers, T. Wilson, B. R. Williams, E. Victor Morgan, G. L. S. Shackle and A. R. Prest, have been reprinted from the *Economic Journal* by kind permission of the Royal Economic Society. All other papers have been reprinted from the *Advancement of Science*. All the papers have been reproduced in full. The few explanatory footnotes which have been added are contained in square brackets. The authors have been most generous in granting permission to reprint their papers. Permission to reprint the Presidential Address by the late Sir Alexander Gray was granted by Mr. John Gray. Permission to reprint the paper by the late Professor H. O. Meredith was granted by his literary executive Mrs. Muriel Forth and by Mrs. Margaret A. Meredith.

I wish to acknowledge that the paper by the late Sir Hubert Henderson was included in *The Inter-War Years and Other Papers; a Selection from the Writings of Hubert Douglas Henderson*, H. Clay (ed.), 1955 and the paper by Sir John Hicks was included in his *Essays in World Economics*, 1959, both books were published by the Clarendon Press, Oxford. J. K. Galbraith's lecture on "The Language of Economics" is included by permission of Granada Television and was originally delivered in Guildhall, London, in October, 1962, as one of the annual Granada Guildhall Lectures. I am grateful to Macmillan & Co. for permission to reprint "The Price of

Growth" by T. Wilson which was included in *Planning and Growth* and published in 1964. "Economics in Unwonted Places" by B. R. Williams is reprinted here by permission of Chapman and Hall, the paper was included in *Technology, Investment and Growth* published in 1967. Permission to reprint "Policy, Poetry and Success" by Professor G. L. S. Shackle and "Economic Model Building for Control" by Professor R. J. Ball was granted by the Liverpool University Press, the essays will be included in *On the Nature of Business Success*, G. L. S. Shackle (ed.) to be published in October, 1968. Permission to include "Sense and Nonsense in Budgetary Policy" by Professor A. R. Prest was granted by Manchester University Press, the essay was included in *Public Sector Economics* which was published in July, 1968.

A Section F Research Committee consisting of Professor G. L. S. Shackle (Chairman), Mr. R. Shaw (Recorder, Section F) and Mr. R. L. Smyth (Secretary) was appointed by the British Association to prepare this volume for publication. The Committee having completed its pleasant task is most grateful to the economists who, over the years, have acted as President and/or read papers to the Section.

R. L. SMYTH

The University of Keele, September, 1968

INTRODUCTION

CENTRE AND CIRCUMFERENCE IN SCIENCE

A *bit of information* nowadays means technically the answer to a Yes or No question. A collection or a system of such answers, somehow circumscribed, can thus give us the notion of a quantity of information. The concept of a quantity of knowledge seems, by comparison, remote and elusive in the extreme. If the scheme of things entire is a unity, if there is in some sense a single secret or principle of Nature, like the randomness of the Democritean atoms flying in all directions, that secret or principle might be the whole of knowledge. Its logical consequences, once it was grasped, might embrace all that is and all that can be. Or that very principle might imply the essential indeterminateness of things. Even a middle state is conceivable, where the classes of events or evolutions were prescribed but their detailed forms arose *ex nihilo*, unpredictable even in principle. If ultimate indeterminacy were the truth, knowledge would be ever-extending in its available quantity, it would have as its scope an ever-growing description of the past. Whatever may be the case, those who seek knowledge by investigation seem to fall into two kinds. There are those who hope to be approaching the ultimate basis of things, and those who are compiling a *catalogue raisonné*, an associative taxonomy or collection of cases. Those of us who work in the so-called sciences of man surely fall properly into the second kind. We unavoidably have our backs turned to those endeavours of more basic sciences to see into the heart of things. Those endeavours may themselves be foredoomed to failure. J. B. S. Haldane is reported to have said that "the universe is not only stranger than you imagine, it is stranger than you *can* imagine". But in the arts and the social sciences, we are not even looking for the way to the heart of things. We are engaged on a vast task of description. What man does may be evidence of what he is, but it is immeasurably too indirect and remote from the sources of his nature to allow us to discover those sources from a knowledge, however detailed, of how he has behaved. Instead we seek a practical theory of his affairs by trying to discern repetitive patterns or stereotypes of his conduct and his institutions. Leaving the centre to others, we are concerned with the *circumferential.* It appears to be good sense, accordingly, for us to maintain an awareness of the limitations of a study confined to the outer rings of the human phenomenon. Humility need not be advocated on ethical or aesthetic grounds alone, it has its strong recommendation as a sound rule of practice.

Amongst economists there have been at times those who saw detailed description of events, institutions and organizations as their only justifiable and proper activity. "Theory" and "analysis" were for them an attempt to put words into the mouth of fact rather than let it speak for itself. Yet even description rests upon classification, classes are concepts, and concepts are thought-entities invented by human beings. There can be no escape from theory. What we, as economists, political theorists, sociologists, psychologists, even anthropologists, have to recognize is that our theories point in a different direction from those of the natural scientists. The biochemist, the geneticist, the molecular biologist, wishes to approach the sources of Nature. We wish to observe, classify and assemble into patterns the most outward, complex and subtle manifestations of Nature, as seen in the conduct and cultural movements of men. Our task is concerned, necessarily and honourably, with the extremities and the fruits of that deeply rooted tree, the natural history of humanity.

If this view is in any way acceptable, it has some consequences for the shaping of economic study. Many an article of faith of the natural scientist must go overboard. Precision, rigour and even consistency will have to make drastic concessions. We should have to recognize that what we can understand are *partial* systems only, systems that can be compared to sailing-boats enveloped in an unpredictable environment of air and ocean. How the boat will behave in given circumstances can be admirably known, it is the circumstances that cannot be known in advance. Economic knowledge is *ad hoc*: and what is *hoc* going to be? We cannot tell, and we must not overlook this limit to our competence, or we shall find that we have given advice concerning the wrong *hoc*. This predicament, I am suggesting, is the consequence of our knowledge being essentially of what lies farthest from the heart of things, the circumferential. I need hardly explain that I do not use this term in any pejorative sense. It simply names an inescapable fact.

The essential difficulty of the economist can perhaps be expressed in another way. As a means of insight into his subject-matter he has invented a number of abstract systems or models. Such a model has elements each corresponding to some aspect or component part of the real scene, and relations between these elements which are supposed to reproduce, in main character, those of reality. Some of these models represent a small part, albeit a typical part, of the entire economic aspect of society. They are called "the firm", "the industry", "the consumer", "an activity", "a market". Others seek to embrace the whole of economic society. They are called "the general equilibrium", "the theory of output as a whole", "a model of multi-sectoral growth", "development economics". Each of the small systems may have persuasive claims to be a valid and illuminating analogue of a small part of the whole reality. It even enables us to make conditional predictions, predictions which start, in principle, with the word "If". But the stipulated condition turns out to be "If the rest of the economy is unchanging" or "If the rest of the economy behaves in a known way", and such a condition may be incapable of fulfilment. Moreover we are tempted to try to put all the small systems together, in their multitudes of incarnations, to compose a comprehensive system. But this composition will not work. The small systems are only valid each on its own. The mortar is lacking to bind the bricks into a building. When we turn to the models which embrace the whole economy, they require different assumptions, and work on different lines from the small systems. And these large systems themselves are again only predictive in the conditional sense. They require stipulations about the other aspects of society, the political aspects, the state and progress of technology, the degree of exposure to suggestion and to news of other parts of a still larger whole. The large economic models, pre-eminently, are superficial. The fatal temptation for the economist is to forget this superficiality, to give instructions for the handling of the sails in oblivion of the tide.

Physics no longer claims complete determinacy down to its

smallest entities. But it can still give precision to its concepts. Economics is debarred from such precision by the nature of its subject-matter. "The general level of prices" is the answer to a calculation, and the formula of this calculation can be devised by each man for himself. "Wealth" is the result of adding together what are, in the last analysis, subjective or personal valuations and judgements of an immense and unlimited diversity of things, each depending for its value on the presence or absence of other items of the collection. "Capital" seems in many discussions to name a scalar quantity, yet it is also a collection of things as various as hand-tools, ships, distilleries, gas pipelines, telephone systems, forests, flocks and herds. Value itself, as a concept with a public meaning subject to arithmetical manipulation, depends on the existence and efficient working of a human institution, the market. It is as though the law of gravity depended on orderly human conduct. Economics is, in some real sense, far removed in the nature of its subject-matter and the inescapable conditions of its pursuit of understanding, from that constancy, consistency, universality and detachment from human desires and interests, which are the characteristic marks and essential foundation of natural science. It is time, perhaps, that some more explicit recognition was given to this situation.

Our science, if we feel obliged to call it such, is different from the fundamental sciences. Like them, it has two methods, the stereotypic and the axiomatic. By a stereotypic method I mean a search for universally repetitive and fixed configurations of objects, aspects, measurements or classes of measurements, assembling and associatting such elements either independently of time or in constant temporal patterns. Such a stereotype can encompass much or little of the field of observation, can be simple or complex, and it is, of course, a construct in the observer's mind, imaginatively discerned and invented by him. But once established, it claims predictive, explanatory and technological power. When some of the elements of the pattern are perceived, we infer that the rest are also present, we predict that they will be found; or when these others are found, we regard them as accounting for those first observed. The flash of lightning predicts the thunder, the jet plane seen flying overhead accounts for the sonic boom. If we can bring into being some elements of the pattern, we may be able to count on the others also being achieved: the match-head under friction will produce a flame.

This is technology, however simple. The axiomatic method consists in adopting a set of propositions as a relevantly complete hypothetical description of some system or some portion of reality, and proceeding by logical inference or mathematics to see what other expressions or reflections of its character must also be true. In the fundamental sciences, the possibility of isolating parts of reality so as to form self-contained systems, and the supposed completeness, self-sufficiency, and internal consistency of the natural systems thus detached, is assumed to guarantee that the two methods will eventually, after patient trial and reformulation, inter-lock in perfect mutual complementation, the axioms suggested by the stereotypes being so designed as to bind these stereotypes into a logical ordering which can be consulted for further suggestions as to what may be looked for. But in the sciences of human conduct and affairs, this detached completeness is utterly lacking. The economic man is *not* a man, he is not a puzzled pilgrim of life, a lover and hater, a voter, a gambler, an emulator, a seeker of more and more knowledge and more and more experience, he is not a snob or a bully or a busybody nor a sensitive soul. Thus the world of the economic man cannot possibly, conceivably, model the world of fully-endowed human beings. There is no reason whatever to expect that the axiom-system based on self-interest, reason, and perfect knowledge will be capable of ordering the stereotypes of real conduct. Our field of study is neither self-contained in reality nor capable of being isolated in experiment. The great, simple and inclusive systems of economic theory can give us insight. It is most questionable how far they ought to be trusted for foresight.

The impression left by the papers collected in this volume, taken as a whole, is of their persuasive practical wisdom and pragmatic nature, and their wide departure from the character of pure science. They appeal to common experience of life, to the business sense which all viable income-earners must in some degree possess, even to instinctive knowledge. They offer no proofs, they are elliptical and informal, they are readable, engaging and highly educative. What, then, is Section F doing in the British Association?

It would be open to us to reduce our isolation by urging the Association to provide a Section for political theorists. It would, I think, be surprised and disturbed by such a request. Philosophy has no section, nor linguistics. Yet linguistics might claim far more uniformity and self-sufficiency of subject-matter than our own. The Association might be asked to re-name its purpose as the Advancement of Knowledge. Or more practically and acceptably, it might divide itself into a Division of Fundamental (Pure, Exact) Sciences and a Division of Policy Sciences: Economics, Sociology and perhaps Geography and even Engineering. At least there is some case for removing Economics from its status as a barely tolerated Cinderella of the Sciences. Let it recognize itself for what it is: a Policy Discipline of elusive and complex texture, not amenable in any straightforward way to the methods of pure science, not given to exact proof nor highly trustworthy predictions, but yet a discipline and a search for order, coherence and insight. And above all, let it resume its full and explanatory name of Political Economy.

G. L. S. Shackle

Liverpool, August, 1968

PART ONE

ECONOMICS

I

ECONOMICS: YESTERDAY AND TOMORROW

ALEXANDER GRAY

Newcastle upon Tyne, September, 1949

THE natural hesitation which I feel in addressing you as President of this section is perhaps slightly alleviated by the reflection that I am now (I believe) entitled to speak to you—if I may lapse into French—as the doyen among the Professors of Economics in these islands. It is an honourable position which I owe solely to the lapse of time—a process which ultimately brings distinction to the meanest centenarian, as a reward for the somewhat negative virtue of not having dropped out by the way. It is rather like Interest (or at least what Interest used to be before 1935), the Reward of Waiting, attainable even by the mentally deficient, who may doubtless qualify by virtue of "long lacking". It is not far short of fifty years since I was first introduced to the study of Economics on a mixed diet of the small Marshall and John Stuart Mill; I have now been professing since 1921. In this section we are not all "academics" (a horrid word); but perhaps we Academics give a flavour to the proceedings. In the circumstances I think it may not be inappropriate if today I speak to you as a Victorian Professor on his last legs. You may consider that in the string of platitudes which I shall doubtless address to you, I am confusedly making a death-bed confession of error; or (if you are more charitable) you may regard me as doing my best to understand sympathetically how, in the very different climate in which he will carry on his activities, my more enlightened successor may regard me.

We could doubtless learn a great deal of the continually changing view of what Economics is supposed to be, and what purpose its study is supposed to serve, by the simple device of reading in chronological order the definitions of Economics given by its leading exponents. But this is a task which today I may not perform on your behalf. A random stab here and there must suffice. Adam Smith is entirely explicit in one passage frequently quoted in better days: "Political Economy, *considered as a branch of the science of a statesman or legislator*, proposes two distinct objects." These objects do not concern us at present; but you will remember that they were, first, to provide a plentiful subsistence for the people, or, as he at once added (suddenly remembering how omnipresent is the danger of misrepresentation), "to enable them to provide such a subsistence for themselves"; and, secondly, to provide a sufficient revenue for the State. But the essential point to note is that for Adam Smith, Political Economy was a branch of the science of a statesman; in other words, it was inextricably intertwined with politics and government, concerned with getting things done. I do not think that the idea of there being such a thing as an "economic law" ever penetrated the crass intelligence of Adam Smith; I doubt whether the word "Law" in this sense occurs anywhere in *The Wealth of Nations*; but when you come to Ricardo, it is hardly too much to say that the primary function of the Economist is to detect and lay bare "Economic Law". Indeed, the characteristic feature of the early part of the nineteenth century was the conscious effort to transform Economics into a wholly independent scientific discipline, establishing laws or generalizations, while remaining perpetually and eternally neutral in a world of conflict. You will find a sufficiently beautiful expression of this simple view in Senior, who chides previous writers for their incorrigible tendency to wander into what he calls the far more interesting, but far less definite, fields by which the comparatively narrow path of Political Economy is surrounded. It is an arresting simile. The economist is a dumb ox, condemned to follow a narrow path which leads through attractively flowery, but not very definite, meadows; but woe to him if he looks over the hedges. "His conclusions, whatever be their generality and their truth"—it is Senior who is speaking—"do not authorize him in adding a single syllable of advice." Much later in the century you will find the same point of view expressed by Cairnes, with comparisons which I find not too happy: Political Economy (he said) stands "neutral between competing social schemes; neutral, as the science of Mechanics stands neutral between competing plans of railway construction . . .; neutral, as Chemistry"—and this is what sticks in my throat—"stands neutral between competing plans of sanitary improvement".

Indeed, in an era of *laissez-faire*, the divorce between economics and politics is perhaps inevitable. Let us for the moment accept the familiar travesty of *laissez-faire*, and assume that it postulates that the ideal State should confine itself to doing nothing, and doing it rather well; but if that is even an approximation to the implications of *laissez-faire*, then it is difficult to see how Economics, however defined, can be subservient to Politics. For though there may be a certain Art in doing nothing, it may be questioned whether there is a corresponding Science.

Doubtless it was always realized that Economics had its neighbours, that there were frontiers and borderlands; and those of us who were properly brought up and learned our "Scope and Method" from Dr. Neville Keynes, at one time in our lives knew all about the ties between Economics and the neighbouring tracts of country occupied by Political Science, Ethics, Psychology, Jurisprudence and many more. Doubtless also the most resolutely recluse economist perpetually violated his own professed principles; for it is as difficult to prevent an economist from giving advice as it is to prevent the notional proverbial woman from talking. Yet, broadly, despite obvious lapses, it is true that the nineteenth century was in the main a period of specialization, when the economist tried to keep himself to himself, and to pursue the peculiar problems of his own specialism.

It is almost a commonplace today that the era of specialization has for the time being ended; that the old frontiers have been largely obliterated, and that in the next generation the economist will have to be much more than an economist. Perhaps his primary task will be to view his Economics in relation to all the other so-called social sciences, and thereby to effect a new synthesis. Let us consider for a moment, very briefly, some of these increasingly non-existent boundaries. The first and most complete disappearance of a frontier is, I think, that between Economics and Politics. For myself, I regard this as having always been a very blurred and indeterminate dividing line; but that is merely a personal point of view. Today it is possible to say more emphatically than at any time since the dominance of mercantilist ways of thinking, that practically every economic problem has become a political problem, and that most, if not all, political questions have their economic penumbra. The more or less complete fusion of economics and politics can be explained on various grounds, even if the various explanations very largely represent different aspects of the same fundamental tendency. You may say that it is due to the coming of the Welfare State; you may say that it is due to the eclipse of *laissez-faire*. In an age which has, apparently, unbounded faith in the competence of the State to do everything and to provide for everything, the decision in economic problems tends to pass to the Government, and economic discussion finds its last asylum in the House of Commons. As an influence tending to the fusion of Economics and Politics, you may attribute something to the delayed impact of Marx, for whom Economics was a first stepping-stone to revolution, which is political, if anything is. The extent to which Economics and Politics have today become intertwined is seen in the fact that what is probably the most fundamental, as it is the most ubiquitous, problem of these times is precisely that of determining the limits of the economic activity of the State—what we expect the State to be, and what we expect it to do in economic matters.

The second frontier which has obviously been trampled upon—or perhaps should be trampled upon even more than it is—is that between Economics and Psychology. We ought never to forget that we are always dealing with human beings, though perhaps we sometimes tend to do so when we wrap ourselves in a cloud of differential equations. But if we are dealing with humanity, then we ought to know everything that there is to be known about the curious behaviour of this most curious human beast. We should remember that we are never far removed from a suffering human heart. Here possibly, as I sometimes think in moments of intellectual pessimism, will for ever be the weak point in Economics, and indeed in all the social sciences. For the heart of man is unsearchable, and his behaviour can never be foretold, moved as he not infrequently is, and moved surprisingly, by motives of which he is himself unconscious. Strictly speaking there is no such thing as Labour, glorified with a capital "L", apart from individual labourers who all toil and sweat at different jobs, and display an infinite variety of temperament, disposition, endowment and circumstance. There is also no such thing as Capital, apart from the individual owners and controllers of the means of production; and these again, I need hardly tell you, are a motley crowd.

The older generation suffered much ridicule—undeserved, as I think—because of what was supposed to be the undue simplification of their underlying psychology. But indeed there is something to be said for them. They realized that if they were to reason about Man, they must first define him; just as, before reasoning about triangles, you must know what a triangle is. And as a result there emerged, or was supposed to emerge, that ridiculous, bloodless scarecrow, known as the "Economic Man"—the man whose every action was determined by a careful balancing of economic considerations. Yet, if he existed anywhere, I doubt not that he was a most exemplary citizen, observing the laws both of God and of Man. He remembered the Sabbath day to keep it holy, being advised by his medical attendant that one day's rest in seven would increase his productivity in the remaining six. He honoured his father and his mother, knowing well how wide is still the testamentary discretion which the law allows to parents. Of the grosser offences he was guiltless, being well aware that a period of incarceration would effectively debar him from the profitable service of his fellows. If he had any weakness, it was doubtless a tendency to covetousness, but such slight shortcoming as he may have been guilty of in this direction was, he felt, no more than was inevitable, if he were to comply with the Pauline injunction to covet earnestly the best gifts. Such, supposedly, was the Economic Man, and though he had his virtues, "Who would not laugh if such a man there be?" Nevertheless, looked at more closely, what the older economists were trying to do was, in their own words and for their own purposes, to "make abstraction" of those qualities which did not affect Man in his acquisition or consumption of wealth. Political Economy was concerned, such was Mill's view, with Man solely as a being who desires to possess wealth, and who can make efforts to that end. Other qualities of the human beast must be ignored, except in so far as they are "perpetually antagonizing principles" to the desire for wealth. And of such perpetually antagonizing principles, there are two. In a very fine phrase, they are "aversion to labour, and the desire of the present enjoyment of costly indulgences". Man, in short, is a lazy brute, and he wants to have a good time *now*; and if we are honest with ourselves, in our private confessionals, we will acknowledge, each speaking for himself, that it is at least a part of the truth, even if we should prove incapable of clothing the confession in the impeccable language of John Stuart Mill. But it was never meant to be a complete picture: still less did that saint of Rationalism intend it to be a picture of the ideal man. Mill, in effect, said: "I cannot tell you what Man is; but this, alas, is a bit of him." And also implicitly the Economic Man was a warning regarding the limitations of the validity of economic conclusions. In a sense Mill also said: "I am talking of one side of Man; but he has other sides, and therefore you had better be on your guard." In these days when we do so much to encourage research, I should like some modern John Bunyan to supplement *The Life and Death of Mr. Badman* by a companion volume on *The Life and Death of the Economic Man.* The research student who is conspicuously distinguished by aversion to labour will find a great deal of the necessary biographical detail in Dr. Hennipman's imposing volume. For if the Economic Man is not dead, at least we seem to have buried him. Yet incomplete and defective as this ogre may have been as an explanation of human action, he was at least an acknowledgement that you do need a psychological foundation. I am not sure that we are further on today. If anyone were to ask me what are the psychological assumptions of modern economics, I should be constrained to give a dusty answer. Perhaps the ghost of the Economic Man, that perturbed spirit, still stalks our ramparts. But of one thing I am certain: a structure of economic theory that is not based on sound psychology is a house without foundation. And therefore your economist must be a psychologist—of a sort.

I must deal more briefly with some of the other disappearing frontiers. In my youth there was much talk of the relation of Economics to Jurisprudence. Apart from all that was then said, about it and about, I suggest that in the new world there are overwhelmingly stronger reasons why ever economist must become something of a lawyer. In the Welfare State, the law provides the machinery for the economic activity of the State; the machinery rests on and is modified by the law. Today the economist must read and, so far as that is practicable, understand a considerable section of the enactments that are being incessantly disgorged from Westminster—even if Members of Parliament themselves are exempted from this exhausting task. It used to be said that the best source-book for a study of mercantilism could be compiled from the Preambles of Acts of Parliament, in days when Acts of Parliament and their preambles were still models of reasoning and of English style. Today one of the chief sources for the economic tendencies of our times is in the Statute Book itself; and an economist must be at least of the competence of a hedge-lawyer to find his way about.

Need I say anything about Ethics, our nearest and our oldest neighbour? You will recall Marshall's saying that Economics is the handmaid of Ethics. Admittedly, handmaidens today are more of a notional race of beings than they were in Marshall's life-time; but the idea is clear and its justification incontestable. Let us admit, even in this Section, that Economics can never be an end in itself; by its very nature and from its birth it is doomed to be a subordinate, a younger sister, a handmaid to someone. At its best Economics is designed to disclose a means to the attainment of some end, to the realization of some way of life, some vision or some ideal. It is for Ethics (we hope) to tell us what the good life is, what justice and equity are, what sort of an existence we ought to try to provide for ourselves and others—if it comes to that, how we ought to behave to each other, a question which not infrequently has curious economic infusions. But those who are concerned with the means can hardly be denied the privilege of having some views on the end. It is, indeed, only in so far as we take some part in the ethical debate that our Economics can acquire a meaning, an inspiration and a driving force. If you ask me to fix a just wage, you must allow me to have some ideas about ' justice". And I think that we economists should perpetually bear in mind that the framework of *The Wealth of Nations*—which we may conveniently take as the source of modern economics—was first presented to raw Scottish undergraduates as part of a course on Moral Philosophy. We economists were conceived in the study of a Professor of Moral Philosophy, and cradled in a Moral Philosophy classroom. Whether you believe in the laws of inheritance or in the potency of early environment, you can hardly deny that it is "natural" for an economist to be a moralist.

And having gone so far—Heaven help me!—may I go still further and suggest that the economist may have to become something of a theologian? Or if for any reason you shy at some of the ordinary implications of the word "theology", let us say that the economist should aspire to a reasoned *Weltanschauung*—for there is always much wisdom in taking refuge in a foreign language, imperfectly understood. Doubtless, it is at times difficult to make sense of this world; yet I suppose it is what we are all trying to do. And unless we are prepared to regard ourselves merely as a company of irresponsible idiots dancing in the void, we must frame for ourselves, if only as a working hypothesis, some sort of view of the kind of cosmos which we inhabit, and of the manner of its governance. The economy of heaven may be dark, as one of our poets suggested, using a very familiar word in rather an archaic sense; but unless we can persuade ourselves that life in some way makes sense, the significance of our economics will likewise evaporate.

I have been led on to this, perhaps rather delicate, subject, because one of the most striking features in the economics of the Founders, above all in Adam Smith and Malthus, was the strong infusion of theology at the roots of their thought. *Laissez-faire* nowadays is a doctrine that has, apparently, fallen so low that, with few exceptions, there be none so poor as do it reverence. In an ignorant age, which to its disgrace has allowed Adam Smith to go out of print, it is commonly assumed to be a godless, damnable doctrine of selfishness and of "devil-take-the-hindmost". But in its origins, as represented by Adam Smith, it is something entirely different. For him the justification of *laissez-faire* is to be found in the perfection with which the Almighty has done his job. Men are unwise and curiously planned—no doubt. But the Creator deliberately made men unwise in certain respects and planned them curiously in others, so that human weakness and folly might be powerful levers to make the great world accomplish its daily round. The folly of men, indeed, reveals the wisdom of God. It may not be popular doctrine in these days, but Adam Smith's answer to the race of planners would have been simple. He would have said that God had already done all the planning necessary, and that your bungling, earthly planners can, at best, merely upset the divine plan. Into these troubled waters I may not enter: I am merely concerned to remind you that if Economics grew out of Moral Philosophy, it is also true to say that in its modern origins, it relied on and drew strength from a system of Natural Theology.

Perhaps I have delayed you too long on this question of disappearing frontiers; I admit that I am tempted to consider one more example, recalling as I do with a fascinated curiosity a second-hand book catalogue I once received in which there was a section devoted to "Political Economy and Crime". But I do not press the point; though there may be something in it. Nevertheless, it is time to bring these conclusions together. The nineteenth century was an age of specialisms. Today the boundaries between the Social Sciences (if we must use the phrase) have broken down. The economic problems to be solved present themselves inextricably embedded in a whole mass of relationships which cut across purely economic considerations, and involve all phases of the manifold problem of men living in society. I do not say that we must therefore cease to be economists. But more than ever, an economist, to be an economist, must be vastly more than an economist. You may recall one of the most memorable of Lord Keynes's asides, where he emphasizes that the Master Economist must possess a rare combination of gifts: "He must be mathematician, historian, statesman, philosopher—in some degree. . . . He must study the present in the light of the past for the purposes of the future. No part of man's nature or his institutions must lie entirely outside his regard. He must be purposeful and disinterested in a single mood; as aloof and incorruptible as an artist, yet sometimes as near the earth as a politician." Such was Keynes's vision of the Master Economist; and to this model the rank-and-file economist should also (if it is not asking too much) endeavour to conform. He must be skilled in many fields; if he is merely an economist, he is damned.

In a world where we have removed the customs-barriers between ourselves and our neighbours—in which the economist, invading the field of Ethics confesses that he has nothing to declare—we shall of necessity pursue our studies in a somewhat different climate. May I approach what has always been a somewhat delicate question in the history of Economics, viz., the relation between pure theory and the direct observation and study of the raw material presented to us by this clamant world? Just as the individual professor of economics spends his life alternately neglecting his lectures and neglecting the world on which he lectures, periodically throwing a sop to his conscience by varying the field of his neglectfulness, so

Economics itself has its periods of devotion to theory and to what, not very happily, is sometimes called "realistic studies". Doubtless what I am saying reflects my own limited tastes and equipment; yet I have a feeling that recently theory has been running away with us. It is in danger of becoming a field for airing and exercising our academic ingenuity. Take this question of "Value"—the central, indeed, at times the exclusive, subject of economic speculation, so much so that at one time Economics was re-named "Catallactics", though I rather think the new name was washed away in the course of the baptismal ceremony. We have discussed the subject of Value for a solid 2,000 years; but it may be doubted whether we have made much progress. Such advance as is periodically made seems, indeed, to consist largely in a dawning realization of the inadequacy of the recently dominant theory. It may be that none of us knows—any more than Marx knew—what we mean by Value: and that in itself perhaps renders the formulation of a satisfactory theory of Value a matter of some difficulty. In my life-time, we have brooded on the margin, when brooding on the margin was still a fairly recent escape from the summation of past costs. More recently we have been sliding down curves of indifference, exchanging cigarettes against tots of rum, according to our varying individual tastes and preferences, or tobogganing over surfaces of indifference when we introduced a third commodity (chocolate) to render life almost unbearably complicated; and, I presume, ploughing our way through the fourth dimension, if we were so rash as to contemplate a world where insatiable Man demands four commodities. Not that I would deny or decry the place of theory, or indeed its inevitability and supreme importance. Man, among other things, is a questioning animal, and it is of the nature of the ruminator to ruminate and of the theoretician to theorize, in accordance with the will of God. And retrospectively, if only as a key to the interpretation of history, nothing can be more important than theory, for in the last resort it is ideas that move men. Lenin rests on Marx; and Marx at least thought that he was a theory of Value. If you care to be fanciful—and I admit that you would be fanciful—you might contend that the Iron Curtain which today divides Europe has as its foundation-stone (if curtains may be allowed foundation-stones) a theory of Value which the West has discarded.

Yet I cannot help feeling that in the next generation of reorientation there may be more important tasks than the elaboration of theory far above the heads of all but the experts, in fields, moreover, in which the experts have quite obviously considerable difficulty in apprehending the drift of the arguments advanced by their fellow-experts. We are privileged (if it is a privilege) to live in an era of intense economic excitement. Never was there a time when so many experiments were being launched in the economic laboratory. Never was there a time of such far-reaching institutional change. The whole structure of society, of government, of the machinery of administration is undergoing rapid and continuous transformation. Perhaps in these circumstances our first duty is to keep our eye on the Coal Board, and on the Ministry of Town and Country Planning —and much more; in fact, perhaps for the next ten years we shall be constrained to revert, somewhat but not overmuch, to a point of view resembling that of the Institutionalists.

In this new world where Economics and Politics are so closely entangled, and where the subject-matter with which we are concerned is so often a matter of dispute in party politics, the position of the economist, if he is to retain his professional integrity, is rather a difficult one. We may not be greatly admired; but, heaven knows, we are made use of. The time which Professors of Political Economy can spare from the neglect of their ordinary duties is in most cases swallowed up by service on Government committees. At the same time our chief function as teachers nowadays seems to consist in training up a race, not so much of economists as of economic advisers, who go forth to hold their own in Whitehall and elsewhere.

This trade or profession of Economic Adviser is one of the most interesting by-products of our new world; and I watch all economic advisers curiously. If we are experts, we ought without doubt to be able to say something worth listening to. But let us, just for a moment, be modest, and acknowledge that we do not possess the final answers, nor are we the repositories of ultimate wisdom. There never was a more foolish question than that which I have had addressed to me: ' Why don't you economists put the world right?" prefaced sometimes by the reproach: "Look what a mess you economists have made of the world!" One might, somewhat feebly, retort by asking why the lawyers, or the moralists, or the Church have failed to put the world right. For, so we hope, we are all employed on the same job. But probably there is a better answer than a vulgar *tu quoque*. If a combination of Aristotle, Adam Smith, Karl Marx, the Archangel Gabriel and Sir Stafford Cripps were to arise, and proclaim, with all the guile of Machiavelli, the distilled essence of economic wisdom, people would not necessarily act accordingly. The problem of government is essentially one of expediency; above all, it is concerned with the practicable, the very urgent question of how to keep going for the next six months. There is no point in offering the country the clotted cream of economic sapience, if Parliament and the electorate will refuse the draught. There is this amount of truth in the old doctrines of Senior and Cairnes already cited. The enunciation of a flawless theory of wages (if such could be formulated) will never still the passions which have given rise to a strike. And accordingly—I am on the point of speaking blasphemy!—the economic adviser should at times be able to forget that he is an economist, and indeed to realize that there may be occasions when he ought to forget his economics. He is doubtless an expert witness; but his chief value lies in the fact that he ought to be a sympathetic observer of the human scene, one whose awareness of certain aspects of life has been sharpened; one who knows what to look for; who knows what questions to ask.

So far I have been concerned in the main with yesterday and today; what about the economic climate of tomorrow and the day after tomorrow? We are moving, as we all know, to a world very different from nineteenth-century Victorianism. It follows that the economist's tasks and his problems may very well be different in the next generation. I need not tell you what are the promised characteristics of this new age, and of this new State. It is what, for convenience, is quite usefully described as the Welfare State, a State responsive to the material needs of all its subjects; providing complete and adequate security against all the sinister contingencies of life; abolishing want and unemployment; giving education up to University standard (and beyond) to all who desire to avail themselves of it. In short it will be what I recently saw described somewhat derisively—I am glad it was by an American writer—as the Santa Claus State. I have also heard it depicted, with even more derision and cattiness, as a world in which the entire population will have breakfast in bed. It will also be a world in which the State, directly or at one remove, assumes responsibility for the conduct of the major basic industries; a world also in which economically the individual will have largely disappeared. Society, indeed, has already undergone a process of coagulation, so that, if we count for anything at all, we count solely as a member of our appropriate group. Moreover, let us not forget that these groups may have conflicting interests.

Now in such a changed world where many things, if not all things, will have been made new, the politico-economic problem may be very different from that to which we older people have been accustomed. By the politico-economic problem I mean the problem of how to live together (always a difficult matter), and how to keep things going. It may seem a perverse thing to say; but just as life in heaven (or in some heavens) may not be altogether easy, so possibly life in the agreeable world of the future may present peculiar difficulties of its own.

There are, I think, three ways in which we may manage to live together in the complete Welfare State: or perhaps it would be better to say that there are three preliminary conditions, any one of which, if satisfied, would enable us to do the trick. The first is that of relying on a degree of compulsion vastly greater than we have yet had the courage or the honesty to admit may be necessary. I am not now pointing out the horrors of the Road to Serfdom, or of what awaits you when you come to the end of the road. In its higher altitudes this is already a well-discussed topic. I confine myself to the superficial and indeed the platitudinous. A State cannot undertake to provide from under the counter whatever anyone may need unless simultaneously it sees that someone is putting under the counter what is required for the purpose. The State cannot promise every schoolchild a glass of milk at eleven o'clock, unless it has directly or indirectly the corresponding number of cows standing at command. May I refer you to John Ruskin, a writer whom ordinarily I would not commend for his economic insight? "Finally I hold it for indisputable that the first duty of the State is to see that every child born therein shall be well housed, clothed, fed and educated, till it attains the years of discretion." (So far, an excellent definition of the Welfare State, even if its concern with Welfare is limited to the years of indiscretion.) "But," he goes on, "in order to the effecting this the Government must have an authority over the people of which we now do not so much as dream." It ought to be fairly obvious that the State cannot guarantee everyone against want, unless it reserves the right, if need arises, to take anyone forcibly and pack him off to Caithness or Cornwall to do whatever requires being done there. And sooner or later the time may, probably will, come when it will have to realize that it must not be too mealy-mouthed or timorous about the exercise of these powers of compulsion with which, on Ruskin's view, the Welfare State must arm itself. The State cannot give what is not there. Indeed, in a sense the State, of itself, cannot guarantee anything or any standard of life. It is an old criticism of the Anarchists that the State is for ever sterile. Properly understood, it is an entirely true statement. It can act only through its subjects; and in this matter of distribution, it can only redistribute what its nationals produce or what can be got from other nations in exchange for their products. And if Plague comes, fortified by the Colorado Beetle, Potato Disease, Foot-and-mouth Disease, blockade by the enemy and the other horrors in the Malthusian repertory, a Government guarantee of a standard of life will get you nowhere. The power of the Government to give is for ever limited by what the people themselves produce.

Indeed, in this matter I am inclined to carry my pessimism still further. It is the tritest and most hackneyed of platitudes that rights must for ever be accompanied by duties; but though we invariably pay lip-service to the well-worn dictum, in fact, our eyes in these days are morbidly fixed on our rights, whereas our duties, after a vague and perfunctory wave of the hand in their direction, are allowed to fade into the background. The Universal Declaration of Human Rights is in this respect an illuminating document. Now in the economic field a right is something that you get from someone else, whereas a duty is what we do for another. And a society in which each member concentrates on getting rather than on giving has lost the roots of its stability.

If then, in the words of the Universal Declaration of Human Rights, the Welfare State is going to provide everyone "a standard of living adequate for the health and well-being of himself and of his family, including food, clothing, housing" and much more, it must, in the last resort, have power to compel its subjects to see to it that the national bins are kept full, and that there are ample reserves under the counters of the national stores.

It may, I think, be proper to note one psychological rock which a frank policy of compulsion might encounter. It may appear a paradoxical, and, indeed, a nonsensical way of putting it, but even a policy of compulsion must rest on consent. The bulk of the population must at least realize the necessity of compulsion, and be willing that others vicariously be coerced. It is because the need for compulsion is so much more obvious in war, that wartime coercion can be so surprisingly successful. But it is otherwise in peace when the need for compulsion is, for so many reasons, much less obvious. We are doubtless learning in these years of austerity and adamantine budgets. Yet I think that our problems have been made harder for us by long insistence in certain quarters on the phrase which speaks of "Poverty in the midst of Plenty"—or more discreetly, "Poverty in the midst of the possibility of plenty". It is a phrase that goes as far back as John Gray. On the contrary, the wolf is ever at the door; and throughout history a large section of the population of the world, taken as a whole, have been down at starvation level. I think that perhaps we may have bemused ourselves with speculations about the so-called Laws of Diminishing and Increasing Returns. Admittedly—*given the material out of which such things are made*—it is possible to belch out motor cars, and utility trousers and gadgets of all kinds, as never before. But let us be crude: Man lives not on motor cars and gramophone records, but by what he puts in his belly. We have doubtless all chided Senior for his somewhat too facile identification of Diminishing Returns with Agriculture and of Increasing Returns with Manufactures, pointing out (quite correctly, and with professorial complacency and superiority) that there are cases where Increasing Returns are manifested in Agriculture, just as in certain circumstances Manufactures may operate to reveal Diminishing Returns. But perhaps in the long run (most blessed of phrases) Senior may not have been so far out. The ineluctable fact is that the human race draws its sustenance from a distressingly thin layer of soil on the surface of the globe, and it is not growing any bigger. Perhaps misguided by the population tendencies of Western Europe, we may have been inclined somewhat prematurely to regard Malthus as a back-number, as a ghost effectively laid by our most admirable and ever-increasing moral restraint. For the world as a whole, population is increasing, and increasing rapidly; the supply of food is not increasing proportionately. One authority tells me that in 1960 world agricultural production may be from 20 per cent. to 25 per cent. above the level of 1930, whereas world population over the same period may show an increase of from 30 per cent. to 35 per cent. Assuredly, we are as yet hardly in a position to speak over-confidently of the arrival of an era of unlimited plenty.

So much for the first method of meeting the future, the method of compulsion and direction—that degree of authority over the people of which John Ruskin alone was capable of dreaming. You do not like it? No more do I, though I am of a more submissive disposition than most. But economically, it might be an efficient system, if the rest of the population were as submissive as I am, which probably they are not. From all we know of the Incas and the Jesuit settlements, it might be for certain placid peoples a highly efficient system indeed, producing on the material level a remarkably high degree of comfort and well-being. If compulsion is to be condemned, it must be on moral rather than on economic grounds; it is to be abhorred, above all, because it involves a denial of personality and an abrogation of responsibility.

But if, disliking the idea of a world resting on compulsion, you ask for an alternative which will preserve our free society, I suggest, as the second of my possible devices for the future that you might consider what can be done towards a solution of the age-long question of Incentive. And in some ways this is the most urgent of all our industrial problems, for never since the finest trumpetings of the mercantilists, has the clarion-call to work sounded so insistently as today. The idea of "Incentives", however, seems to involve the acceptance of the view that the natural man does not love work, or that he does not love it or endure it cheerfully, except in moderate doses. Yet apparently this innocuous proposition seems to be one which it is rather dangerous to advance in certain circles. For moralists tell us that we ought to love our work, and tend to think that if we have not yet reached that stage, the fault lies not in Man, but in the organization of labour. As Fourier said in one of his illuminating flashes of vision: "Morality teaches us to love work; let it then known how to make work lovable." And as you may have discovered in your miscellaneous reading, any suggestion that mankind as a whole have in their make-up a something which leads them to regard work as no more than a second-best way of passing the time, is at times roundly described as a foul slander on our fellow-men. Yet I am unrepentant. I am sufficiently under the influence of Jewish mythology to believe that work is a curse, and I take refuge under the broad wings of St. Thomas Aquinas, who somewhere has tersely summarized Man as an animal *laborem fugiens*. What I would reject as a "foul libel" would be the suggestion you may also have encountered that Man is as lazy as he dare be without risk of being found out. Searching my own heart in a desire for a just delicacy of statement, and contemplating a life-long struggle against what Godwin called the "allurements of sloth", I would confess for myself that I have been just about as lazy as my self-respect would allow. That, when I come to think of it, is rather a nice formula, tossing the ball back to our friends the moralists.

Work, for the present, then, I assume to be something which soon comes to be avoided, except for a small happy section of the community whose work and whose play merge into each other—the small body of insincere cranks who in *Who's Who* describe their recreation as "More Work". We work because we must; we consent to do more work, because of additional inducements and incentives. But in the new world to which we are moving the question of incentive, of overcoming Man's disinclination to work, will of necessity become vastly more difficult, just because the older incentives in their harsher form must become enfeebled as we seek to guarantee security and a reasonable standard of life in all circumstances.

Doubtless the problem of incentives should be considered along with the allied question of the removal of disincentives, if we may lapse into the barbarous jargon of these times. I am not sure that the Authorities realize how powerfully in certain circumstances the present Income Tax arrangements operate to restrict effort. The fact that payments in respect of overtime may bring into the group that pays Income Tax a worker who would otherwise be exempt leads him to assign the whole of the tax exclusively to that portion of his earnings that come from the extra hours worked. He complains that whereas he has from time immemorial been paid time-and-a-half for work outside normal hours, he is now being fobbed off with three-quarters time: he is, in fact, being paid at a lower rate for his overtime than for his ordinary day's work. There is, of course, a catch in it; but if you discuss the matter with him, unless you are a very good dialectician, he has a fair chance of persuading you that he is right.

Waiving the question of the removal of such "disincentives" which I mention merely to complete the picture, it remains true and regrettably true, that the only effective incentives are of a material character, with an appeal to the individualistic and competitive instincts of mankind which we are supposed to be eradicating. You may ring the changes on higher rates of pay and ingenious bonus payments; you may bring in shorter hours; but you are still moving on the material plane and appealing in one way or another to the desire of gain and comfort. Nor do you escape (entirely, or at all) this material character by giving better seats at the Opera, or tours to the Northern Capitals, on the *Kraft durch Freude* principle. And as I said, precisely because we are moving into a better world, this problem of incentive must become more difficult; it may, indeed, turn out to be the acid test of the stability of our future economy. We have the firmest assurances that the Government will in future accept the task of maintaining full employment, though doubtless "full employment" may be variously defined. The testing-time which will reveal whether the State has at all times and in all circumstances the power to fulfil this undertaking still lies ahead. But if full employment is defined, as it sometimes has been defined, as a world in which there are more jobs than men, then I tremble as in the presence of a nightmare. I am aware that I am again endangering my life, for I have already read the words of ecclesiastical dignitaries, censuring the cruelty of those who would drive men to work under the lash of hunger. One ought to be able to assume in bishops a knowledge of the Book of Genesis. The whole of Man's existence on earth has been a struggle for the conquest of bread. In a world where there are *more* jobs than men, it is fairly obvious that two things will happen. First, and by definition, a number of jobs will remain unfilled, and it is not difficult to say which jobs these will be. Man, *more suo* and *laborem fugiens*, will avoid those tasks which, for any reason, are regarded as unattractive, unpleasant or unduly arduous, though it may quite possibly be that without these a city may not stand. And simultaneously, higher up the scale, employers in desperation will spend their days enticing away the employees of others by the offer of higher wages, so that in the end we may say of wages, in the words of Isaiah (in his metrical version):

On eagles' wings they mount, they soar.

It is sometimes instructive to see on a small scale what may later happen on a larger. Today you have a fairly good illustration of a world of more jobs than men, if you take the market for domestic service. Domestic servants, so far as they survive, having read their Bernard Shaw, make a bee-line for widowers' houses—elderly widowers, with no children about the place. I do not blame them; I should do the same myself. An elderly widower who spends all his evenings at the Club provides a haven of peace compared to anything that can be offered by a harassed young woman with four children. Also the elderly widower is more squeezable in money matters. At present, accordingly, the survivors of the race of domestic servants flock to the houses of those who in many cases might be better dead, and avoid those homes where the need is the sorest. This is almost a parable of what would take place in a world of more jobs than men; and the only possible remedy is clear. If there is a danger that certain essential tasks may remain undone because no one is willing to undertake them, the State, even if professedly shunning compulsion, would have to devise means of coercion. And so by another route, you are brought back to compulsion which we have already considered.

While on this question of incentive in this present transitional world, and with men as we still know them, I should like to allow myself a passing observation on two points in partial criticism of the tendencies of our time. First, am I perverse in sometimes feeling that today we are tending to be far too impatient of any suggestion of inequality in any sphere of life? I am still enough of a Saint-Simonian (and for that matter, a Fourierist) to consider that it is only by admitting a certain measure of inequality, something of the nature of a hierarchy, that we shall be able to get anywhere at all, or be able to make the machine march. The only place where there is absolute equality (just as it is the only place where there is absolute security) is in the grave. There is, I think, no harm in a certain degree of inequality, on two conditions: first, that the resultant disparity should not be offensive; and secondly, that there should be no barrier in the way of the somewhat-less-favoured of today becoming the somewhat-more-favoured of tomorrow by their own efforts, and (admittedly) by such an admixture of luck as you will never eliminate from life. Life always has been, and always will be, something of the nature of a race; and the young at least would have it so. But there is not much fun in taking part in, or in watching, a race where in advance the umpires impose handicaps which will effectively ensure that all the competitors will arrive simultaneously at the winning-post. In fact, incentives won't work, unless you are prepared to allow some inequality of one kind or another. And there is this further point. We turned to the possibility of devising effective incentives, in order to avoid compulsion and to preserve our free society. But, indeed, though Liberty and Equality have been for a century and a half yoked with Fraternity in a curious and uneasy Trinity, nevertheless, Liberty and Equality are natural enemies. It is the dilemma which vexed William Thompson for a life-time—a dilemma from which he never escaped. For if we are to be free, and if we exercise our freedom, we must be free to be, among other things, unequal. On the other hand, if we are to be equal, it will be only because we are forcibly compelled to be equal, and denied the liberty of surpassing our fellows.

The second general point which I would merely mention in all this question of incentive and work is whether we may not have been striving somewhat too zealously and automatically in the direction of a shortening of the hours of work, regarding this as an end desirable in itself and in all circumstances and apart from all other considerations. It is a curious situation that a time marked by unremitting calls for increased activity should also be marked by continual strivings for reductions in the hours of work, and in some cases in the number of days in the working week. I am aware that I am again in danger of seeming to speak with the voice that betokens the heart of the callous slave-driver, and therefore I must tread delicately. I have already admitted that work is, in our professional jargon, a disutility; but those of us who have intermittently lapsed into work will probably agree that it is not such a loathsome thing as might be imagined from the unguarded talk of men taking their Sunday ease in their inn. It is not nearly so objectionable as, for instance, idleness spent in boredom. I am merely concerned to suggest a doubt as to the correctness of the assumption which we seem to make that every reduction in the hours of work must of necessity be a blessing in all cases. Doubtless at this point we pass the invisible frontier between Economics and Ethics; but I would like to suggest that the question whether a diminution in the hours of labour is or is not a blessing depends in part on the use made of the additional non-working hours. Ideally I would like a reduction in the hours of work to march hand-in-hand with a more intelligent use of the hours of leisure. A mere increase in the number of hours when a man does not know quite what to do, when he is merely a nuisance about the house, is probably a curse rather than a blessing. For assuredly, leisure unless it is filled with some occupation that almost assumes the dignity of work has, like other things, diminishing utility.

I have offered you compulsion; but you say that if possible you would prefer to retain your freedom. I have suggested that you endeavour to solve the question of Incentive in a free society; but you tell me that there may be something illogical in our new society in relying on incentives which, at their worst, as in *Taylorismus*, are unlovely, and which are of necessity material in their nature, with an individualistic appeal, inevitably differentiating if not dividing men. The third course—I promised you three—is to enrol yourself frankly among the followers of Lenin (for this purpose) and wait in faith for the emergence of a better Man, for the universal prevalence of a higher order or morality than that now to be found among us; when in consequence the worker will no longer (the words are Lenin's) "calculate with the shrewdness of a Shylock whether he has not worked half an hour more than another, whether he is not getting less pay than another"; when "the necessity of observing the simple fundamental rules of human intercourse will become a habit". Admittedly this is a long-term policy and a long-term hope, and postulates in the words of Lenin "a person unlike the present man-in-the-street".

How far we can make ourselves fit to live in a better world by evolving a higher type of morality is presumably not an economic question. Nevertheless, I may not omit it today, because in the past —Louis Blanc is a useful example—it has so often been hoped that our economic difficulties would be solved in some such way. Nearly all our ardent reformers have confidently trusted that in a better world where all things are held and operated on behalf of the community, a higher order of morality would prevail. When workers could feel that they were working for their fellow-workers and not merely for the gain of another, they would adopt a new code of behaviour. Admittedly it will be a slow process, even on Lenin's own showing; and therefore perhaps we should not be impatient. I doubt whether so far anyone who in the past would have swindled the Railway Company has started like a guilty thing upon a fearful summons on observing that the letters "L.N.E.R." had been replaced by "B.R." Also we have made doubtful progress towards industrial peace; for apparently employment by the State or by a National Board does not necessarily mean bliss and content for all concerned. There is a devastating sentence in the second Annual Report of the Coal Board. It tells with restrained gratification that there were no official strikes during the year; "but," it adds, "there were 1,635 unofficial strikes where men stopped work in defiance of their Union." One-thousand-six-hundred-and-thirty-five! One is reminded of the love affairs of Don Juan: "And in Spain, a thousand-and-three." Here surely, in the cold statistics of the Coal Board, is an illuminating figure significant of the economic and psychological friction prevailing in our society. It will assuredly take some time before we are all prepared to crucify Self to such an extent as will qualify us for admission to Lenin's heaven.

And so I leave it—somewhat inconclusively, like certain modern composers who end without even asking a question, but merely because they have exhausted their time or their paper. Compulsion, shall we say, is detestable and ultimately immoral. Incentive is essentially a species of bribery, relying on the competitive instincts and leading us back to what some would have us regard as the jungle of individualism. I am all for the evolution of a better Man, and for that matter of a better Woman; but it is a slow process for frail creatures whose years are three-score-and-ten. Perhaps in the end there *is* a conclusion, though it is not an economic one. It is that before we can be trusted to live in the New Jerusalem, we must first of all be fit to walk the streets of the New Jerusalem. And as applied to our transitional times, I would suggest that despite all superficial appearances, the New World into which we are moving is not going to be a world which will make everything easy for everybody by giving everybody everything. If it is to work, it will be a world which will make vastly greater demands on everyone. It will demand that most difficult of all things to attain, that plant of very slow growth, a higher standard of public and private morality in all things, and in particular the suppression of Self. For socialism is parading under a false name, unless it means an order of things in which we forget ourselves in our zeal for the good of society and of our fellows, and in which speculation as to our place in the queue is the last thought that occurs to us. And it is not I, but Lenin who says so.

2

FIFTY YEARS OF ECONOMICS

H. O. MEREDITH

Belfast, September, 1952

ECONOMICS today is recognizably the subject I began, under the title Political Economy, in the autumn of 1899. If you should open Marshall, or J. B. Clark, or Böhm-Bawerk, you would not find yourselves in a different intellectual universe, while even the Schmollers and Sombarts, or our own Ashley and Cunningham, were economists in our sense: their dream of a new economics issuing ready armed like Athena from the head of Zeus may have faded, but only in one accidental respect has the importance of history receded: we no longer suffer from such paucity of contemporary record as made men eighty years ago turn eagerly to history to supplement deficiency of data. Whether the ratio of data to the number and urgency of problems has also risen is not, perhaps, so evident: it seems, at times, that the economic universe is expanding and that the faster we run the further we are left behind.

The standard case in economics is still what it was: a community in trade with an outside world. In this standard case, however, both outside world and community have altered and much of the difference between modern and late-Victorian economics is explicable as an attempt to adjust the subject to these alterations. Consider first the outside world. There was in the nineteenth century a long-term stable dynamic of expanding exports from industrialized areas partly to new countries which were producing reciprocal supplies of food and raw materials, partly to old where traditional handicraft goods could be displaced by machine products. Under these conditions the elasticity of international exchange and finance was so large that Marshall considered reasoning in regard to inelasticity to be an intellectual toy. Given this general presumption an economist tended inevitably to regard his outside world as a cushion, stable itself and a stabilizer for his community: he knew, and needed to know, little more about it than Mr. Podsnap's aphorism: ' Foreign nations do, as they do!" About his community an economist might be more curious for usually it was interest in some accident or aspect of his community which had attracted him to economic studies and one thing leads to another. Inelasticity was a working tool of some importance in community short-period problems of price or wage adjustment. But here also a seemingly stable dynamic of long-period trends cushioned the economist against over-concern with minutiae of cause and consequence. The short period might be largely neglected as not significantly affecting the long, whilst even in the longest of long runs it was only the individual, not all of us, who died: in the Marshallian forest there were no forest fires.

The contrast with all this in our contemporary standard case is indeed remarkable. Our outside world is less a cushion than an explosive bed of Procrustes oscillating between alternate phases of rack and amputation: it is vital that we should know as much as may be about it. In our community, again, we have lost assurance of long-term trends and search painfully among short-period accelerations to discover which to encourage, which to contain. One way and another we clearly need fuller detail and more exactitude of knowledge not merely because like any other body of inquirers we wish to know more but because the nature of our problems seems to have altered, presenting us with more unknowns, demanding more equations of greater precision more elaborately arrayed.

Let us pass to a further change which fifty years ago was only beginning. Private enterprise had then no visible rival as a means to efficient organization and technological advance. Now it is confronted with a formidable competitor. First Germany, then Japan, then the Ministry of Munitions, and so on to Stalin's five-year plans and such pale simulacra of planning as our own right or left intermittently entertain. Briefly the past half-century confronts us with the suggestion that centralized propaganda and discipline backed by force may achieve results which probably could not have been obtained otherwise and certainly could not have been obtained so speedily in cases where speed is essential. A key-experience was, I suggest, the failure of private enterprise in England between 1914 and 1916 with its consequences in the establishment of the Ministry of Munitions and all that went with it on both sides of the Atlantic. Had Lenin in 1920 been challenged by an English economist to say why he was so certain that Russia needed socialism he might well have answered: "Your own recent history demonstrates its necessity: you tried private enterprise and it failed; you switched to centralization backed by force and it succeeded: do you blame me if, needing an even greater and swifter change-over than you in 1914 required, I follow in the path where you have led?" It would not have been easy, I submit, for our economist to answer effectively. He must have tried, I presume, as many of us did try, to belittle our experience, to argue that war is abnormal, that what happens in it is no guide to what is desirable when normality returns. If only "normality" (in that sense) could return! It has taken some of us (I by no means exclude myself) thirty years to discover that normality (i.e. things following some line or pattern) is not a cause but a consequence or (shall I say?) an expression of underlying equilibria, that if the equilibria which it expresses be sufficiently anarchic their normal expression will be chaos.

I have tabled these, perhaps too self-evident, generalizations because it seems to me on looking back that the course which economics has taken has not been determined solely by its own endogenous momenta but has been influenced significantly by change in its subject-matter. This seems to me to be true alike in the field of observation and in the field of theory, of the transition from description to econometrics and of the shift of emphasis from statics to dynamics. But first I must say something of the great and growing demand for economics which has promoted training of economists and output of economic literature on so vastly expanded a scale. That this has not been due wholly to exogenous forces is evident if only because it began earliest and has gone farthest in the United States which finds itself still, relatively speaking, carefree at home and confident abroad. It was America that first invented and produced in significant quantity the expert in economics as opposed to the economic pundit. Nevertheless growth in the demand for economists in America no less than here has been accompanied by a shift in the kind of economics demanded. We are asked less and less to light beacons towards which courses may be set, more and more to illuminate environmental fog. Those hard-headed businessmen, those hard-driven civil servants, those hard-bitten politicians, who enlist our services, ask us primarily neither where to go nor how to get there but what the given situation is, what accelerations it contains, how these accelerations are reacting on one another, are increasing, or are diminishing. What they value in us at the council table is our gift for showing that one suggested course is a cul-de-sac, that another returns upon itself, that a third may conceivably lead somewhere, briefly—our power to keep the heads about the table turning until discussion has milled around sufficiently to generate some agreed decision. There is a hint of paradox in the fact that whereas when some century ago the few economists in England were esteemed authoritative their market value approximated to zero, today the marginal demand price for a far larger number of substantially less prestige is comfortingly high. This paradox is, however, easily resolved. Men may trust economists less but they need or at least feel that they need them more, are less certain that they know already all that economics can teach. Whether they will continue to feel this lies largely in our own hands: it is a hopeful sign that they also approach their work today with a fuller sense of its difficulty, are less inclined to think little of one another and less of everybody else. The men who remind me most today of what economists sometimes were, are, low be it spoken, the communists: they are as irascibly cocksure that all will go well provided profit-making is abolished as Mr. Podsnap was provided it were indulged. There is, in fact, in Russia today a "glad confident morning" feeling reminiscent of our own 1860s; the language that voices it seems to echo Gladstone's paean of "prosperity advancing by leaps and bounds". By the same token, if I may judge from what I spell out painfully in *Ekonomiki voprosi*, their economics however structurally compact is, from our point of view, vestigial.

To take such a place at the council table as I have indicated, an economist needs today a more and more detailed knowledge of contemporary economic fact, a more and more elaborate theoretical insight into interaction through and across time. Where his predecessors dealt mainly with things in the round, for him the dispersion of a mass is often as important as its total. His function is no longer one of sensing overriding tendencies from some point outside the battle. He must enter the mêlée and submerge his mind in a welter of strategic planning and tactical manoeuvre.

It would be misleading to suggest that nothing of this was sensed or surmised in 1900 or for that matter in 1870. In England, at least from the career of Jevons and the contemporary beginnings of Marshall, there was agreement among economists of every school or tendency on the need for more factual knowledge and for broader and deeper analysis. By 1900, if there was not much doing in analysis, the tide of information was rising. The Royal Commission on Labour had, as he told the world later, re-educated Marshall, Booth had organized and published his *London Survey*, Beatrice Potter had explored co-operation, the same Beatrice with Sidney Webb had delved deeply in Trade Unionism, Rowntree had turned his microscope upon the poverty of York. Nevertheless the total flow of orderly organized information was small, the technique of investigation, statistical or other, was rudimentary, the standards of economists whether in observation or in analysis was amateur rather than professional. Consider, for example, the Fiscal Controversy: seen in retrospect it is, surely, a melancholy business, wherein those arrayed on the one side do not know how to argue their case, while those on the other fail to see that there is a case to be argued. How little of all that literature has survived or deserved to survive! Marshall's *Memorandum*, perhaps, and Pigou's *Preferential and Protective Import Duties* on the one side: on the other, Balfour's *Essay on Insular Free Trade* and Bickerdike's paper on *Incipient Import Taxes*.

The progress since those days alike in analysis and in observation is indeed stupendous. The mere quantitative increase of published economics is daunting apart from what sleeps, for security or other reasons, in the files of government offices and business houses or in unpublished dissertations on the shelves of University libraries. I have been glancing recently at the bibliographical notes in the *A.E.A. Survey of Contemporary Economics* and cannot sufficiently congratulate myself on having so long passed the age of attempting to keep up to date. And after all, what even American economists read (and their erudition has always astounded me) can be but a fraction of what there is for them to read even if they should confine themselves (as Americans by no means tend to do) to what is available in English. On this side of the Atlantic also, though erudition now as ever is by us less highly esteemed, I am impressed when I meet my juniors by the dozens of books and articles which they discuss and have evidently at least glanced at as compared with the tiny number I had heard of, let alone read, when I was their age. Moreover, though I find contemporary economics less and less intelligible, I seem to sense in it an ever-rising standard of professional competence. New notions are taken up and debated and after suitable dust of conflict something reasonably definite emerges: a new brick is added to our tower of Babel.

The leading part in this growth of a profession of economics has been played by America with England a good second, and Scandinavia and Holland hard on our heels. The coming greatness of U.S.A. economics was seen by Marshall on his second visit to that country. He was impressed he said, speaking of their economists, "not so much by the force as by the promise of force". Germany at that time might have seemed a more likely candidate for the first place but in economics as in other matters the fatalism of German intellect, its chronic *ich kann nicht anders*, has prevented great minds from getting sufficiently together for fruitful intercourse. If any of my hearers doubt this let him cast his thoughts back to the great debate at Dresden in 1932 on Probleme der Wertlehre when eleven schools of thought were most competently expounded and no one listened *effectively* (the operative word) to what anybody said. On Russian economics I will say something later: here one word more on the United States. The conditions of American life from the War of Secession onwards protected their economists from that sense of the unimportance of the short period which was our bane in England. They had confidence in the future of their community, in a sense more confidence than had we, but far less feeling that how their future would shape itself was independent of what happened from day to day. And, on the other hand, what was happening was more arresting and exciting, was calling more urgently and obviously for examination and control: witness, for instance, the evolution of transport and banking and the emergence of a "trust" problem. Furthermore, the activity and mobility of American life, the fact that the individual graduated often through several occupations in widely separated localities before he settled down, bred a habit of mind in which it seemed natural to take stock of situations and be guided by measurement and ratiocination rather than by pressures of circumstance and tradition. Let us add that, for one reason or another, Americans are (shall I say?) less reticent than we are, have less horror of washing linen whether dirty or clean in public, less feeling that individuals and associations have a right or a duty to keep their own counsel, to refrain from confession of weakness or boasting of success. Lastly, the American academic tradition much as it owes to Scotland and England has drawn far more than our own on European sources: there is a catholicity in American economics which we can but admire, our own tending still to smell too strongly of Cambridge, of the London School of Economics, of Glasgow, or where not.

You will not, I hope, be expecting from me a *catalogue raisonné* of this vast expansion in economics, or a detailed exposition of its star events. I shall content myself with a perhaps too personal account of "how it strikes a contemporary" who however incompetent to keep up with and comprehend what was going on about him yet never wholly lost interest in it and did manage to pick up some crumbs from those groaning tables. Let me begin by stating that I am constitutionally sympathetic to one of the most obviously important developments, namely our abandonment of the Marshallian doctrine that the proper place for theory is at the back of the mind, that it should make only occasional appearances on the stage to forge short links of argument, our transition to the view that it should sunbathe in the shop window with every jot and tittle exposed to full glare of publicity. I always wished for as complete a theoretical model as possible of the economic universe, one moreover that would fall into its place as part of an even wider synthesis enclosing the whole of human desire, activity, satisfaction. Such was my dream, and so was I attracted to Jevons, to J. B. Clark, to Wicksteed, to Irving Fisher, to Schumpeter, craving for a complete blueprint of the skeleton which Marshall preferred to keep, not precisely in a cupboard, but masked behind flesh of fact and apparel of tradition. I ought, it should seem, to have rejoiced as the pendulum swung over more decisively in my preferred direction, as Pigou exposed Marshall's skeleton and developed its knubblier parts into progressively more delicate articulations, as elements of Lausanne and Vienna infiltrated the London School of Economics, as more and more complicated geometry and algebra invaded the textbooks, as issue after issue of the *Review of Economic Studies* and *Econometrica* slipped into their places on library shelves. I ought, I say, to have rejoiced and in a sense I have, but my delight has been partial and embarrassed. It *is* shy-making for a professor to realize as the years go by that more and more of the new work in the subject to which he is accredited is to him unintelligible. If only I had been taught, or been able to teach myself, mathematics! I made attempts but could never reach a sufficient standard. The statement, for instance, that the number of our equations should neither exceed nor fall short of the number of our unknowns conveys, as nearly as is possible, nothing to my mind. With that you might judge that I should be well advised to let the matter rest, but I have not even tried to persuade myself to do so. It seems to me too evident that the whole progress of economics during my life-time has been bound up with mathematical talent and training. Had Marx soaked his youthful mind in mathematics instead of in Hegel his impact on the world might well have been less, but we should not still have been waiting for some indication that his majestic intuitions and ant-like industry had initiated a branch of science that was capable of growth.

Let me record, shortly, my sense of what may be gained from trying to think mathematically despite failure to acquire manipulative technique. It might seem the merest common sense to suggest that if two forces x and y co-operate in producing a resultant z we should not expect to double z by doubling x or y while leaving its fellow unchanged. Yet how haltingly and gradually did this common sense infiltrate economic thinking, from its beginnings in Ricardian rent theory, through the misty origins of diminishing marginal utility, and so at last to the august generalization of the diminishing marginal productivity of individual factors! Looking back I see how my own mind, over a period of say twenty-five years, repeated a process which had taken economics say a hundred years, which is now I imagine traversed by representative students in five years, by the *élite* in five months, by an exceptional freak in five days. I cannot doubt that Marshall was fundamentally mistaken when he wrote: "The chief use of pure mathematics seems to be in helping a person to write down quickly, shortly and exactly some of his thoughts for his own use": he did not realize that without his own mathematical bent and training his mind could never have formulated these thoughts precisely enough to be written whether down or up. No: there is no going back from the dictum of Jevons: "economics deals throughout with quantities; it must be a mathematical science in matter if not in language".

A mathematical approach must evidently stimulate interest in defining precisely concepts of national income and accumulation and in national accounting generally. It was not for nothing that Irving Fisher spoke of his work on Capital and Income as "a kind of philosophy of economic accounting". Briefly, mathematical economics has always in view just such a blue-print or complete model of the economic universe as I adumbrated earlier. Marshall no doubt had such a model but he kept it deliberately in the background and it was not until I read Pigou's review in 1907 of a new edition of the *Principles* that I realized, or thought I ought to try to realize, the cardinal role of the national dividend concept in that great work. My own readings of the *Principles* had left me uncomfortably vague as to what was and what was not income whether national or individual and it was Irving Fisher and Pigou who did most to clear up my perplexities. I have never quite got to the end of them and some not too recent suggestions of Professor Hicks have opened new vistas of uncertainty. I used to think and teach that Adam Smith's distinction between productive and unproductive labour was sheer muddle, but I now suspect that as in the somewhat analogous case of Marx's theory of value there may have been a real problem behind an unconvincing solution.

Concern for precise formulation measurement and subdivision of the national dividend has played a notable part in the evolution of theory. Unless we conceive of it as a quantitative magnitude, as long as we think of it vaguely as an emanation from similarly misty aggregates of productive forces it is not easy to proceed to the notion of the part played by amount and composition of the national dividend at one moment in shaping its amount and composition at the next. A door to that development was opened by Keynes in the *Treatise* when he formulated his first equation in terms of total output savings and investment, deriving from it a definite sum of positive or negative profit encouraging or discouraging increase of total output. Doubtless at that time Keynes was thinking mainly of price levels and fluctuations and was only at the beginning of the train which led to his General Theory. Nevertheless the link of implications seems to be clear as also the dependence of the whole catena on a mathematical approach.

I am concerned to emphasize this point because it connects the whole movement in economics for which the name of Keynes has become a symbol with the prodigious pioneering of Irving Fisher—the greatest name, if a foreigner may presume to judge, in American economics. He takes us back, of course, some twenty years before my period but his work from the very outset and his whole approach to the subject were essentially modern. The pioneer treatise on mathematical economics, the pioneer model mechanism for exhibiting theory, the treatises on capital and income, on interest, on the purchasing power of money, the "Grand Old Man" of the econometric society, the man incidentally who in a college textbook twenty years before Keynes's *General Theory* insisted that the study of value is inseparable from the study of money. Keynes, I feel, was less a professional economist than a superman whose orbit happened to intersect our pedestrian proceedings. Neither the *Treatise* nor the *General Theory* shows either the erudition or the thorough grounding of a professional however truly each of them towers above such standards in freshness and force and forensic ability. It was, in fact, largely because he was not an economist or, as I personally should prefer to put it, because he was so much more than an economist, that his impact on the subject was so important. Coming from outside us, but speaking sufficiently our language, he gathered eclectically what was serviceable to his purpose and, throwing what he gathered into what Bloomsbury would have called "significant form", at once inspired and focused debate. It is this peculiarity in his work which justifies common use of such a term as "the Keynesian revolution" for an advance in economics which has embodied the work of numerous writers in many countries and was not due to or even predominantly inspired and directed by any one man.

I pass to another movement which is even more difficult for a non-mathematician to grasp and delineate, namely the shift of emphasis from static to dynamic theory. What I seem to see here is not that problems which used to be regarded as dynamic have risen in importance relatively to those which were aligned to statics but that the nature of what was treated by statics has so altered as to demand dynamic treatment, while much of what was regarded as dynamic has dropped out of the picture for the time being. It cannot, I suggest, be accidental that contemporary dynamics contains so little reference to the work of Marshall and J. B. Clark though the former professed a dynamic economics *pur sang* while the latter restricted statics to short period problems. If we inquired after the origins of modern dynamics we should be led back, I think, primarily to Wicksell, behind him conceivably to Sombart and Böhm-Bawerk, behind them to Marx. It may, however, be doubted whether these or other possible lines of development are worth examining: it seems more probable that our modern movement has sprung from those changes in the economic universe which I sketched in my introduction. Marshall, it will be remembered, deprecated the importance of J. B. Clark's distinction between static and dynamic problems, arguing that dynamic theory is inclusive of statical as the special case where accelerations are reduced to zero. It might have been retorted that he himself kept his accelerations so low that his dynamic theory differed but little from a static and there may well, I imagine, be readers of Marshall who tend to think and speak of his work as statical, forgetful that in his own view the billiard balls and the basin were slowly, slowly, oh so slowly, changing shapes and sizes and shifting ever so slowly this way and that. It may be noted also that in his biological analogies Marshall was eminently of the older Darwinian school, was thinking of the accumulation of infinitesimal changes through epochs of geological time. *Natura non facit saltum* was his motto, on which Schumpeter remarked aptly some forty years ago, in accordance with neo-Darwinism, that evolution *geradezu sprungweise fortgeht.* Clark again in his dynamics was not, I submit, a modern, however important his work may have been in clearing the way. For him dynamics found its field in the long period, to the short statics were appropriate. Why? Surely because he, equally with Marshall, believed that short-period oscillations in the main cancel out and are of negligible importance in the long run. May it not be that it is because this view seems no longer to be tenable that economists more and more find it necessary to include accelerations and acceleration of accelerations in *all* their work with the result that theory is from top to bottom more and more dynamic and by the same token constrained to briefer and briefer time periods through the increasing difficulty of predicating anything with certainty about the remoter future?

This brings us to the threshold of the high theme of econometrics, if I am right in supposing that econometrists aim to clear economics of equations based upon psychological postulates and to found it upon direct inductions from objectively observable and measurable phenomena. This movement has done something and there is good ground for hoping that it will do much: it may be useful, however, to define a difficulty which it, in common with all other schools, has, whether at the outset or ultimately, to face. If economic consequence worked itself out wholly in the economic field as physical seems to do in the physical, the road to a perfectly objective science of economics would be open. The facts, however, seem to be otherwise. It is generally agreed that part of the causation and part of the consequence of every economic event occurs in the non-economic field, but not all of us draw the inference that the whole economic consequence of an economic event cannot be ascertained by a purely economic calculus. The economic consequence will always include a repercussion-element mediated back from the non-economic into the economic field: for complete accounting, therefore, even of economic consequence only, a calculus which covered both fields would be necessary. In so far as such reactions are important, and it is probable that in some critical connections they are very important, economics must remain an art and cannot become science, must rely not on measurement and reasoning but on judgement and intuition.

There is much else I should like to speak of, there are many names I should like to mention, in what may well be my last at all formal utterance on economics; but what I have said may have suggested all too sufficiently the kind of things I might have said, had time permitted, on other relevant topics. I shall conclude by offering a few remarks on a very vexed question—namely, that increasing difficulty of economics, which, however it may attract us by challenging our powers, yet also occasions most of us at one time or another more than one kind of head- or heartache. Speaking with all due humility it does seem to me a pity that so able a man as myself should have found so much of the subject beyond his power of comprehension: yet I have felt obligated to state what seems to me a convincing defence of its increased and increasing complexity. This would not matter if the problems with which it deals were such as the average man can safely leave to wiser heads than his. Economics is a socio-political subject and if the nit-wit abandons it to the wise-acre each of them will ultimately find himself in the cart. Is there any hope of escape from this dilemma? There may be some here who remember twenty-five years ago a plea for simpler economics addressed by Edwin Cannan to the Royal Economic Society. It was a moving plea, but it has not stayed the march of complication. Cannan could see things simply because he was in the best sense a simple soul with clear-cut convictions and unwavering faith. We, by comparison, have divided souls, have been told that in the long run we are all dead, have more than a suspicion that our apple-cart may be overturned before the long run arrives. It is this creeping fog of doubt and sense of immediate urgency which involves us in more and more elaborately difficult effort to measure in detail our day-to-day environment, the direction in which each part of it is moving, its speed of movement. Briefly, if we want (and we ought to want) to simplify economics we must begin by simplifying life. I do not mean that we should strive to become "simple lifers" in the escapist sense of denying life in order to avoid its perplexities, but by a real process of restoring men's faith in the long run and giving them better grounds for it. It may well be that economics has a part to play here in the next fifty years no less important than the honourable if modest part it has played during my working life in the gestation of the Welfare State. If society can assume a form in which problems of day-to-day adjustment are less acute it will matter less what precise adjustment is reached in particular cases: rougher observations and cruder theories will suffice: there will be less need for ultra refinement. Unfortunately it is all too easy to confuse ease of adjustment with enhanced power to thrust the weaker to the wall or less resistance on the part of the weaker to going there. And further it is not sufficient to set up true valuations: they will not operate satisfactorily unless they are felt to be true. There is, none the less, some hope in the paradox that in a world where everyone valued everything correctly and felt that it was so valued there would be no need of a theory of value. We need economics the more the more current valuations are or seem to be unsatisfactory. Doubtless it is for this reason that economics is (from our point of view) vestigial in Russia, the *communis opinio* there, or what passes for it, feels that current valuations are, broadly speaking, so right, or so little wrong, as to leave little room for argument and little need for elaboration of observation or theory to support argument. Difficulties and disputes there must no doubt be but—*solvuntur ambulando*. This state is admittedly the outcome of a centralized power, a systematized propaganda, a ruthless official discipline, beyond everything which we experienced in either war. It is claimed, on the other hand, that representative Russians are less frightened of Stalin than they are of private enterprise, and knowing what one does of Russian conditions before and since the revolution it would not surprise one if this claim were justified. What concerns my discussion more is the fact (as it seems to me to be) that Russia has developed a will to work in a disciplined way, a flexibility of economic organization, and an enthusiasm for technological advance, which have enabled her not merely to make a creditable appearance at Helsinki but to carry through an economic metamorphosis incomparably greater and swifter than history can show elsewhere. The nearest parallel perhaps to the Lenin–Stalin episode is the career of Mahomet. He had their power of propagating split-atom mass enthusiasm, but his problems of reorganization were not fundamentally economic. Some comparable degree of simplification might be forced upon us swiftly by some adequately disastrous emergency as it was forced upon Russia by the inability of Czarism to meet the German challenge. Without such compulsion we cannot, or at any rate men of my age cannot, reasonably choose to do more than move towards it by such gradual changes as will leave us feeling free. The Welfare State, we may hope, is a first step in the right direction, attacking some of the most menacing of our inelasticities, but much more will be needed before it will be possible for us to feel like St. Paul that a new discipline has begotten a new and larger liberty. Until that transition is accomplished I am afraid that economics must continue to be difficult and that economists must expect to hear men mouth against them intermittently the jibe of the poet:

> "They use the snaffle and the curb all right,
> But where's the bloody horse?"

3

CAN THERE BE A VALID THEORY OF WAGES?

RICHARD G. LIPSEY

Lister Lecture,[1] Norwich, September, 1961

I HAVE been asked in this paper to explain to the non-economist what I, as an economist, do and why. In a nutshell I can say that, as a practitioner in the field of economic science, I search for stable patterns of human behaviour in the economic sphere. Such behaviour patterns provide the basis for making the testable predictions without which there can be no science. In some cases we search the data directly to discover stable behaviour patterns which we suspect, for one reason or another, to exist; in other cases we *postulate* them, then *deduce* what their consequences would be, and only then search the data to see if these consequences can be observed.

The view that economics can be a discipline which deals *in a scientific manner* with human behaviour is not one which is universally accepted. Indeed some of the strongest opponents of this view are to be found amongst professional economists in government, business and universities. What I wish to do here is to consider in general the major arguments advanced for the view that economic *science* is impossible, then to show how I would go about meeting these objections in the context of one particular practical problem, the determination of the general level of money wages.

The subject-matter of economics is the ordinary person; and the ordinary person is very sensitive about his image of himself. The idea of laws—especially the eighteenth- and nineteenth-century idea of laws which grind forward inexorably with mechanical

[[1] Lister Lectureships were established by the British Association in 1958. They are designed to give young scientists an opportunity of reporting on the nature and significance of their work].

accuracy—applying to himself seems to rob the ordinary person of those facets which he regards as distinguishing him from the animal.

Human beings, it is argued, have "free will"; they are capable of changing their behaviour in quite unpredictable ways. Consider trying to predict such a simple thing as when an individual will board a bus or an underground train on his journey home from work. Whether he leaves early or late will depend on a vast number of things, things which have happened to him from without, so to speak, such as how much work is put into his IN tray and how many friends stop to chat with him during the day; and things which have happened from within, such as his own state of mind and body. Even if we could know and sum up all these influences, the individual could confound our predictions by an utterly capricious change of mind—*an exercise of free will.* Similarly, for such things as the wage bargain, the outcome depends on a vast number of factors—who the arbitrator is, who the union negotiator is, many facets of the climate of opinion, accidental occurrences, and on top of all this it can be influenced by utterly capricious acts on the part of the negotiators. Surely, it is argued, such occurrences cannot be subject to stable behaviour patterns which can be used for prediction. Sometimes economists content themselves with listing all of the factors which might influence the outcome of some phenomenon; but such "theory" does not get us very far and is often discouraging in that it paints a picture of an impossibly complex world in which simple stable patterns of behaviour appear to be most unlikely.

When contrasting the social and the natural sciences the general public and the professional economist usually look to classical physics and astronomy as models of science. Here the contrast is heightened by the nineteenth-century view of the physical world as a machine grinding forward with precision and inevitability. But even when a more subtle view is taken of these sciences, the great success of the impersonal scientific method in the study of the physical universe leads to gloom and often even defeatism on the part of the economists. Few economists who do look to science for guidance know much about chemistry and even fewer know anything about biology and other sciences which have problems much more akin to those of the Social Sciences but which have enjoyed undoubted success none the less.

Here then is the picture which seems to present itself: chaos and unpredictability in human affairs—in the simple case of the decision to go home, and in the economic case of, say, wage determination; this is contrasted with an orderly mechanical view of the physical world.

But there are certain general considerations which must make us mistrust this dichotomy between natural and social sciences. Although individual behaviour is very difficult to predict, group behaviour often shows remarkable constancy. Set people to measure the length of a room, and one person's errors are virtually impossible to predict; but ask many to do it and, by drawing a frequency distribution of the actual errors, you produce one of the most remarkable and beautiful of all constants, the *Normal Curve of Error*. We can in fact predict with amazing accuracy how *the group* will make errors. You cannot predict when one person will begin his journey home, but *en masse* this behaviour is wonderfully constant. The unpredictability of the individual is reduced to the regular graph of loads carried on public transport from hour to hour. On a normal day such charts can be used to predict with a high degree of accuracy how many people will travel from place to place at any time of the day. Also if you make a change, say, raise fares for journeys commenced between 5.15 and 5.45, you will reduce total travel in this half-hour period, and such a change will be clearly observable on the graphs. Here we have a stable change in human behaviour attributable to the *cause of the alteration in fares* (although of course John Jones, or any other single individual, may sometimes travel between 5.15 and 5.45 and sometimes travel outside of this period for reasons almost impossible to predict).

Now this should make us wonder if the same considerations might not apply to the wage bargain and other economic events. But in these cases we find not only individual behaviour which is difficult to predict, but also changing institutional circumstances so that, even if wage negotiations should show stable reactions to things like the level of unemployment in, say, the 1890s, we would hardly expect it to show the same reactions in the 1930s, let alone the 1950s. Surely the rise of unions and employers' organizations, the change in the level of negotiations (from the plant to the nation-wide bargain) and the increasing concern of government through such means as compulsory arbitration must mean that wages react to given circumstances in a very different way now than they did in the past.

Thus, it is argued, each historical period is unique and we cannot hope to get a theory applying to more than a few years at a time.

Now these are powerful arguments for the unpredictability of human behaviour in economics but, on the other hand, we do have general knowledge showing that we can get somewhere with a scientific inquiry into at least some spheres of human behaviour. How then should we proceed? Clearly the answer to our particular question about the possibility of finding stable, hence predictable, patterns of human behaviour in the economic sphere must be sought from empirical data. *A priori* arguments have been inconclusive; we cannot rule out stable behaviour in general because we have already found it in some cases, but we do not know how much we shall find and where we shall find it. We therefore frame the working hypotheses that group human behaviour shows stable patterns and that these patterns do not change in response to institutional variations. We then test this hypothesis against the data and abandon it only when forced to do so by the data.

Let me now try to illustrate all of this by making reference to the work that has been going on in the last few years, and in which I have played some small part, on the determination of the level of money wage rates. The general theory is that the level of demand for labour is an important determinant of wage changes.[1] More specifically it can be argued that, when there is positive excess demand for labour,[2] wage rates will rise, the larger the excess demand the faster the wage rise; and when there is excess supply wages will fall, the larger the excess supply the faster the fall in wages. Now the level of unemployment (i.e. the percentage of the labour force unemployed) is a reasonably good guide to the level of excess demand for labour, unemployment and excess demand varying inversely with each other.[3] We may thus look, to test our theory, for a relation between the level of unemployment (U) and

[1] To the non-economist to whom this may seem an obvious platitude it must be pointed out that this was not the prevailing view a few years ago and that it is still not accepted by many economists.

[2] Excess demand for labour is defined as: Demand for labour *minus* supply of labour; negative excess demand is often called excess supply.

[3] For a theoretical consideration of the precise relation see my "The Relation Between the Level of Unemployment and the Rate of Change of Unemployment in the U.K., 1861–1957: A Further Analysis", *Economica*, February, 1960, Section II (1). Since, even when there is large excess demand, labourers do change jobs, unemployment always exceeds zero.

the rate of change of money wage rates (W). The theory recognizes that many other factors affect the wage bargain but cuts through all of these to assert that demand is a most important factor and that we can get a long way by relating wages explicitly only to demand and by summing up the effects of all other factors in an error term, ϵ.

A casual glance at the time series for these two variables suggests that there is some relation. Now, in order to investigate this further, we can draw a scatter diagram plotting U on the horizontal axis

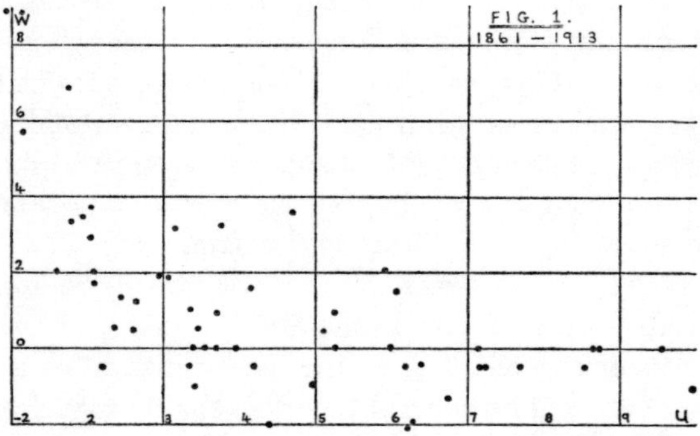

and W on the vertical one, where each dot represents the figures for unemployment and the change in wages for one particular year from 1861 to 1913 (Fig. 1). Now this graph is indeed very disappointing; there seems to be some sort of a vague relation but it does not seem to be a very strong one.

At this stage mental attitudes become critical. If we believe in the arguments against constant human behaviour patterns, we say, "just as I thought", and we give up. Many people have in fact looked at a scatter diagram containing more or less the information given in Fig. 1 and then given up. But, if we believe that there is a stability to be found, then we go back to the data and we try again.

We might then reason somewhat as follows: the near chaos is only apparent, there *must* be some order here. But there is not much order in what I see, so I must have left out some critical bit of information. Well, in Fig. 1 all points appear the same, but of course, they actually occur in a time sequence. Let us try dating

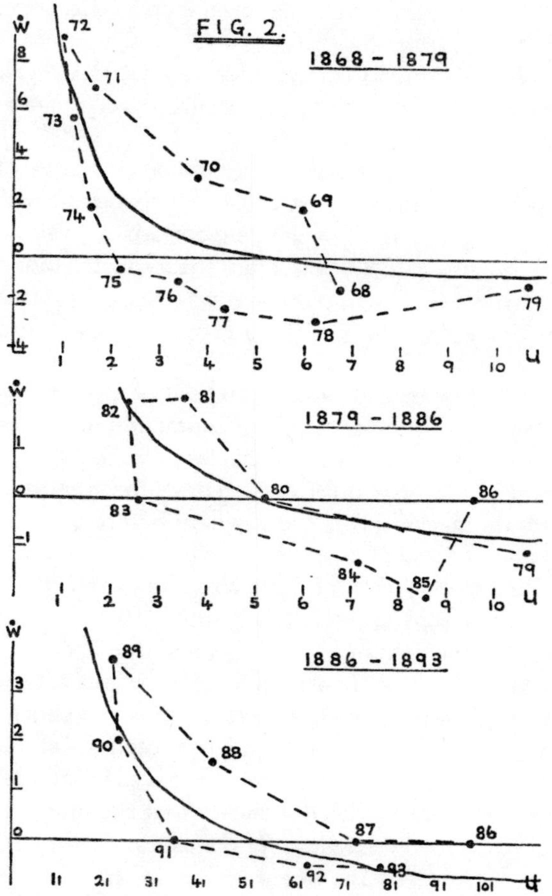

the points and observe the sequence in which they occur. When we do this we observe the most remarkable phenomenon. The points form very clear LOOPS, three of these loops being illustrated in Fig. 2. It will be seen that, on the upswing of a trade cycle when U is falling, W is high, while on the downswing when U is rising W is low.

We now fit a curve to all the points for the years 1861–1913.[1] This curve, which is shown in Fig. 2 describes the average relationships

[1] There are clear theoretical reasons for using a curve and not a straight line. See Lipsey, op. cit., Section II (1).

between *W* and U. When we relate each loop to this curve we find the following:

(1) Each complete loop corresponds to one trade cycle. (Over the nineteenth century these cycles occurred very regularly, each cycle lasting about eight to ten years.)

(2) The rising part of each loop lies above the curve of average relationship and the falling part of each loop lies below it. This indicates that, for any level of demand for labour, the wages rose faster when unemployment was falling (i.e. on the upswing of a cycle) and slower when unemployment was rising (i.e. on the downswing of a cycle). Now our original chaos has resolved into truly remarkable order!

Professor Phillips of the London School of Economics was the man who originally discovered this phenomenon of the loops.[1] He put forward a theory to account for the loops which, in my opinion, was incorrect.[2] But this does not matter; the important breakthrough was the discovery of order where before there seemed to be only chaos. The next stage is, of course, to advance a theory explaining this order; this Phillips also did. After that the new theory must be tested and, if it is refuted, this means that new knowledge (the observations which refuted the theory) has been brought to light. A new theory must then be put forward which explains the original phenomenon, but which is also consistent with the newly discovered observations which refuted the earlier theory.

The stage at which we now find ourselves is as follows: the observations seem to conform with our theory that the rate of change of money wages is related to the level of the excess demand for labour. We also have discovered the phenomenon of the loops, a relation between the rate of change of wages and the *rate of change* of unemployment. In this case I cannot as yet report to you a really satisfactory theory to explain this phenomenon. But now let us return to the theory of the relation between *W* and *U*.

We have found that, in the period before the First World War,

[1] A. W. Phillips, "The Relation Between Unemployment and the Rate of Change of Money Wage Rates in the U.K., 1861–1957", *Economica*, November, 1958.

[2] One cannot be dogmatic on so difficult a subject as yet; but see my forthcoming "A Test of Some Hypotheses Concerning the Relation Between the Rate of Change of Money Wages and the Rate of Change of Unemployment", to be published in *Economica*.

the rate of change of money wages was indeed related to the level of unemployment (with the proviso that the relation was different when unemployment was rising from what it is when it was falling). The next step is to discover how this remarkable relation has behaved over time. In Fig. 3 we draw the curve describing the average relation between *W* and *U* as it existed in the nineteenth century and we then draw in the points indicating the actual post-First-War observations.

Immediately after the First World War we observe what looks like near chaos again. Wages shoot up by more than 25 per cent per annum in 1918 and 1919 and then fall in 1921 and 1922 by almost the same amount. These movements appear to be unrelated to changes in unemployment. In fact they reflect two things:

(1) a tying of wages to the price level which seemed a good thing from the point of view of the unions when prices were steadily rising during the war;
(2) a violent set of fluctuations in the level of retail prices due mainly to even more violent fluctuations in primary prices throughout the world.

Then, after the immediate post-war chaos, things settle down again—but unfortunately they settle down at a very high level of unemployment. It will be noted that the points for the last half of the 1920s lie reasonably close to the curve.

Now this was the period in which England had gone back on the gold standard at what was then an overvalued rate of exchange. This meant that it was necessary to force down the British price level before a balance between exports and imports could be obtained. In the event, wages and prices fell very slowly and the gold standard was abandoned before the necessary reduction in the price level was accomplished.

The prevailing view then and now about the failure of the gold standard experiment in the 1920s was that it was frustrated by institutional changes occurring about the time of the First World War. In the nineteenth century, it was argued, wages would have fallen rapidly in the face of such heavy unemployment and, once the reduction in wage costs had been effected, prices would soon have followed. But around the time of the First World War all of this was changed because of changes in institutions. The rise of really

FIG. 3.

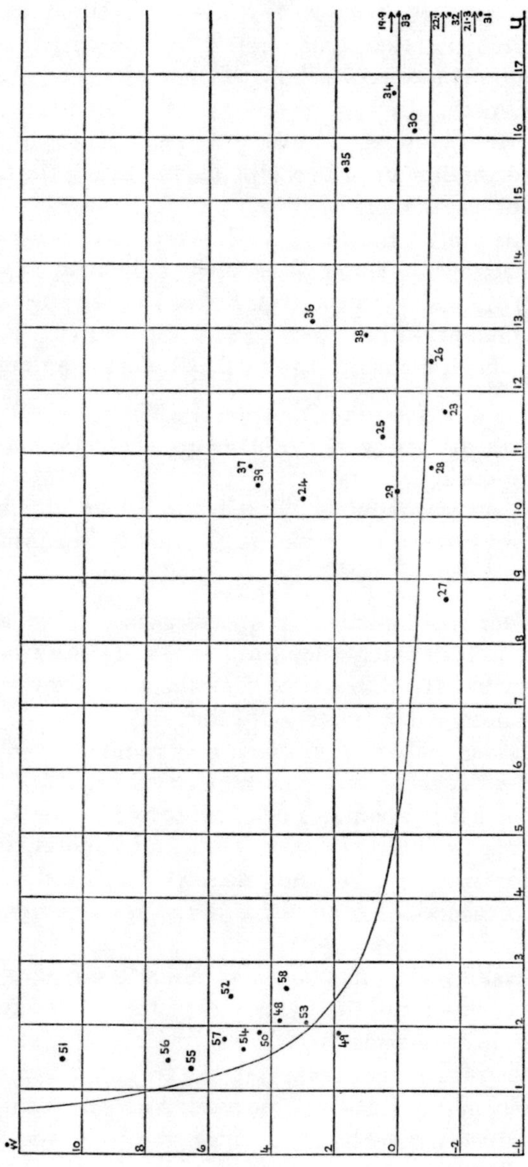

effective unions made wages very inflexible downwards and this policy of forcing down wages and prices, which would have worked in the nineteenth century, was frustrated by the changes. Clearly, and this was the important general inference, every historical period is unique and the experience of one period is no guide to that of another.

No one had bothered to lay out the data—although it was readily available at the time—and do an analysis such as I have just reported, so it was easy enough to hold this view. However, when Phillips did his analysis he found that the outcome of the disastrous experiment of the 1920s could have been predicted with considerable accuracy on the basis of the nineteenth-century experience. Phillips comments as follows on his analysis:[1]

> The decision to check demand in an attempt to force the price level down in order to restore the gold standard at the pre-war parity of sterling prevented the recovery of business activity and unemployment remained fairly steady between 9·7 per cent and 12·5 per cent from 1925 to 1929. The average level of unemployment during these five years was 10·94 per cent and the average rate of change of wage rates was —0·60 per cent per year. The rate of change of wage rates calculated from the curve fitted to the 1861–1913 data for a level of unemployment of 10·94 per cent is —0·56 per cent per year, in close agreement with the average observed value. Thus the evidence does not support the view, which is sometimes expressed, that the policy of forcing the price level down failed because of increased resistance to downward movements of wage rates. The actual results obtained, given the levels of unemployment which were held, could have been predicted fairly accurately from a study of the pre-war data, if anyone had felt inclined to carry out the necessary analysis.

This again is a case in which mental attitude is critical. If one believes the general *a priori* arguments about changes in institutions, one never seeks to compare different periods and one accepts quite uncritically the interpretation of the 1920s based on *changing* behaviour patterns. If, on the other hand, one accepts the working hypothesis which I suggested, "institutional variations do not upset stable behavioural patterns", then one does seek to predict the 1920s using the data for the nineteenth century; in this case the results would be satisfactory; even, however, if they are not then one has

[1] Phillips, op. cit., pp. 294–95.

discovered, by refuting the hypothesis, the direction and magnitude of the actual effects of institutional changes.

Now let us move on to consider two other time periods; that of the Great Depression in the 1930s and the period following the Second World War. In the very depths of the Great Depression, the years 1930 to 1932, unemployment was 16 per cent., 21 per cent. and 22 per cent. and the change in wage rates was approximately that predicted by the pre-First-War relation. Then from 1932 to 1939 unemployment fell every year (with the exception of 1938), but, even by the outbreak of the Second World War, unemployment had not fallen below the figure of 10 per cent. which signalled the depths of a severe depression in the nineteenth century. During this period of recovery, wage rates rose in spite of the very high average levels of unemployment. An inspection of the figures shows that although movements in W do not appear random in relation to U, the relation is very different from those experienced previously.

Here then our simple theory that there is a unique and stable relation between W and U has been refuted by observations over the whole recovery period of the Great Depression. What then are we to think? First, we might look for some simple explanation which saves the theory of a unique relation between W and excess demand. I have in fact tried to do this in my earlier article, putting forward the hypothesis that the rise in the average level of wages was caused by wage rises in certain sectors in which unemployment was very low. Since wages rise faster when U is low than they fall when U is high it follows that if unemployment is very unevenly distributed (as it was in the 1930s) W can be rising for the whole economy even though the average level of U is quite high. This theory preserved a unique stable relation between W and U for each sector of the economy while abandoning it (as the evidence had shown it must be abandoned) for the whole economy. Unfortunately, careful tests[1] showed this theory not to be in conformity with the evidence. Apparently more radical departures are necessary.

Next one should notice that the late 1930s constitute the only set of observations that we have of the recovery of the economy from so severe a depression. It is always possible that the behaviour of the economy is radically different in such a depression than it would be otherwise. Theories of this sort would require another depression

[1] See my forthcoming article already referred to.

as severe as that of the thirties to be tested. Fortunately we will probably never get another chance to do such testing.

All that one can say at the moment is that the 1930s constitute a refutation of the simple hypothesis and provide a challenge for explanation by some other hypothesis. One can take refuge in the "principle" of historical uniqueness and dismiss the thirties as a unique period never to be repeated and forget explanation. On the other hand one can try to find an explanation which preserves the general theory which does so well in most periods but which accommodates the 1930s as a special case. Such a theory is bound to have testable implications other than the ones that we already know. My own theory of sectorial inequalities was one of this sort and it was refuted by testing some of its other implications; it is along the lines of developing another theory of this sort that I am now working.

Now let us glance briefly at the figures for the 1950s. It will be seen that they lie pretty close to, but generally above, the curve fitted to the nineteenth-century data.[1] What are we to make of these observations? First there is quite clearly (and statistical analysis confirms this) a relation between *W* and *U*. The general hypothesis that there is such a relation continues to conform to the facts. Second, the observations definitely lie above the curve fitted to the nineteenth-century data, so that the simple hypothesis of a unique and stable relation is refuted.[2] Here at last we may have found the

[1] A plot of the crude unemployment figures as they are currently reported lies pretty well on the curve! It is generally agreed, however, that the definition of *U* has altered. The plotted figures for the post-war period have been corrected in an effort to make them comparable with those of the pre-war period. The corrections made are those that were suggested by G. Routh, an expert on the statistical data. See G. Routh, "The Relation Between Unemployment and the Rate of Change of Money Wage Rates in the U.K.: A Comment", *Economica*, November, 1959. Recently Professor Phillips has suggested to me that Routh's arguments about the changing definitions of *U* are incorrect and that *U* as measured in the nineteenth century is comparable with *U* as measured in the period following the Second World War. Should Phillips prove to be correct then a re-interpretation of the evidence will be necessary.

[2] This statement is not quite accurate. The observations show what actually happened to *W* and *U*. These occurrences are the result of a large number of *behavioural relations* between variables such as *W* and *U*. The *fitted relation* shown in the diagram is a *predicting relation* which predicts *W* from *U*, given all other associated changes which occur in the economy. It is just possible that the *predicting relation* has shifted without any change in the basic *behavioural relation* (showing the direct influence of *U* on *W*). Indeed contemplation of the effects of known changes in the economy on the fitted relation between *W* and *U* shows this to be a distinct possibility.

influence of changing institutions. Increased union power may mean that, for any given level of demand for labour, wages are now pushed up faster than previously. The shift in the relation (the average W over the period was 5·2 per cent. while the average predicted from the curve is 3·2 per cent.) would then be a measure of the quantitative importance of institutional shifts. Should this hypothesis of changing union strength pass other tests and be accepted (in the tentative sense in which any hypothesis is ever accepted), then we would have to abandon our original hypothesis that institutional changes had no effects on the relationship. But how much better to abandon the hypothesis after it has been carefully tested and how much better to have some *quantitative* idea of the amount by which these institutional changes have affected the behaviour of the system; how much better all this is than the position in which we find ourselves if we do not conduct the experiment at all on the grounds that institutional changes *must surely have upset the relationship*.

But another interpretation is possible. During the twentieth century cost-of-living adjustments have become important in wage determination. During the period following the Second World War the cost of living has been rising continuously. It is just possible that the same relation as existed earlier between W and U still holds but that the upward deviation of all the points represents the added influence of cost-of-living adjustments. There is, for example, little doubt that the extreme deviations in 1951 and 1952 were associated with the cost-of-living changes which were consequent on the Korean War. Clearly the various possible hypotheses have to be formulated carefully and tested comparatively before we can assess the significance of this shift. This is one of the tasks on which I am at present engaged.

This has been a very, very brief report on a series of hypotheses and empirical investigations in the field of aggregate wage determination.[1] I have been trying mainly to strike a note of hope for the scientific study of events in the economic sphere. But it is most important to note also the very severe handicaps under which economics does function as contrasted to the natural sciences. Some of the most severe problems are associated with the data. It is often

[1] The report has necessarily been on a somewhat intuitive level. The actual investigations have used more precise theoretical and statistical tools.

necessary to formulate and test a theory in the face of no more than ten or twenty observations. The theory on which I have been reporting can be tested against observations over the last one hundred years, but this is rare. Few series go back this far, some start after the First World War, some in the 1930s, many not until after the Second World War and, in many cases, we have no observations at all. In the course of my work it has sometimes become necessary to test the theories by testing their implications about the data for individual industries;[1] here it is often not possible to get annual observations before 1945, and where a series can be pushed back into the inter-war period, a really major effort is required to do so. This poverty of data is often a discouraging thing, but on the other hand it seems to me that it should be a great cause for hope as to the future of our science beyond our own life-times. Economists too often forget the myriads of observations carefully collected over *centuries* which preceded the development of the Ptolemaic cosmology, to say nothing of the revolutions of Copernicus, Kepler, Galileo and Newton. That economics has managed so much on the basis of a few observations collected over a few score of years should be a cause for great encouragement. For those of us who do not accept the defeatist arguments about the uniqueness of each historical period the prospect of future economists having at their disposal even a small fraction of the data available to Renaissance cosmologists is a most heartening thing. In the meantime, however, we stumble along with our desperately imperfect sets of observations.

Another data problem is that connected with the absence of controlled experiments in economics. Some economists have felt that, because of the impossibility of controlled experiments, economics could not be an empirical science. It is a mystery how this view could have been held in the presence of the obvious counter example of the science of astronomy. Controlled experiments obviously give tremendous advantages: they allow one to manufacture relevant evidence at will and they present the evidence in such a way that it is usually easily interpreted. The absence of controlled experiments means that we must wait for the passing of time to throw up evidence relevant to our hypotheses and on occasions we must wait

[1] See, for example, R. G. Lipsey and M. D. Steuer, "The Relation Between Profits and Wage Rates", *Economica*, May, 1961.

a very long time indeed. Also it is often necessary to treat our data with elaborate statistical techniques in order to interpret it correctly; too many things are happening at once for our evidence to be easily and straightforwardly interpreted.[1]

One is left, at the end of all this, with a feeling of the possibility of a truly scientific study of human behaviour in the economic sphere and with an attitude of optimism about the long-term development of such a science. In the past, economists both amateur and professional, have: (1) taken too much to heart the difficulties of predicting individual behaviour and forgotten the remarkable group stability in many human fields; (2) been very discouraged by contrasting social sciences with an outdated, nineteenth-century view of physics, when a look at other sciences, or even a more critical look at physics and astronomy, would have given more cause for optimism; (3) been too easily convinced, *a priori*, that every historical sequence is unique. When in fact we take a look in a sphere most affected by these defeatist arguments we find evidence of simple behaviour patterns, remarkably stable over, what in economics, is a very long period of time, and, when complete stability has not been maintained, we find what looks like a reasonable chance of developing and extending our theories to cover these more complex patterns of behaviour.

[1] Having enough real difficulties with data there is no need, as is so often done, to invent non-existent difficulties. It has been argued to me, for instance, by several eminent economists that the whole of the theorizing and testing which I have reported is worthless because the wrong variable is employed. The theory uses *wage rates* which are the standard rates agreed at the union–management bargain; it is argued that *wage earnings*, which are the actual amounts earned allowing for bonuses, overtime, short-time, etc., should be used instead. To argue in this way is to ignore the facts that an empirical relation has been discovered between wage *rates* and unemployment, that a theory of the dependence of *rates* on unemployment has been put forward, and that this theory has passed tests other than the ones reported here. It also ignores the fact that, although *a priori* reasoning can suggest many reasons why rates and earnings might not move together, they do in fact stay, over any long period of time, remarkably close together, so that any theory which explains one will go a long way towards explaining the other. To dismiss a successful theory on the grounds that something else might have been made the subject of the theory is typical of the *a priori* and cavalier manner in which empirical evidence has been dismissed by so many economists.

4

THE LANGUAGE OF ECONOMICS

J. K. GALBRAITH

Granada Lecture, Guildhall, October, 1962

AMONG the social sciences, and indeed among the reputable fields of learning, economics occupies a special place for the reproach that is inspired by its language. The literate layman regularly "proclaims his discontent with the way in which economists express themselves". Other scholars emerge from the eccentricities of their own terminology to condemn the economist for a special commitment to obscurity. If an economist writes a book or even an article in clear English he is praised for avoiding jargon—and also for risking the rebuke of his professional colleagues. And economists themselves, in their frequent exercises in introspection, regularly inquire whether they are making themselves intelligible to students, politicians or the public at large. Committees empanelled to consider the matter invariably urge improvement.

My purpose in this paper is to go into these charges and assess their substance. My ambition is to put a period, or at least a semicolon, to this discussion. For I hope to show that the transgressions of the economists in the matter of communicating their thoughts are not especially grave. Some of the fault lies in the attitudes, including the insufficient diligence, of those who lead the attack. Some is in the sociology of the profession and may not be peculiar to economists.

The language of economics is commonly indicted on three different counts. It is of some importance that these charges, which often are mixed together, be kept separate. They are:

1. That the concepts and terminology of economics are complex and artificial and exceedingly confusing to the layman.

2. That economists are bad writers. And it is said that obscure

and difficult language may even enhance a man's professional standing.

3. That arcane concepts and obscure language are symptoms of deeper disorder. So far from seeking communication with the world at large, the tendency of economics is to divorce itself therefrom and construct an unreal universe of its own.

I shall take up these several charges in turn. Each calls for a progressively more detailed examination.

II

That economics has a considerable conceptual apparatus with an appropriate terminology cannot be a serious ground for complaint. Economic phenomena, ideas and instruments of analysis exist. They must have names. No one can reasonably ask a serious scholar to avoid reference to index numbers, the capital gains tax, the consumption function, acceleration effects, circular money flows, inflation, linear programming, the progressive income tax, the pure rate of interest or the European Common Market. Nor should he be expected to explain what these are. Education in economics is, in considerable measure, an introduction to this terminology and to the ideas that it denotes. Anyone who has difficulties with the ideas should complete his education or, following an exceedingly well-beaten path, leave the subject alone. It is sometimes said that the economist has a special obligation to make himself understood because his subject is of such great and popular importance. By this rule the nuclear physicist would have to speak in monosyllables.

A physician, at least in the United States, does not tell you that a patient is dying. He says that the prognosis is without important areas of encouragement. The dead man becomes not that to his lawyer but the decedent. Diplomats never tell or ask. They make representations. Economists have similar vanities of expression and an accomplished practitioner can often get the words parameter, stochastic and aggregation into a single sentence.[1] But it would be hard to prove that the working terminology of the subject is more pretentious or otherwise oppressive than that of jurisprudence, embryology or advanced poultry husbandry. One indication that

[1] Arcane terminology and esoteric concepts do play a certain role in the prestige system of the subject to which I shall return.

it is not is the speed with which the important words and ideas—gross national product, compensatory fiscal policy, GATT, international liquidity, product differentiation—pass into general use.

I turn now to the quality of writing in economics.

III

Anyone who wishes to contend that economists are bad writers is faced with the fact that no learned discipline unconnected with literature or the arts has had such distinguished ones. Everyone has his own test of good writing. I would urge a multiple one in which particular excellence in one respect is allowed to offset lesser achievement in others.

Thus power and resourcefulness of language are important, as are purity and distinction of style. The latter means that writing is identified with personality—that it does not have the rigid homogeneity sometimes associated with scientific prose. Nor should it. Language has many dimensions. It does not convey meaning more accurately by being completely flat.

Good writing, and this is especially important in a subject such as economics, must also involve the reader in the matter at hand. It is not enough to explain. The images that are in the mind of the writer must be made to reappear in the mind of the reader, and it is the absence of this ability that causes much economic writing to be condemned, quite properly, as abstract.

Finally, I doubt that good economic writing can be devoid of humour. This is not because it is the task of the economist to entertain or amuse. Nothing could be more abhorrent to the Calvinism which underlies all scientific attitudes. But humour is an index of the ability to detach self from subject and this is of scientific utility. In considering economic behaviour it is especially important for, needless to say, much of that behaviour is infinitely ridiculous.

An impressive number of English-writing economists qualify strongly by these standards. At the head of the list, if I may digress for a moment into literary criticism, I would put Adam Smith. In both purity of style and certainty in his command of language he is inferior to J. S. Mill. But he is effective and resourceful in exposition and far superior to Mill in imagery and humour. Smith knew that a trip into the pin factory to see the division of labour in operation would establish the importance of the phenomenon for good. (Pins were also an excellent selection. Something more important might have been dismissed as a special example of scientific management occasioned by the social need for the output.) Similarly, a less amused man would simply have condemned merchants for a wilful tendency to conspire against the public. The merchants would have replied, not without indignation, and being men of influence and admitted respectability, their view would have prevailed. Their critic would have been dismissed as a scold. But Smith assembled them for the most innocent and convivial divertissement and then found them relentlessly impelled into designs for bilking the public. Neither anger nor sorrow were in order; only reflection on man's inability to resist the opportunity to turn an improper penny. In this form the indictment has never been lifted. To this day, in the United States at least, even a brief exchange of words between two competitors is assumed by observers to be costing someone some money. Such craftsmanship was far beyond the reach of Mill.

To the list of truly talented writers I would also add Thorstein Veblen. His prose lacked everything that Mill's possessed—it was graceless, difficult and often highly contrived. But it too had vitality, versatility and imagery. As Smith's merchants remained permanently under suspicion of restraint of trade, so Veblen's rich never recovered from the sardonic disdain with which he analysed their impulse to vulgarity. The manners of an entire society were altered as a result. The phrase "conspicuous consumption" ruined the real estate market in Newport. "Conspicuous leisure" made it difficult for even the daughters of the rich to relax.

The list of distinguished as distinct from talented writers—the elder Mill, Malthus, Henry George, Alfred Marshall and (subject to some reservations to be mentioned presently) Lord Keynes—is also a considerable one. So it would be difficult, on the general evidence, to find fault with the literary qualifications of the English-speaking economists.

IV

Perhaps, however, this does not quite settle things. It will be said that when economists have gone to the technical heart of the matter, as did Ricardo in *Principles*, or as they have come up against the full complexity of modern economic problems, as did Keynes in *The General Theory*, they have become much less lucid and accessible. Some will surely think it significant that the best writer by my accounting was so nearly the first. Were Smith or Mill writing today, they would be relegated to the annual economic surveys of the *New York Times* or to the coloured pages inserted at intervals by *The Economist* as, one is told, its surrogate for sex.

This confuses the problem of complex exposition or scientific perception with bad writing. Ricardo's problems were no more difficult than those which were lucidly discussed by Malthus or Mill and he did not go into them very much more deeply. Ricardo's reputation as a bad writer is amply deserved. He was, in addition, an unscientific one. His prose was awkward, uncertain and unpredictable as to meaning conveyed, and it was his habit to state strong propositions and then qualify them to possible extinction. His natural price of labour was such as to "enable labourers, one with another, to subsist and perpetuate their race". But within a page or two the application of this heroic (and historic) law was suspended in "improving" societies of which contemporary England was obviously one. The notion of subsistence was also enlarged to include conveniences, these being any luxuries to which the worker had become or might become accustomed. And the population theory on which the proposition depended was modified to exclude Englishmen although it was deemed to have full force and effect for the Irish. This is neither good writing nor good scientific method. It is bad writing based on incomplete thought.

The writing in Keynes's *General Theory* justifies similar if somewhat less severe comment. Keynes has been widely acclaimed as a master of English prose. A good part of this applause has come from economists who are not the best of judges. More rests on his handling of easy subjects. But the test of a writer is not whether he can produce a Philippic on the Versailles Treaty or the hard money policies of Winston Churchill, or an agreeable memoir on an academic contemporary, but whether he remains with a difficult subject until he has thought through not only the problem but its exposition. This Keynes did not do. The *General Theory* is an acrostic of English prose and the fact that it was an important book should not cause anyone to say that it was well written or even finished. Though new, the theory was still of the same *genre* as that presented with competence by A. C. Pigou and a certain churchly eloquence by Alfred Marshall. Other writers—Mrs. Joan Robinson, Professors Hansen, Harris and Samuelson—turned Keynes's ideas into accessible English, thus showing that it could be done. A better writer—patience has a certain standing as one constituent of genius—would have done the job himself.[1]

I would conclude, therefore, that ideas of the *General Theory* are within the competence of clear English supported by the necessary knowledge of economic terminology and concepts. There is one further and final question, which is whether clear and unambiguous statement is the best medium for persuasion in economics. And here, I think, one may have doubts.

V

Had the Bible been written in clear, straightforward, non-contradictory language, and had the language been constantly modernized to accord with contemporary taste, it would almost certainly have been, or have become, a work of lesser influence. In the familiar or King James version it has three compelling qualities. The archaic constructions and terminology put some special strain on the reader. Accordingly, by the time he has worked his way through (say) the Book of Leviticus he has a certain vested interest in what he has read. It is not something to be dismissed like a leader in yesterday's newspaper. Too much work has gone into it.

The contradictions of the Old Testament also mean that with a little effort anyone can find a faith that accords with his preferences and, within limits, a code of behaviour which is agreeable to his tastes. Thus heretics and sinners are not extruded; they are accommodated a little later on.

[1] Those who think this underestimates the difficulty of the ideas with which Keynes was dealing will do well to notice the carelessness of his non-technical expression in this volume. The following is from a summary of his position in an early chapter: "The celebrated *optimism* of traditional economic theory, which has led to economists being looked upon as Candides, who, having left this world for the cultivation of their gardens, teach that all is for the best in the best of all possible worlds provided we will let well enough alone, is also to be traced, I think, to their having neglected to take account of the drag on prosperity which can be exercised by an insufficiency of effective demand." (*The General Theory of Employment, Interest and Money*. London. Macmillan & Co. Ltd., 1936, p. 33.)

Finally the ambiguities of the Scriptures provide the occasion for debate over what is meant. This also is most important for attracting belief, for in the course of urging a particular position the disputant, often unknowingly, becomes committed to the larger Writ.

Difficulty, contradiction and ambiguity have similar advantages in economics. Anyone who worked his way through Ricardo, Marx or Keynes was likely to justify the effort by according the author at least an element of belief. Ricardo and Marx were sufficiently replete with qualification or contradiction so that the reader could provide himself with the interpretation he preferred.[1] All three were richly productive of argument as to intended meaning. Many hundreds, and even thousands, read these authors less for wisdom than because they wished to participate in a reasonably impressive way in the exciting, fashionable or politically imperative arguments over what was said.

The case of Keynes is especially interesting because prior to the publication of the immensely difficult *General Theory*, he had advocated many of its conclusions—in particular its antidote for depression—in clear English in both the United States and Great Britain. He had not been greatly influential. He won influence by involving economists in a highly professional debate on technical concepts and their interpretation. His practical recommendations did not play an important part in this discussion. But the participants then carried his practical programme to Washington and Whitehall. Would a simple, clearly argued brief such as later produced by (among others) professor Hansen have been as influential? My reluctant inclination is to doubt it.

Yet the clear writers also had influence. And ambiguity is a tactic which not everyone should try. Economists will seize upon the ill-expressed ideas of a very great man and argue over what he had in mind. Others had better not run the risk. Here I can perhaps be allowed to advert briefly to personal experience.

[1] No great figure since biblical times has lent himself to such varied interpretation as Marx. This arises partly from the manner of expression, partly from contradiction inherent in some of the ideas and partly from the fact that so much of his work was uncompleted at his death and conflicts that might otherwise have been cleared up by revision or deletion were carried into print. But it is also important to bear in mind that Marx is the only writer since biblical times for whom reinterpretation is not a scholarly pursuit but a profession.

In the years following World War II, drawing on the Keynesian Revolution, the substantial revision of the ideas and empirical view of monopoly in the previous decade, and my own experience as principal wartime price-fixer in the United States, I produced a small book on the strategy of resource mobilization in the market economy.[1] It was of modest technical difficulty—about that of a non-mathematical article in *The Economic Journal*. I then thought, and I continue to think, that it formulated the problem of resource mobilization accurately and comprehensively for the first time and that it corrected ideas about the strategy of fiscal policy and control which were seriously and perhaps dangerously in error. My high opinion of the book was shared by three or four other economists who chanced to read it. Alas, these were all. The book sank without trace. I reflected deeply on this experience, and the investment of time involved. I concluded that the only safe and certain way to engage the attention of my professional colleagues was to capture the interest of some part of the literate public at large. A professor of economics who was asked with sufficient frequency, "How do I answer Galbraith?", would then have no recourse but to read him. On the whole I am not discontented with the outcome of this experiment.

VI

So far I have been dealing with (by broad definition) classical rather than contemporary writing in economics. The time has come to consider the complex language and the difficult mathematics of the current contributions not only to *Econometrica* and *The Review of Economic Studies*, but also of many of the articles in *The Economic Journal* amd *The American Economic Review*. And here the question ceases to be purely one of language. These articles are obviously beyond the reach of the intelligent layman. Is it possible that they are also out of touch with reality? Doubt is not confined to non-economists and it transcends ideology. Professor Samuelson, in his recent presidential address to the American Economic Association, noted that three previous presidential addresses in succession had been devoted to a denunciation of mathematical economics and that the most trenchant had encouraged the audience to standing

[1] *A Theory of Price Control.* Harvard University Press. Oxford, 1952.

applause.[1] Three years ago, while on a visit to Soviet economists, I spent a long afternoon attending a discussion on the use of mathematical models in plan formation. At the conclusion an elderly scholar, who had also found it very heavy going, asked me if I didn't think there was still a "certain place" for old-fashioned formulations of the labour theory of value.

The full answer invokes much less the language or method of economics than its sociology. Once this is understood the layman can view what he does not understand with some equanimity. And members of other scholarly disciplines can concentrate on the oddities of their own guild.

Professional economists, like members of city gangs, religious congregations, public schools, aboriginal tribes, fashionable regiments, craft unions, clubs, learned disciplines, holders of diplomatic passports and, one is told, the intellectually more demanding criminal pursuits, have the natural desire of all such groups to delineate and safeguard the boundary between those who belong and those who do not. This has variously been called the tribal, gang, club, guild, union or aristocratic instinct.

The differentiation of those who belong from those who do not is invariably complemented by a well-graded prestige system within the tribal group. And—a vital point—the two are closely interdependent. If the members of the tribal group are sufficiently conscious of the boundary that separates them from the rest of the world, the tribe becomes *the* world to its members. Its limits and the mental horizons of the members are coterminous. This means, in turn, that the prestige system of the tribe is the only one that has meaning to a member and it is all-important. The most honorific position in the tribal group then becomes the most honorific position in the universe. If the school is all that counts, then the head boy is a person of the greatest possible grandeur. In the Barchester Close the eminence of the Bishop was absolute because no one was aware of the world beyond. Among the professionally erotic, the position of a famous film star is similar. Everything within, in each case, depends on the exclusion of what is without.

The prestige system of economics is wholly in accord with these principles. It assigns, and for good reason, the very lowest position

[1] "Economics and the History of Ideas", P. A. Samuelson, *American Economic Review*, March, 1962, Vol. LII, No. 1, p. 2.

to the man who deals with everyday policy. For this individual, in concerning himself with the wisdom of a round of wage increases or the need for an addition to the deficit, is immediately caught up in a variety of political and moral judgements. As such he is a threat to the sharp delineation which separates the tribal group from the rest of society and thus to the prestige system of the profession. Moreover, his achievements are rated not by his professional peers, but by outsiders. This causes difficulty in fitting him into the professional hierarchy and argues strongly for leaving him at the bottom.[1] [2]

A very low position is also assigned to economists who, even though forswearing any interest in practical affairs, occupy themselves with related disciplines—urban sociology, political theory, cultural anthropology, juvenile delinquency. The reason is the same. These men are also inimical to the tribal delineation and their achievements depend on the judgement of non-economists and thus cannot be integrated into the established scale. An economist who concerns himself with sociology is assumed by his colleagues to be escaping the rigours of his own subject and by sociologists to be showing slightly broadened tendencies of mind.

At the higher levels, economics divorces itself fully from practical questions and from the influence of other fields of scholarship with the exception of mathematics and statistics. One can think of the

[1] In the United States, at least, a similar disposition is made of members who, being good or entertaining teachers, are accorded the applause of their students.

[2] Thus during his life Keynes was held in rather low regard. In his *History of Economic Analysis*, which is an authoritative view of professional precedence, Professor Schumpeter affirms this judgement and bases his disapproval on Keynes's insistent advocacy of practical measures. (He condemned Ricardo on similar grounds.) In 1936, the year of the publication of *The General Theory*, the Harvard Department of Economics was asked to make up a list of the world's leading economists to be honoured at the Tercentenary celebrations of that year. The suggestion that Keynes's name be included was dismissed as eccentric. At the time of his election to the United States Senate, Professor Paul Douglas had a very high position in the prestige system of the profession and, indeed, had just completed his term as President of the American Economic Association. While economists continued to take pride in his accomplishments, and especially have welcomed his demonstration of the versatility of their craft, he was promptly demoted in professional rank. No grave professional importance could any longer be attached to his writing or his stand on technical issues. From being a leading economist he became the leading economist in politics. This resolution of the matter is certainly a sensible one. To fit a United States Senator into the prestige system of the profession would be without workable precedent and otherwise would be very difficult. Better to compromise on purely nominal rank.

full prestige structure of the subject in terms of a hollow pyramid or cone, the sides of which, though they are transparent and with numerous openings at the base, becomes increasingly opaque and impermeable as one proceeds to the apex. Positions near the apex, those of greatest prestige, are fully protected from external influence. Work near the top is pure in the sense of excluding questions of practical application and purely economic in that it excludes the influence of other disciplines. If practical application is unimportant, parameters and variables can then be accommodated to the analytical techniques which are available or which the scholar wishes to use. This work is not mathematical *per se* but it lends itself well to mathematical treatment. Needless to say, communication is closely confined to those within the pyramid and advancement to higher levels within the pyramid is wholly by the agency of the occupants. The standards of accomplishment which lead to recognition are thus self-perpetuating. It is no criticism of this work that it is unrelated to the real world. The divorce therefrom is an inherent feature.[1]

VII

It is no part of my present task to pass judgement on this prestige structure or to compare it with that of other learned disciplines. In a world where for pedagogy and other purposes a very large number of economists is required, an arrangement which discourages a certain proportion from rendering public advice would seem to be well conceived. Much of the discussion, in the upper reaches of the pyramid, can be criticized as idle—models unrelated to reality are constructed, commended, criticized, amended and then completely forgotten. But, as often happens, there is no ready way of separating the valueless work from the possibly valuable and the effort would be intrinsically damaging. It is the good fortune of the affluent

[1] This explains why professional economists of the highest standing can and often do come forward with proposals—for the abolition of corporations or trade unions, the outlawing of oligopoly, the enforcement of free competition, therapeutic unemployment, cathartic deflation, elimination of central banks, ending of income taxes—of the most impractical sort without damage to their reputations. No particular store is set by ability to assess such measures in their political and social context. The man of prestige has naturally learned to be indifferent to irrelevant measures of achievement.

country that the opportunity cost of the economist is low and hence it can afford all kinds. For instruction the models are valuable. The oldest problem in economic education is how to exclude the incompetent. A certain glib mastery of verbiage—the ability to speak portentously and sententiously about the relation of wages to productivity or central bank policy to the price level—is easy for the unlearned and may even be aided by a mildly enfeebled intellect. The requirement that there be ability to master difficult models, including ones for which mathematical competence is required, is a highly useful screening device.[1]

What is clear from this brief view of the sociology of the subject, and this is the matter of present importance, is the view which the intelligent layman and the inquiring scholar from another discipline should take of contemporary economic literature. The relevance of much of this writing is not great. Much of it, and more especially that exchanged in the upper levels of the pyramid, may with good conscience be ignored.[2] Since so far from being addressed to outsiders it is designed to exclude them, the outsiders should take the hint. In any case, the outsider is presumably interested in economics as it bears on matters of practical policy or as it is related to other disciplines. These matters are consciously excluded within the upper levels of the pyramid. The work at the non-prestiginous lower edges does not lend itself to highly technical and mathematical treatment. This is the part that is important to the outsider; while he may not find it easy, he is not excluded.

As I noted at the outset, I would not excuse anyone from mastering the basic ideas and terminology of economics. He must expect

[1] There can be no question, however, that excessive and prolonged commitment to mathematical exercises in economics is damaging. It leads to the atrophy of judgement and intuition which are indispensable for real solutions and, on occasion, leads also to the habit of mind which simply excludes the mathematically inconvenient factors from consideration.

[2] He may take comfort from the fact that the most esoteric of this material is not read by other economists or even by the editors who publish it. In the economics profession the editorship of a learned journal not specialized to econometrics or mathematical statistics is a position of only moderate prestige. It is accepted, moreover, that the editor must have a certain measure of practical judgement. This means that he is usually unable to read the most prestiginous contributions which, none the less, he must publish. So it is the practice of the editor to associate with himself a mathematical curate who passes on this part of the work and whose word he takes. A certain embarrassed silence covers the arrangement.

also to encounter good economists who are difficult writers even though some of the best have been very good writers. He should know, moreover, that at least for a few great men ambiguity of expression has been a positive asset. But given the foregoing, he may then conclude that what remains wholly mysterious is most likely to be, for him, unimportant.

5

ECONOMICS IN UNWONTED PLACES

B. R. WILLIAMS

Southampton, August, 1964

ONE hundred years ago the President of the Economics and Statistics section of the British Association was William Farr, M.D., F.R.S. Farr, after a training in medicine, joined the Registrar General's office. He published many papers on general statistics, prepared life tables for insurance, wrote the greater part of the Census Reports of 1851, 1861 and 1871, and resigned when, at the age of 72, he failed to obtain the post of Registrar General.

Farr had a rather naïve belief in the power of statistical tables to solve the difficult problems of Political Economy, and the power of numerical evidence to determine public policy. In his Presidential address he asserted that because "statistics admits of many practical applications this naturally commends the study to the minds of Englishmen"; that "the statistical argument in favour of free trade is accumulating; it gains fresh force in every table, and will in the end lead all nations to exchange their products freely"; that statistics "enables Governments to count the cost of war and to weigh its results against expenses".

Although much of his approach has a curiously old-fashioned air, his emphasis on the need for "results–expenses analysis" has not. Cost–benefit analysis, as we now call it, has become very fashionable in academies, and had more notice been taken of Farr's plea for adequate statistical information we would be in a better position to make use of such calculations to guide decisions on public expenditure. Public expenditure is over one-third of national expenditure, but to most of it we cannot apply the market test of whether results (in the form of sales) are greater than the expenses of production. To find out whether the Government should be spending more or less than £450 million on research and development, £1,000 million on education, £250 million on highways and so on, we have to develop special ways of calculating a results–expenses balance. Failure to take account of this balance leads to the wrong use of resources and to less growth in output per man-hour, and less material satisfaction than we could achieve.

Cost–Benefit Analysis in the Public Sector

The modern interest in cost–benefit analysis started, I understand, within the U.S. Army and then spread to the highway and natural resources engineers. In Britain the growth of interest has been more recent, and the area of public expenditure for which reasonable cost–benefit calculations have been made is very small indeed.

Owing mainly to the work of the Road Research Board, there is now a considerable amount of worthwhile information about the social return to be expected from capital invested in the M1 motorway, the relative merits of investment in new motorways and other road works, and the net social benefits likely to accrue if taxes paid by users of motor vehicles were more closely related to costs of road use. We also have the Beesley–Foster cost–benefit analysis of the new Euston–Victoria line,[1] and the Buchanan report on *Traffic in Towns*, concerned with "the long-term development of roads and traffic in urban areas, and their influence on the urban environment". Although Buchanan used an arbitrary "town planner's" version of cost–benefit analysis, and concentrated on the means and costs of *curing* traffic congestion at the expense of the means and costs of *preventing* it, he produced a very important report; not least because it was commissioned by the Ministry of Transport.

It must be admitted that the cost–benefit analyses of the M1 and the Euston–Victoria line were made after the investment decisions had been made, and that rural motorways still constitute a higher proportion of new road construction than cost–benefit analysis can justify. However, an important start has been made, and perhaps

[1] See, for example, *Road Research Technical Papers*, 46 and 48, 1960, and BE 246, 1963; *Road Pricing*, Ministry of Transport, 1964; Foster and Beesley, "Estimating the Social Benefit from Constructing an Underground Railway in London", *Journal of the Royal Statistical Society*, 1963.

before very long cost–benefit analyses will be undertaken to inform and, we may hope, to improve the decision process.

So far as I know, there are no very good British examples of cost–benefit analysis in the fields of defence and health. Nor, despite Adam Smith's ancient demonstration of the similarities between investment in people and investment in machinery, are there good calculations of actual and potential rates of return to investment in education to act as a guide to educational expenditure of various kinds. True, the Robbins and Newsom reports have both produced strong general arguments for believing that the benefits to be gained from greater expenditure on education would exceed the costs. The arguments were, however, too general to provide a useful guide either to short-term priorities in expenditure or to the long-term objectives. For that we need a much more detailed study of the effects of various kinds and lengths of education on both personal development and economic growth.

It would be absurd to suggest that economists and calculators can use cost–benefit analysis to take the difficulty out of decisions to spend on health and education. They cannot. In both cases only part of the expenditure can reasonably be classified as investment. The consumption part—on which for obvious reasons practitioners in both fields tend to place a rather excessive emphasis—throws up problems of valuation which the calculators cannot solve. They can only work out the numerical implications of different value judgements and so make the decision process more informed. They can also calculate the rates of benefit–cost surplus on alternative programmes. Indeed, until this is done, we cannot make sensible choices between alternative uses of scarce resources. We may simply go on believing that there are *right* solutions that we must adopt regardless of cost. This is a form of lunacy which has come to be exposed, though not yet cured, by thought about the problems of expanding rapidly the numbers in higher education.[1]

The application of cost–benefit analysis to expenditure on applied research and development should be rather easier. For unless we

[1] I have examined some of the implications of treating Universities as multi-product firms in "Capacity and Output of Universities", *The Manchester School*, May, 1963. For some of the financial implications of this form of analysis, see Carter and Williams, "Proposals for Reform in University Finance", *The Manchester School*, September, 1963

equate even applied research to opera and such delights, we can measure the potential benefits in fairly simple commercial terms. However, cost–benefit analysis of public expenditure on applied research and development has developed very slowly. For the most part Government expenditure on research and development has been based on a popular, but quite unproved, belief that if research and development as a percentage of net product is high, that is good for growth. Not only has there been little attempt to measure the benefits,[1] but in measuring the cost of the operation the side effects on the deployment of scarce scientific manpower—which is used both for creating new science and technology and for applying science and technology to industry—have been neglected. The possible significance of this can be demonstrated by a few rough calculations relating to Germany and Britain. The stock of qualified scientists and engineers is about the same percentage of working population in both countries. But whereas Britain is spending nearly 3 per cent. of net product on research and development, Germany is spending a little over 1 per cent. Allowing for the higher cost per scientist and engineer engaged in British research and development, it appears that Britain uses twice as many qualified scientists and engineers as Germany in trying to create new science and technology and half as many in trying to *apply* science and technology to industry. There is now a good deal of evidence that the British deployment of scientific manpower has actually hindered the rapid application of "science" to industry. We need scientific manpower to use science in industry, but we need not, and cannot, grow all science at home. To refer to Germany as an example of "Prosperity Without Science" (as does *The Economist* of 22nd June, 1963) is to misunderstand the whole process. A country may use a great deal of science without making any attempt to add to scientific knowledge by research. A great deal of confusion has resulted from failure to distinguish between the stock of scientific and technological knowledge and the activity of adding to that stock by research and development.

The absence of appropriate cost–benefit analysis shows not only

[1] For an attempt, see R. Ewell in *Chemical & Engineering News*, 1955, pp. 2980–6. For critical analysis see F. Machlup, *The Production and Distribution of Knowledge in the United States* (Princeton, 1963), and B. R. Williams, *Investment and Technology in Growth* (Manchester Statistical Society, 1964).

in general Government decisions on public expenditure but also in Ministerial decisions on the operation of public enterprises. We can use the case of electricity to illustrate this point.[1] There seems little doubt that the large Government outlay on research has been a factor of importance in decisions on the power plants to be used. The Government made available to the Atomic Energy Authority large sums for the development of nuclear reactors, in the expectation that there would be a handsome pay-off in the form of cost-reducing power stations and export business. In 1955 when coal was expected to remain in short supply it was decided to install 1,500–2,000 MW of nuclear capacity by 1965, and in 1957, when oil supplies were thought to be at risk, this figure was revised to 5,000–6,000 MW. When it became clear that the nuclear reactors would be very far from economic the 5,000 MW programme was extended from 1965 to 1968. Because of these investment decisions, the generating costs of electricity are something like £20 million a year higher than need be.

There appear to be three explanations of this costly policy. First, in the calculations of when nuclear stations would become economic, nuclear engineers made no (or quite insufficient) allowance for progress in the design of conventional stations. This has been, predictably, considerable. Their judgement was as impetuous as that of the English cricket journalists who heard that the Australian team was the weakest on record and took it for granted that England would retain the Ashes. In most interesting things there is more than one variable. The second reason is that the capital cost of nuclear stations is much higher than in conventional stations. Because of this, higher interest rates pushed up nuclear costs more than conventional costs. The third reason, given in the White Paper on nuclear power, is that it has been made "less economic by the increased emphasis on earning a proper rate of return". This extraordinary statement needs some explanation. One cost of production is the depreciation of the plant used, which is higher in nuclear than in conventional stations. However, until 1957 the Ministry looked

[1] The reports of the Select Committee on the Nationalized Industries make it clear that investment decisions have often been irrational. For an analytical summary of practices and a comment on the rather mixed-up White Paper on "The Financial and Economic Obligations of the Nationalized Industries" (Cmnd. 1337) see Merrett and Sykes, "The Financial Control of State Industry", *The Banker*, March and April, 1962.

at returns on capital before depreciation.[1] When after 1957 it started to take depreciation into account this constituted a very nasty blow to the estimated economics of nuclear power.

It would be easy to draw up a very long list of cases in the public sector where cost–benefit analysis has been neglected. For instance, the aircraft industry for much of the post-war period had such lavish Government aid that it was responsible for one-third of our total research and development expenditure. Yet it contributed less than 5 per cent. to our exports, and nothing spectacular in the way of new technologies to other industries. However, concentration on the public sector would be misleading. For cost–benefit analysis has also been neglected in the private sector, though the neglect has been less publicized.

Cost–Benefit Analysis in the Private Sector

There is another good reason to examine cost–benefit analysis in the private sector. This is to make it clear that the basic concept of cost–benefit analysis is not new. It is as old as economics itself. All firms and households are involved in some sort of cost–benefit analysis as part of the normal business of life. The only distinctive thing about the recent growth of cost–benefit analysis is the attempt to measure net social benefits for goods and services that are not sold, or sold under special conditions.

In the classical theory of competition it was supposed that firms would be forced to base their actions on profit calculations. Now these profits are simply the excess of benefits, in the form of revenues from sales, over costs. Profits were given the important functions of providing an incentive to effort and inducing investment in additional capacity where revenues exceeded costs. The important feature of this investment process is that it undermines profits, and so gives firms an incentive to invent new methods or new products. Where one succeeds others copy; the restoration of profits proves short-lived; and the pressure to innovate becomes strong again. The classical economists placed great faith in this built-in pressure

[1] See *Report and Proceedings* of the Select Committee on Nationalized Industries: Electricity Supply Industry. In answer to questions 155–57 it emerged that the Ministry looked for a gross and not net return on average net assets "to give credit to an industry like the electricity supply industry which had a more prudent depreciation policy".

to efficiency and innovation. They also assumed that each household knows best how to spend its income and from this followed the conclusion that cost–benefit analysis could be left to firms and households. Thus the whole classical theory of competition implied that firms and households made cost–benefit analyses, and that they based their conduct on them.

But competition does not always exist. Where it does not, making the best use of productive resources requires the guidance of cost–benefit calculations of a kind that are not made by firms as part of the ordinary business of life. The problem of measurement becomes public. Some such measurement is required, for example, whenever the State decided to regulate a monopoly, whether private or public.

In any case, it is now clear that throughout the economy, pressures to efficiency and innovation may not be very strong. The mere presence of many producers, and the absence of agreements to restrict trade, does not ensure such action.[1] Impressive evidence of a large degree of slack in the British economy is to be found in the files of industrial consultants. When Professor J. Johnston examined a sample from these files, he found that where quantitative assessments were both feasible and recorded consultants were able to suggest lines of actions which brought average productivity increases of over 50 per cent.[2]

Now it is true that the use of industrial consultants (and of internal operational research teams) costs money, a fact which cost–benefit analysis must take into account. But there is plenty of evidence that in thousands of firms a cost–benefit analysis would show the wisdom of incurring the cost.

Further striking evidence comes from a recent publication by the British Productivity Council, *Sixteen Studies in Value Analysis*. "Value analysis", a technique said to have originated in the General Electric Company of the United States, is a form of cost–benefit analysis. Many firms use "work study" in an effort to cut production costs of a given product. Value analysis simply goes further by not taking the product as given. It analyses the product's function,

[1] I examined the reasons in a paper read at the British Association meeting in York, and later published in the *Yorkshire Bulletin of Economic & Social Studies*, December, 1959.

[2] "The Productivity of Management Consultants", *Journal of the Royal Statistical Society*, 1963.

and then seeks the minimal costs of providing for that function. The return on the cost of the value analysis is often very high. In one U.S. defence programme the return was sixty times the cost. The British studies suggest a typical return of twelve to fifteen times the cost.

What of the more general search for new methods which competition is supposed to ensure? Do typical firms give enough attention to it? C. F. Carter and I looked into this for the Science and Industry Committee (formed at the Belfast meeting of the British Association), and we reported in *Industry and Technical Progress* that they do not.

This is a complex matter. In some industries the search cannot go far without a large outlay on research and development; in other industries it is the inventions of others (of, for example, the makers of machines, machine tools, scientific instruments, chemicals) which matter. But even in the science-based industries, research and development expenditure alone is not enough. Both the choice of worthwhile projects and the final application of science to industry depend on having qualified scientists and technologists in production departments. Furthermore, even in industries with high rates of expenditure on research and development, many of the opportunities for innovation come from outside the firm—from another industry or country. In all industries, then, it is important to watch for outside changes and to identify opportunities, and this also requires skilled scientists and engineers. Within firms, as well as nationally, too little thought has been given to the best use of scientific manpower, and there has been insufficient attention to costs and benefits in alternative uses.

Competition is also supposed to force firms to invest in all projects where, after allowance for risk, the prospective rate of return over cost is greater than the relevant rate of interest. Yet the upshot of many inquiries into investment decisions is that relatively few firms, even in the competitive sector, so act.[1]

Some firms do not even calculate the prospective rate of return over cost, preferring to take action only if "the case is so obvious that calculation is rather pointless". This must mean that they miss

[1] For some recent evidence see *Report of the Committee on Turnover Taxation* (Cmnd. 2300) (H.M.S.O., 1964). See also Andrews and Brunner, *Capital Development in Steel* (Blackwell, 1951); Carter and Williams, *Industry and Technical Progress* (O.U.P., 1957).

many worthwhile investment projects. The majority appear to use a pre-tax average rate of return above cost, in association with a minimum rate of return which they find acceptable. It is remarkable how often this pass or cut-off rate proves to be 15 per cent. Yet a 15 per cent. cut-off rate of return is arbitrary, and even in a given period it is irrational to use a 15 per cent. cut-off rate for both replacement of plant with hardly any interruption of earnings, and investment in a new product which takes several years to work up to a profitable rate of output.

The calculation of pre-tax benefit is also misleading. The impact of initial allowances, investment allowances and development-area grants can vary greatly between projects with the ratio of fixed to total capital and the location of the investment. A cash-flow analysis concerned with the present value of prospective receipts and payments (including tax), and not a pre-tax average yield calculation, is needed. The failure to use a cash-flow analysis has led both to the choice of many wrong projects and to an under-estimation of the profitability of investment, particularly in re-equipment. A sudden shift to cash-flow analysis would probably face the Chancellor with an embarrassingly abrupt investment boom.

Social and Private Costs

I come now to a different sort of cost–benefit problem, elaborated by Marshall and Pigou. Differences between social and private costs (and benefits) call for some sort of public control over the commercial activities of firms, whether public or private. If smoke from factory chimneys inflicts an uncharged loss on the community as injury to health, buildings and plants, and expenses for cleaning, the social costs will be greater than the costs to the firms concerned. So too with alcoholic liquor if the costs of alcoholism, road accidents and the additional police and magistrates due to drunkenness are not charged to the industry. So too with tobacco if its side costs in the form of lung cancer and heart disease are not charged. If a transport firm used the Queen's Highway quite free its own costs would be less than the social cost to the extent of the physical deterioration of the highway and the additional road congestion.

By contrast, a firm that spends money on training or research may get less benefit from them in the form of lower costs or greater sales than does the community. For the trained labour may go to another firm, and research may lead to new processes or products which other firms adopt, without paying to the firm that incurred the cost the difference between the return to the firm and the return to the community.

Where social and private costs differ, and these differences are not the same in each industry, the competitive system can only allocate productive resources properly if taxes and bounties offset these differences. Otherwise production will be too large where private cost is less than social cost, and vice versa.

Little attention has been given to the *measurement* of differences between social and private costs and benefits for, e.g. alcohol and tobacco. Of course, excise duties on tobacco and alcohol are high, and until fairly recently it probably seemed obvious that they more than covered the difference between social and private cost. However, with the rise in the incidence of lung cancer and heart diseases and the growing evidence of widespread alcoholism, this should no longer be taken for granted. A systematic statistical study is needed. In saying this I do not imply that we should simply measure the loss of earnings and medical costs due to drug addication and throw that cost on the industries. Where prohibition is not appropriate (as with smoke nuisance) a great deal of medical research and health education is called for, and this should be included in the social cost.

For road transport, efforts have been made to calculate whether parking and licence fees, and petrol duties, do compensate for the differences between private and social costs. These differences vary between country, trunk and city roads. Transport economists have insisted that because taxes on road transport do not conform to these differences, potential social gains are there to be gathered in by an appropriate system of pricing. Recently the Ministry of Transport appointed an expert committee to examine the economic and technical possibilities of pricing road use according to costs. The Committee concluded that practical pricing methods could probably be devised and that the measurable net gain to the community would be in the order of £100–£150 million a year. There is much more work to be done in the field, but *Road Pricing* is a most encouraging start.

Where social benefits are greater than private benefits, a case can be made for bounties. Industrial expenditures on research and training are assumed to generate a social-benefit surplus and are given favourable tax treatment, though little effort has been made to measure the assumed surplus. I have come to doubt whether there is a general social-benefit surplus from industrial research. Given our very large research expenditure and low growth, and the signs that we have placed excessive emphasis on the use of scientific manpower in research, we should consider whether blanket tax allowances for research have contributed to that maldistribution. I suspect that they have, though the effect is likely to be very much smaller than that of large Government research grants to particular industries made without the aid of cost–benefit calculation.

Why the Neglect ?

The neo-classical theory that, subject only to differences between private and social costs, firms in following their own interests would promote the public good, was not based on the idea of a spontaneous harmony of interests. The theory was only applied to competitive conditions. It was based on the idea that competition would force firms to act as if there were an identity of interests. Competition is simply a form of social control. In the absence of competition we need other forms of social control.

Competition is now a less pervasive form of social control than in the nineteenth century. The reason is that technical conditions of production have changed. The folk wisdom contained in the saying "necessity is the mother of invention" has been weakened by the change in the nature of invention. Nowadays typical inventions grow out of expensive applied research and development activities (not necessarily at home), which in turn grow out of expensive processes of higher education and pure research. For the inventive process we cannot now rely on competition. If the State creates the basic conditions by providing for education, basic research and even applied research and development where there is reason to expect a "pay-off" but the necessary scale cannot be managed by the public or private firms in the industry, then competitive pressures can play an important part in the speedy and efficient application of science to industry.

Once the basic conditions of industrial innovation are provided for, it is quite possible to have strong competition with only a few producers. But without a strong sense of opportunities to innovate, and at least a suspicion that competitors know how and intend to use them, competitive pressure, even in multi-firm industries, is not likely to be strong. In this case there is bite in the quip that competition is not severe because businessmen only have to compete with other businessmen.

In some industries it is not simply the conditions of invention that have changed, but also the conditions for exploiting inventions. The scale of expenditure involved in developing, for example, a supersonic airliner is such that Britain and France found it necessary to venture jointly. In atomic power it is beginning to seem that we should have ventured jointly. Going it alone forced what may prove to be a very expensive gamble on the most likely form of nuclear development.

Although competition cannot be such a pervasive and creative form of social control as it used to be, we have not created an effective substitute for it. This is because far too few people have realized that competition is an effective form of social control only if competitive pressure is associated with an opportunity to innovate. From the need for greater Government action to create the conditions of effective competition in a wide range of industries, and the need for new forms of social control in sectors of industry (including much of the public sector) where the competitive mechanism cannot operate, follows the need for a radical overhaul of the Government machinery. The Civil Service, as at present organized and manned, cannot cope with many of the problems of modern industry.[1] I have emphasized the need for more cost–benefit analysis to guide decisions. Such cost–benefit analysis may often be very complicated indeed, and require the co-operation of scientists, technologists, economists and statisticians to provide the basic detailed information and expert judgements on which the forecasts should be based.

The need for a more adequate provision "for the organized acquisition of facts and information, and for the systematic application of thought, as preliminary to the settlement of policy and its

[1] There is now a considerable literature on the shortcomings of the Civil Service. See, e.g, B. Chapman, *British Government Observed* (Allen and Unwin, 1963). See also P. D. Henderson, "The Use of Economists in British Administration", *Oxford Economic Papers*, 1961, and Merrett and Sykes, op. cit.

subsequent administration" was emphasized in the Haldane Report on the Machinery of Government (Cmnd. 9230, 1918). On the grounds of "the proved impracticability of devoting the necessary time to thinking out organization and the preparation for action in the mere interstices of the time required for the transaction of business" (para. 13), the Haldane Committee recommended (para. 14) that: (*a*) in all Departments better provision should be made for inquiry, research and reflection before policy is defined and put into operation, and (*b*) that for some purposes the necessary research and inquiry should be carried out and supervised by a Department of Government specially charged with these duties, but working in the closest contact with the administrative Departments concerned with its activities.

The establishment under the Lord President of the Council of the Department of Scientific and Industrial Research to develop and organize the knowledge required for the application of science to industry was in accordance with part (*b*) of this Haldane doctrine. But apart from small statistical sections within some Departments and the post-war creation of the C.S.O., part (*a*) of the doctrine was practically ignored. Not surprisingly, therefore, Departments are badly placed to perform the tasks which fall to them. For example, the Ministry of Transport as at present constituted and manned is not competent to make cost–benefit calculations and is badly placed to make wise long-term decisions about inland transport policy. It has no research section itself and has to rely for advice on the Road Research Laboratory of D.S.I.R., the research organs of the airlines (under the Ministry of Aviation), and British Railways. The Ministry of Power is no better placed—perhaps worse placed in that the activities of the A.E.A. (which include the final development of nuclear reactors) are matters for the Ministry of Science.[1]

[1] See paragraph 402 of the *Report* of the Select Committee on Nationalized Industries: Electricity Supply Industry, where it is reported that when the A.E.A. decided to build a particular prototype of a heavy water reactor the C.E.G.B. was not told in advance. When it expressed misgivings and asked how the Authority evaluated schemes in competition with others the Authority declined to show the papers. When the Ministry of Power took up the matter with the Authority it was simply told that the Authority and not the C.E.G.B. was charged with the responsibility to develop nuclear reactors.

For suggested reforms in scientific policies, see C. F. Carter and B. R. Williams, "Government Scientific Policies and the Growth of the British Economy", *Manchester School*, September, 1964.

There is a further problem which is well illustrated by the private proposals to dam Morecambe Bay and Solway Firth. Here are two projects having little hope of acceptance without a wide-ranging public cost–benefit analysis. These dams would create vast supplies of fresh water and give a good line for a northern motorway avoiding Shap. They would greatly improve the prospects of depressed areas in North-west Lancashire and West Cumberland, and create an excellent opportunity for new town developments. Yet, such projects very seldom originate from the public sector, and when they come up are simply referred to inter-departmental committees which lack the ability and the will to evaluate them. This doubtless helps to explain why Britain has such a poor record in resource development. Despite our less doctrinaire attitude to Government intervention, we have not produced anything remotely like the Tennessee Valley Authority.

The related failure to develop public cost–benefit analysis of possible lines of action and to adapt our social controls to new technologies, is an important part of the explanation of our failures in economic growth. So, too, is straightforward lack of understanding of a kind that can be cured by investment in the appropriate forms of education, so long, of course, as we manage to sell the potential output to the right people. When businessmen and civil servants choose investment criteria which are not in the interests of growth in output per head it is not usually because they have offsetting interests. It is usually because they don't know better.

It is now accepted that we need a great increase in business education. But the magnitude of the problem is such that it cannot be left to a few business schools who will take in students at the post-graduate stage and after ten years in industry. Training in appropriate forms of cost–benefit analysis in, for example, the engineering schools will be every bit as important. And, if we are to move quickly, educating the existing top managers will be even more important. There is room at the top for a great deal of education in the uses that can be made of modern techniques for making plans, choosing rationally from among them, and exercising control; room also for education in the conditions required for the proper use of these techniques.

When the British Association programme was printed I was asked several times whether the "unwonted" in the title of my address was a misprint for "unwanted". It was not, though I doubt whether it would have mattered. Strong resistances to cost–benefit analysis come from those who fear that such analysis might lead to a smaller expenditure on what they are interested in, from those who are used to making decisions in situations where "quick decisions are more important than right decisions" (though the need for a quick decision is frequently the result of failure to think ahead), and from those who desire to operate within a given administrative framework, even when that administrative framework is too restricted for the problem in hand. This is not surprising. But given that our resources cannot be stretched to do all the things we would like, there is a continuing need to discover and explain the costs and benefits of different lines of action, and to see that our social control systems help resources to flow into the appropriate channels.

6

POLICY, POETRY AND SUCCESS

G. L. S. SHACKLE

Nottingham, September, 1966

REASON or imagination; probability or poetry; the search for solutions or the search for beauty. These are the contrasting theories of the conduct of affairs which I begin by suggesting to you. To each there corresponds a general policy of life, a general prior assumption dictating attitude and method. There are those who believe that life consists of a series of imposed situations to each of which there is one right response, and there are those who think that we ourselves impose upon the material chaos a psychic order of our own invention, not seeking to solve a problem but to conceive a work of art.

A problem is a set of conditions abstracted from circumstance. We are asked to say what these conditions, *and these only*, imply. A solution of the problem is a suggested state of affairs which conforms to the stated conditions. In life at large; in politics or business, in human affairs in general, who abstracts for us a set of known conditions and arranges for the exclusion and non-operation of any others? Who limits our field of action to a *given* state of technology or of basic science? Who preserves this field inviolate from the effects of other contemporary or future human choices?

Business is the making and pursuit of policy. Is the nature of things, the so-called human predicament, such that we face an endless examination in arithmetic, each hour presenting its sum, and the subsequent hours or years marking our answer right or wrong? If so, policy-making is problem solving, there is an algebra of business which only needs to be supplied with a sufficiency of information to guarantee success. Or is the logic of things such that no such sufficiency of information can ever exist? Is policy-making, by necessity, an originative art? Art is the manipulation of constraints. The poet is confined to the use of words whose meaning is supplied by tradition and convention. The musical composer can only exploit the possibilities of sound, whose properties are given by Nature. Light and pigment condition the realizations of the painter. Art is not arbitrary, unconstrained caprice. But the required knowledge may be knowledge of what can be done rather than of what must be done. I wish to draw suggestions about the basic nature of business policy-making from some purely logical considerations.

The man who bets on the fall of a pair of dice does not have to invent the rules of the game. The physical character of the dice in all relevant respects is known to him. The relevantly distinct things that can happen as the result of a throw are all fully specified and completely listed, and they are known to be completely listed. They are classified under eleven heads, the relative frequency of occurrence of which, on the assumption of symmetrical configuration of each die, can thus be calculated. The same is true if he bets on the turn of a card. In a horse-race things are not quite the same. It is hardly conceivable that even if he were given access to every racing stable involved, and able to inspect the course under every condition of weather, he could list every possible combination of circumstances which could prevail in the race. Even with a computer, could he do it in time for the race? Of course, it would be no use taking so long over his listing of phases, over writing down all the different sets of circumstances, that the race was over before he had found which horse had most such sets in its favour. But even a horse-race is simple compared with investment in new business enterprise. Where is the card of runners, limiting his choice to a finite and quite small set of pre-specified enterprises? And where is the book of rules, making it even logically possible to know the phase-space, the complete list of everything that can happen, and to assign to each enterprise, either by statistical experience or by appeal to considerations of symmetry, as with a pair of dice, the ratio of the phases favourable to that enterprise to the total of all possible phases? There can be no list, known to be complete, of possible forms of business enterprise, for the variety is always already limitless and always known to be increasing. And when a man has imagined such an enterprise in all the detail required for ordering the purchase of land, the design of buildings and plant, the engagement of staff, the signing of contracts for supplies of materials and power, the organizing of sales and publicity, can he then list all the distinct *life-histories-to-come* for this business, including every one such history which, for all he can tell at this moment of imaginative invention, might come true?

The decision to invest his money in a new business enterprise requires a man, in principle, to start by inventing a variety of enterprises, specifying each in considerable detail as to products, technologies, scale, location, markets, suppliers, finance, associates in management. Then for each such figment he must begin to consider the things that can happen to it, if he does bring this particular figment to realization. And this task is endless. The variety of political developments in the world at large, which could affect a given kind of business, is plainly beyond any man's reckoning. The variety of other businesses, rivalling his own in this or that respect and in this or that degree, which could be set up is without limit. These possibilities in the sphere of political and commercial circumstances may, none the less, perhaps be conceived to be drawn from a hat the broad nature of whose contents is within conjecture. But what of scientific discovery and technological invention? An invention, a discovery, is by its very nature something logically incapable of being known about in advance. Nor can we set bounds in advance to the possible effects of a discovery. New knowledge is destructive. It also, of course, can open up untold riches. But it overthrows more or less radically and completely the structure of ideas we have hitherto relied on. It throws light from new, unsuspected directions, it makes *everything* look different, it upsets all calculations, it states new axioms, it leaves nothing as it was. Unless we believe ourselves to know already all there is to know, we have to recognize that our lives float on a fathomless depth of unconjecturable revelations and inescapable surprises. It is no use telling oneself: "I will prepare my mind for *anything*, I will not be taken by surprise." I, and you, *will* be surprised.

Later I shall want to place great stress and relevance upon the *unlistable* character of the general field of possible outcomes of investment, which the mere boundedness of our available time, the mere presence of a deadline, combined with the intolerable diversity even of known possibilities, imposes on us. This *unlistableness* is increased and multiplied beyond conception by our consciousness of limitless things still waiting, and for ever waiting, to be discovered. But first, a definition and an axiom.

By *decision* I mean an act of moral, or if you like, of psychic, commitment. A man who has taken a decision has created within himself a structure whose alteration or abandonment would be felt as wounding and hurtful, as a defeat, as a negation of himself in some degree. A decision is a step which, although it takes place entirely within a man's mind, is in some sense and degree irretraceable. Most often he doubtless makes it irretraceable in a more ordinary sense by making it public, by giving as a hostage his signature and reputation. But the crucial event is a private one, an act of thought. Leading up to this focal and final act there is doubtless a more or less prolonged, more or less laborious, systematic, resolute, resourceful, rich, efficient, imaginative, daring, anguishing succession of preparatory steps. We may if you like include within the meaning of decision the whole process from start to finish: the apprehension of some incompleteness of policy or programme; the first statements of possible completions, the sketches of schemes; the setting up of a range of questions concerning each of these schemes and the gathering, analysis and interpretation of facts to answer them; the crucial, extra-logical act of judgement and choice; the making public of what has been chosen. Decision, then, is choice, but it is choice amongst *thoughts*. Before a man can choose a course of action he must imagine the possible, the available courses. Before he can know which to choose he must imagine, for each such course, as many as he can of its possible outcomes. Decision involves imagination, it is an act of imagination, it is choice amongst the products of imagination. The apparent power, precision and penetration of the modern mathematical and statistical techniques of choice are in themselves a testimony to this elusiveness of the objects of choice. To call them objects is, indeed, itself misleading. They are *figments*. My first proposition is that decision is choice amongst the products of imagination.

All that we know or can know concerns what is past. Even the sense-stimuli which are now coming in at my eye or ear were initiated some fraction of a second, at least, ago. They report to me what *was* the case that time ago. As the cosmologists are always explaining to us, the light-pulses or radio-pulses which reach our telescopes started out at various instants over a vast span of time, thousands of millions of years; some of them, such as those reflected from the moon, only leaving her a second and a half ago, while others from the boundaries of the observable cosmos started when our world was new. What our instruments see is a picture of the evolution of the universe, an immense panorama of the past. On a mundane scale the same is true of our daily and momently observation of our social and economic world. The news we get is only relatively new. What it reports *has* happened, even if it is a live television broadcast. Nothing on the television screen nor on the retina of our eye ever gives us direct, objective information about the future. Everything we know about the future is an inference, the end of a reasoning process, whether the reasoning is sound or not. But *decision* is wholly concerned with the future. Decision is choice of future action aimed at results which we look for in the further future. Thus, decision cannot be choice of facts. We do not find displayed before us a range of entities which, at one and the same time, are facts already realized and therefore observable, and are also hypotheses, figments, imaginations of what might come true in some future remote or immediate. "Choosable actualities" is a contradiction in terms. Hence our deep concern with the nature, means and method of that reasoning which can perhaps carry us from knowledge of the past, including the most immediate past which we call "the present", and including what I have just made up my mind to do, or what, for the sake of argument, I suppose myself to be about to do, to inferences about the future. The questions for the investigator of *decision* are:

1. Does the past repeat itself? In what sense, and in what circumstances, does it do so? How can we tell whether it will repeat itself? For to know that the past is going, in known respects, to repeat itself, is to know some part of the future in those respects.

2. When the kind or degree of repetition that we can rely on are only sufficient to *circumscribe*, and not to *describe* with precision and certainty, those aspects of the consequences of present action which concern us, how can we adapt our policy-decision to this lack of knowledge?

The prime instrument of science is what I like to call the *stereotype*. We arrive at a stereotype by way of the concept of a *circumstance or subject of measurement*. In physics we can measure time-lapse, distance, mass, pressure, temperature, electric charge and so on. Confining one such type of measurement to a defined type of place, object or set of circumstances we get a *class of measurements* or a *variable quantity*. A particular member of such a class of measurements is a (numerical) *value* of that variable. When, in many repeated observations, we find values of several distinct variables associated in patterns which have some ostensible stability, constancy or fixity about them, we may call such patterns *stereotypes*. A stereotype may consist in the simultaneous occurrence of a particular value of a first variable, a particular value of a second variable and of a third, and so on, through some stated list. For example, a particular species of living creature may be identified by the association of a certain set of measurements (the idea of measurement can be readily extended to include colour and other characteristics of a rather complex kind). Or the stereotype may take the form of a mathematical function, that is to say, a rule which permits only certain sets of values, one from each of a list of variables, to be associated together, without, however, confining us to just one value of each variable. And the particular measurements which are associated may, in any case, be deemed to be made simultaneously, or at distinct and separate instants of time, or to consist of a cumulation of measurements made over some stretch of time. Thus, we may have as our stereotype of sequential pattern of situations or events, a segment, or piece, of history. If, by continual and wide-ranging observation, we establish such stereotypes as part of our intellectual equipment, we can thereafter both explain or account for what is past, and also predict what is to come. We have, indeed, in the stereotype, a *theory*.

Scientific explanation and scientific prediction are in essence one and the same. We observe some circumstance or set of circumstances and we say: That situation would arise if certain other circumstances were also present or were antecedent to it. Then we look for those circumstances and the finding of them *explains* our first observation. Or we observe certain circumstances and we say: Circumstances of that kind have appeared in the past to be regularly associated, or to be regularly followed, by such and such a further circumstance. Thus, we *predict* that further circumstance. In both types of operation, in both explaining and (scientifically) predicting, we are relying on *fixity of pattern* in things, on the notion of *stereotype*, on history repeating itself. Prediction and retro-diction are one and the same operation, the act of arguing from what is known directly, as by an eye-witness, to what is believed to be the necessary completion of a larger, recurrent, whole.

How do we settle upon the list of circumstances, measurements or variables that shall appear in our stereotypes or functions? One test of successful choice is, of course, the firmness with which the resulting pattern insists on presenting itself over and over again. If such patterns are the means and expression of our recognition of repetition in history, that is to say, repetition in the structure of the natural or the social world, it is evidently a prime requirement that these patterns, in a fixed and precise form, should turn up over and over again. Let me turn aside for a moment to justify my suggestion that repetition in history, and repetition in nature, are one and the same. In so far as what happens in the world is determined (shaped and steered) by the nature of the world (and surely we could make no sense of things if we did not accept that something of this sort is part of the truth), then sequential constancy of events or situations, so far as it occurs, is an expression and result of structural constancy, and the two aspects are in some measure one and the same. Now one way of explaining the breakdown of such repetitiveness, when it occurs, would be to say that some influence, not included in our list of variables, had *interfered* with their inter-relationship and disrupted the pattern. Might not this sort of interruption, in the same sort of way by the same "outside" influence or factor, be observed over and over again? And if it were so observed one way of dealing with the situation would be to include this influence, hitherto left out of the list of associated variables, in a new, enlarged and rebuilt stereotype or function. Thus, we can say that stability of the pattern depends on our having successfully included in it all the influences or measurement-classes that *actively* play a part in the phenomena we are concerned with.

This brings us to the crux. Where is the extension of the list of variables to stop? Is one of our stereotypes or our functions to swallow the whole of Nature or of human affairs? What limit is there to the inter-connectedness of things? Does everything that happens, and every situation that comes into being, flow as a necessary consequence from what has gone before? Is history a complete, all-inclusive and rigid structure of determination? The very purpose of our theorizing inhibits us from carrying this line of thought to its natural conclusion. For if everything that happens is the only thing that, in the existing circumstances, could happen; if every event or state of affairs is the uniquely possible sequel of its antecedents; then there is no room for decision in the sense of a human originative act. To be meaningfully studied as an *art*, decision must in each instance *start something new*. This novelty implies the cutting of the thread of control of the future by the past. But if every decision cuts this thread, what ground or means is there for reckoning the consequences of a decision? We appear to confront a dilemma. Either decision, in the sense of a history-making act, does not exist; or else these choices amongst rival available acts are inevitably made without the logical possibility of calculating the outcome of each such "option".

No escape from this dilemma can be tidy, rigorous and exact. Broadly it appears to me that the existence (in the logician's sense) of decision as an *inceptive act of reasoning choice* pre-supposes a *partial* connectivity of events. There is a texture in the world which prescribes, not what *will* happen but what *can* happen. But if this is the only supposition concerning the basic texture of affairs which will assign to decision the meaning of an act and art of originative choice, our endeavours to shape and improve this art must be based on that supposition, and not on the supposition of theoretical perfect calculability.

I referred at the outset to the game of throwing dice, where all the things that can happen as the result of a throw can be classified under eleven heads. This list of things that can happen is known to be complete. In other games a gambler may have to spend time in working out the list of things that can happen and the number of these phases, as a proportion of all possible phases or things that can happen, which favour each head. But in all such games the rules of the game make possible a listing of contingencies which is complete and known to be complete. Life in general, and business life, provide no such rules of the game, no such complete statement of underlying conditions from which a certainly complete contingency-list can be worked out. The first task of the systematic decision-maker in a given field of action is to specify some rival courses of action amongst which he will choose. This task itself may be an inventive one, involving the reduction of infinite basic diversity to a finite and small number of discrete "options". But that is only the beginning. For each such rival option he must then write the list of its possible sequels, and here there can be no end to the business. The phase-space is unknown. He cannot know how many ways there are in which a given, specified option could achieve this or that degree of success, or in which it might incur this or that degree of disaster. What he can do, I am suggesting, is to classify these various degrees of success and disaster under headings such as "perfectly possible", "perfectly impossible" and perhaps also "slightly surprising", "rather surprising", "very surprising" if they came true. Let us divide this scheme into two stages, and consider first the implications of treating all degrees of success or failure, all *outcomes*, as either "perfectly possible" or "perfectly impossible".

Perfect possibility means, in this scheme, a judgement made about some hypothesis by an individual decision-maker, expressing the fact that he knows of no circumstance which could block or impede the realization of that hypothesis. To adjudge perfect possibility to some hypothetical outcome of an available course of action does not, in my use of the term, imply any degree, however slight, of positive belief that this outcome will prove to be the truth. It means only the complete absence of any positive degree of belief or assurance that it will *not* prove true. Perfect *impossibility* is the judgement that some hypothesis conflicts with general laws and the nature of things, or else with the prevailing circumstances, so that the decision-maker cannot accept it into his picture of *how things are* without disrupting that picture and rendering it self-contradictory and meaningless. Now it may well be felt, so far as I can tell, that these two categories of "perfectly possible" and "perfectly impossible" are not by themselves sufficient for the classification of all the kinds of judgement that one might want to make about a hypothesis. May not the known prevailing circumstances, or one's general conception of the nature of things, place difficulties in the way of an hypothesis without disabling it completely? I shall be glad in a few minutes to take the view that this is so, but meanwhile let us confine ourselves to just one grade of possibility, so that all hypotheses which make this grade are on the same footing in regard to their adjudged power to come true. When, within this frame of thought, two hypotheses of the outcome of some course of action are both regarded as possible, will they necessarily command from the decision-maker equal degrees of attention and interest? Will he necessarily be equally concerned with them? To use the expression which I have found apt, will they both have over his mind the same degree of *ascendancy*? I think not. For one of them may represent a state of affairs more to be desired, or more to be disliked, than the other.

I think we can go further. I would say that there are bound to be, amongst the outcomes which most readily present themselves to the decision-maker's mind as possible ones, when he contemplates some important act of, let us say, business or financial investment or political strategy, some which he deems to be improvements of his existing situation and some which seem to be deteriorations of it. Indeed, how do we assess the felicity of the "existing situation" in which at any time any one of us finds himself? Surely it depends largely on its promise or its threat. We have yet one more case of what some economists call the bootstraps argument. What a thing is worth now depends largely on what people are expected to value it at in future. Its value "hauls itself up by its own bootstraps". Such a principle applies to investments (in the financial sense) and to fine paintings and to land. Our "existing situation" seems to be a feasible starting-point for the attainment of a highly desirable and brilliant situation, as some more or less clearly visualized date in the future; or it can, perhaps, just as well, if we are candid with ourselves, lead to serious predicaments and misfortunes. But in so far as one or other of these possibilities comes to impress us, we shall be inclined to raise or lower our estimate of our "existing situation". If, at some time, we conclude that all available courses of action expose us to some degree of misfortune we shall reckon our present situation correspondingly poorly, and by that very act of judgement we shall see the favourable possibilities in a more glowing light. Our "existing situation", indeed, is always suspended between the collection of favourable imaginable outcomes of our available acts, on one hand, and the collection of their unfavourable imaginable outcomes, on the other. If so, when we contemplate any particular policy or action-course which is open to us we are likely to be able to arrange the outcomes we can readily envisage for it in order from bad (in some quasi-absolute and not merely relative sense) to good, in a similar sense. And of these outcomes thus arranged, under our present supposition that all are equally possible, only the best and worst will really concern us.

Let me briefly restate our assumptions by way of arguing this last idea. We are supposing the decision-maker to have in mind some list of imagined "biographies" for the future of some contemplated enterprise. These biographies he classifies into a series of groups, all those in any one group being equal to each other regarding the goodness or badness, let us say the desiredness or undesiredness, of their outcome. The groups themselves, containing in general various numbers of these imagined or hypothetical biographies, are arranged in order from most undesired to most desired. Let us give concreteness to our ideas by supposing the enterprise to be a businessman's proposal to construct a new plant, and the desiredness or undesiredness of the outcomes to be accordingly the notions of various sizes of profit or loss, each understood in the sense of a flow of trading profit discounted to a sum of present value. Now since we are allowing no distinction between what is less possible and what is more possible, but are supposing the decision-maker simply to place all biographies that occur to him under the heading of possible or impossible, it follows that those in the "possible" class are distinguished from each other in his assessment only by their various degrees of desiredness and not at all by their degrees, which are all equal, of capacity to come true. When he asks himself "What outcome, what profit or loss, *will* this enterprise yield?" his answer must be, "I have no ground for selecting one amount rather than another." But when he asks himself "What profit, and again what loss, *can* this enterprise yield?" the relevant answers are plainly the greatest profit and the greatest loss amongst the groups containing the *possible* biographies. The *interior* groups, or rather the outcomes associated with them, are of no concern to him. When you ask an athlete "How high can you jump?" he may say "Six feet." But he does not think you will be interested to hear that he can also jump five feet, four feet or six inches. When we classify outcomes simply as possible or impossible it is the best and the worst that matter to us.

Now let us ask ourselves whether *possibility* is really a matter of yes or no. The possibility of some imagined situation or event, the capacity of such a thought-construct to be realized, to be matched by actuality, is something which some individual adjudges to it.

The whole relevance and meaning of the notion of possibility belongs to a time earlier than that at which the hypothesis in question is to be tested. It would be pointless to speak of possibility if we knew for certain that the suggested state of affairs would, or would not, come into being at the date suggested for it. Only in ignorance can we speak of possibility. But this ignorance is not absolute. We have some insight into the nature of the world and of men and their society, and we know something of the *existing* state of affairs at the moment when we are doing our thinking. We can discern *paths* from this existing situation to the one which we hypothesize for some stated future date. One question which concerns us is whether there is time, between these two dates, for any such path to be followed by the course of history. Can we make things move fast enough to get there? Again the path itself can be doubtful without being certainly impracticable. There can, for various such reasons, be *degrees* of adjudged possibility.

Let us therefore suppose our decision-maker to make a double ordering of his hypothetical biographies of his proposed enterprise, first allotting each to some one rung on a ladder of degrees of possibility and then arranging the hypotheses allotted to any one such rung in order of their desirability from highly undesired to highly desired. On any one possibility-rung, the hypotheses will doubtless again fall into groups, within each of which all hypotheses will be of equal desiredness. We can therefore speak henceforth of *outcomes*, each outcome, say each suggested amount of profit or loss, corresponding to an entire group of biographies. Amongst the groups on any one possibility-rung, the same principle will apply as amongst those which were classed as "possible" when only a single degree of possibility was supposed to be distinguished. On any one possibility-rung only the best hypothetical outcome and the worst will concern the decision-maker. But there is in our more sophisticated model an added difficulty. If one single outcome is to stand for the promise, and one single other outcome for the threat, of the enterprise, how is the selection to be made from the whole set of "bad" extreme outcomes and from the whole set of "good" extreme outcomes? For there will be one such good, and one such bad, extreme for each of the many rungs.

Let us first notice that as we shift our attention from greater to lesser degrees of possibility, the worst outcome on each successive rank will be worse than that on the preceding rank, and the best outcome on each successive rank will be better than that on the preceding rank. For by accepting more serious obstacles to realization we are able to imagine "biographies" which would otherwise have been excluded; and some of these formerly excluded biographies will imply larger losses, or larger gains, than any of the biographies which stand on a higher level of possibility. Now there appear broadly to be two types of selective schemes by which the decision-maker can be supposed to adopt one of the extreme bad outcomes and one of the extreme good outcomes as the pair of representative outcomes for the enterprise. One of these schemes consists in his asking himself what is the lowest level of possibility at which he need take seriously the corresponding threat of loss, and which is the lowest level of possibility at which he can take seriously the corresponding promise of gain. These two levels of possibility will not in general be one and the same, for a threat is still a threat and a disturbing thought even when we feel that its coming true would be highly surprising, but a promise has not much ascendancy over us if its realization is too obviously disabled by the existing situation or the nature of things. This first scheme is cautious and defensive. It selects the lowest acceptable degree of possibility without regard to the size of the corresponding loss or the corresponding gain. These two levels of lowest acceptable possibility then determine the representative or "focus" gain and loss. The second scheme makes the acceptable degree of possibility depend on the size of the hypothetical loss, or of the hypothetical gain, which that degree of possibility would bring into view. We remember that the lower the possibility, the larger is the greatest loss, or the greatest gain, which that degree of possibility requires to be envisaged. Size of loss, and size of gain, are decreasing functions of degree of possibility. Now it can be suggested that the decision-maker will treat as a single entity, or *expectation-element*, the combination of a given degree of possibility with its corresponding largest hypothetical loss, or with its corresponding largest hypothetical gain, and that the power of any such entity or expectation-element to claim his attention and secure a voice in his decision will be a function of each of these composing characteristics. This *ascendancy*, or power to arrest attention, exercised by an expectation-element at either extreme of a possibility-rank, will surely be an increasing function of the size of loss or gain, and an increasing function of the degree of possibility, which size and degree, however, are decreasing functions of each other. Shall we not find, then, amongst the hypotheses of loss, one which, taken together with its degree of possibility, has a greater grip on the decision-maker's mind than any other? And likewise amongst the hypotheses of gain, one which, taken together with its degree of adjudged possibility, has a more powerful ascendancy over his mind than any other? If so, these two hypotheses can, under this second scheme, be regarded as the representative pair for the particular enterprise.

The appeals to intuition, observation and reason which I have advanced have led us, if you accept my claims, to a scheme for representing each enterprise, that the decision-maker's imaginative ingenuity has constructed in his mind, by a pair of entities of a type which I call expectation-elements. Each expectation-element is an amount of monetary gain or loss, or a quantifiable success or misfortune of some other kind, coupled with a ranking in respect of its possibility. If we could regard possibility as not merely rankable but measurable in some additive unit, each expectation-element would have the form of a *point* or *vector*, that is, something requiring *two* numbers to state it. As it is, our foregoing argument has enabled us to include degrees of possibility within the considerations operating in the decision-maker's mind, while leaving ourselves with expectation-elements which can each be regarded, not as a vector but as a scalar, a single number. But we still have, for each enterprise, two such numbers. Our final step must therefore be to show how these again can be in effect reduced to one number.

It is practical and reasonable to regard the focus-loss, in absolute terms, as depending on the nature and scale of the enterprise concerned. Thus, by choice of an appropriate kind, or an appropriate size, of plant or enterprise, he can adjust the greatest amount he stands to lose, that is, his focus loss, to the amount which, given the size and character of his assets, he can "afford" to lose. When by this test he has listed a number of enterprises of various kinds, he can finally choose that one which offers the largest focus gain.

I have now put before you my central scheme of thought. There are some refinements, some intensifications of the argument, which, if you wish, can be found set out elsewhere. Without embarking upon them, may I briefly suggest the answer to one question which must have arisen in your minds. Why has the word *probability* made no appearance in this discourse? In what I have been saying, the essence of the answer to this question had been provided from the very outset. It resides in the *unlistableness* of the sequels, or biographies-to-come, which can in general and in the abstract be deemed possible for any one policy or strategy now adopted. To reckon probabilities we must have a list of sufficiently specified contingencies, which list must be known to be complete. A long series of trials with a system, such as a pair of dice or a pack of cards, known to be unchanging in its relevant characteristics, might enable us, if we did not know it in advance, to discover the complete list of phases at the same time as we found out the relative frequencies of occurrence of outcomes corresponding to sets of these phases. But this known constancy or stability of the system is a special circumstance. It prevails in games of chance, which, without it, would scarcely be games. It prevails to some extent in those matters which are insurable, for without such assumed approximate constancy there could be no successful insurance. But does it prevail in business, in questions of investment in new plant when the background is an endless proliferation of new knowledge, new techniques and new markets?

When a man has to admit to himself that the sequel to what he is about to do may be A, or B, or C . . . or G, *or something else*, the admission contained in these last three words, that although he can specify some hypothetical sequels, there must always remain endless others of which he can form no conception, because they involve decisions yet to be made or knowledge yet to be discovered, and because the deadline for his own decision leaves him no time for searching these depths, we may say that he has to include in his list of hypotheses of the sequel to his act, a *residual hypothesis*. It is a black box, containing he knows not what. The assignment of probabilities to various outcomes of an experiment requires the listing of every distinct thing that can happen as a consequence of it, within the boundary of what is interesting and relevant to the decision-maker's concern. It requires these "things that can happen" to be not only all present in the list, but to be things which can be considered equally possible with each other. When the whole field of possibility has thus been divided into "equi-possible" phases; that is to say, when the phase-space has been completely stated;

then for each outcome; let us say each size of profit or loss; the number of phases favourable to this outcome has to be compared with the total number of all phases. How can such frequency ratios be calculated if the total number of phases cannot be listed and the phase-space cannot be stated? In such a case the ordinary concept of frequency-ratio becomes very nebulous and elusive.

But if, on these grounds, we find probability an unsuitable language for expressing the decision-maker's final and climactic task: the comparison of rival policies when (as he always must if decision is an *originative* act and thus releases the future from the governance of the past) he entertains plural and rival hypotheses of the outcome of each such policy: none the less probability, in the objective and statistical sense which centres on the concept of relative frequency, has its indispensable part in decision-making. For in modern natural and also in humane or moral sciences probability is a vital tool in establishing those stereotypes or functions by which the decision-maker must judge what sequels to any given action or policy are possible in this or that degree. Modern natural science and modern sciences of human nature, conduct, institutions and policies are very largely statistical sciences. Physics and genetics are essentially statistical. There is little need for me to stress the dependence of social inquiries upon statistical method. But in all this, statistics is a means to knowledge. My suggestions have been concerned with a means of insight into the policy-maker's essential activity: the exploitation of an essential lack of knowledge, the profiting from indeterminacy.

In everyday language and in that of the policy sciences, *decision* includes two quite contrasted meanings. Two contrasting psychic activities, two attitudes to life and two different types of mind are involved. There are truth-seekers and truth-makers. On one hand, the pure scientist deems himself to be typically faced with a problem which has one right answer. His business is, in the map-maker's language, to get a fix on that problem, to take bearings from opposite ends of a base-line and plot them to converge upon the solution, the truth-to-be-found. On the other hand, the poet–architect–adventurer sees before him a landscape inexhaustibly rich in suggestions and materials for making things, for making works of literature or art or technology, for making policies and history itself, or perhaps for making the complex, delicate, existential system called a business.

Management theory has today become deeply, necessarily and rightly sold on mathematical methods. The policy is to make the manager into a scientist. He can be taught a number of conceptions or procedures by which, accepting certain constraints, certain "givens", he can work out a solution. The manager is taught, in fact, to programme himself as if he were a computer. But computers only do what they are told, however surprising the answers they sometimes produce. Problem-solving is the bread and butter of life, and we shall starve without those who can do it. But besides those who can see ahead of them the one right answer we need those who can see around them a million possibilities. We need the radial, as well as the axial, type of mind.

PART TWO

ECONOMIC POLICY

7

THE PRICE SYSTEM

H. D. HENDERSON

Bath, September, 1948

A YEAR ago, my predecessor in my present role, Professor Dennis Robertson, devoted most of his address to a review of the controversy which was then active about the potentialities of economic planning. I had made my own contribution to that controversy, the Rede lecture which I gave in Cambridge and which I was moved to write, partly by what seemed to me the incoherence of the planning ideology which was prevalent, and partly by the suspicion that planning appealed to many as having the properties of a magic charm which would enable us, not to solve, but to shirk our problems. Since then the ideologues of planning have remained mostly on the defensive, while their opponents, marching under the banner of a return to the price system, have launched a general assault. I had better confess at once that this revivalist ideology seems to me marked by the same defects which repelled me in planning ideology, that is to say, incoherence, and wishful thinking. The phrase "the price system" is bandied about as though its meaning were self-evident, and as though it, too, had the properties of a magic charm. I propose in this address to examine it closely; and in order to minimize the risk of misunderstanding, I begin with a recital of first principles.

In its most general sense the price system is an inevitable outcome of the use of money. Wherever goods and services are bought and sold for money, there must be prices; and these prices must always exert a powerful and pervasive influence. Price provides the principal criterion for resolving every problem of economic choice, both the problems of an individual arranging the distribution of his personal expenditure, and those of a manufacturer in organizing his processes of production. Rationing and allocation schemes may narrow the area of choice, both for the consumer and for the producer; but where choice exists it is exercised by constant, if often tacit, reference to the price criterion. In fact, the problems of choice which arise in ordinary private and business life, even in a highly controlled society, are very numerous; though they are nothing like as numerous as the problems which *might* arise, if they were not settled decisively, by a subconscious appeal to the price criterion, without, so to speak, coming into court. We do not actually have to worry our heads about replacing our china dinner service by more durable gold plate. Nor does a publisher have to spend a moment in considering whether to print his books on paper or on parchment. But, if there were no such things as prices, there would be an infinitude of such questions which someone would have to settle somehow.

The influence of the price system in this sense is far more pervasive than that of the profit motive. A private trader or manufacturer, operating in a highly competitive market, may be more vividly conscious of price considerations and more quickly responsive to them than the conductors of a publicly owned industry, but the latter do not and cannot leave them out of account. Their actions may diverge from those suggested by the price criterion, either from inattention or inertia, or because of decisions made deliberately for good reasons or bad. But in all their decisions, the price criterion is an essential factor. It is the needle which points out the course to follow where there is no reason to deviate from it. And here, too, the questions which call for deliberation are only a small fraction of those which escape attention because the answer given by the price criterion is categorical and obvious.

This then is the first proposition which I wish to emphasize: that even when our economic activities are subject to a multitude of physical controls, and even if most of our major industries were to be nationalized, the influence of the configuration of prices which exists at any time remains strong, far-reaching and fundamental. It is important, therefore, that this influence should be a healthy one, that the configuration of prices should be such as to pull in directions which accord with the public interest. The price criterion may work very badly, as we have plentiful present reasons to know, if the relations between different prices are, to use a common phrase, distorted. We want price relations that are right, so far as that object is attainable. Unquestionably, this desideratum was unduly neglected in our governmental policy a year or two ago. Indeed there seemed then to prevail in Ministerial circles a curious unwillingness to notice the influence of prices, an averting of the eyes which was almost prudish, or perhaps it would be better to say, reminiscent of the mental habit of Mr. Podsnap: "the forces of the price system are un-socialist; therefore, we refuse to acknowledge their existence." They exist none the less for that; and it is always important to have them working for, and not against the public good.

Here, however, we must be careful not to beg a major question. In the matter of price relations, as in many others, it is easier to be sure that certain things are wrong than to know at all precisely what is right. In times of large-scale economic maladjustment, is there really such a thing as a right price for any commodity or service or factor of production; or are there merely widely separated limits within which the price should lie? If there is such a thing as a right price, how is it to be determined and established?

At this stage, I think I can most conveniently develop my argument by considering the answer that would be given to these questions by those whom I call for convenience, the ideologues of the price mechanism. In broad outline, their answer would be as follows: Trust to the forces of a free market, operating under conditions of effective competition, and with the minimum of interference by the State. The right price will then be secured by the interplay of demand and supply on price, and of price on demand and supply. This will be for any particular commodity the price at which demand and supply will be in equilibrium; and the establishment of equilibrium prices throughout the economic system will carry with it the corollary that the relative prices of different things will be right, in the sense that their pull will be in the directions that are needed for the most efficient use of the productive resources of society. Something of this sort is what is usually meant by those who call today for the restoration of the price system.

I have stated this view, of course, in a crude and summary form. Perhaps nobody would associate himself with it without adding various qualifications or reservations. All would concede that due allowance must be made for the so-called "wastes of competition". Some regard these wastes as comparatively unimportant, others as extremely important; and differences of judgement upon this matter form one element in controversies about nationalization versus private enterprise. Again most economists would admit or affirm that large inequalities of income or wealth impair the claims that can be made for the results of a freely working economy; though those whom I call price-system ideologues tend to repudiate the inference that this may justify such expedients as controls or rationing schemes, and to insist that the appropriate remedy is to do more than is done already to abate the inequalities of wealth by redistributive fiscal measures. I say no more about these qualifications or the issues which they raise, but pass to a large reservation which brings us much nearer to the questions which I wish to examine.

The strongest advocates of a free economy are nowadays increasingly inclined to concede that, before it can be expected to work well, a prior condition must first be satisfied. A rough adjustment must be established between aggregate supply and aggregate demand; otherwise a freely working economy may result in inflation, if demand is overstrong, or in a prolonged *malaise* of depression and unemployment if it is too weak. Now this is a considerable admission. First it implies that if aggregate demand and aggregate supply are out of balance, or at any rate, if aggregate demand is greatly in excess of aggregate supply, controls and allocation schemes may be needed after all. Second, it implies that one of the reasons why they may be needed is that otherwise the prices brought about by a freely working economy may be far from right. Third, it implies that the necessary equilibrium between aggregate demand and aggregate supply cannot itself be ensured by trusting to the automatic responses of a free economy. This task, it is recognized, can only be discharged by deliberate policy, perhaps taking the form of a budget surplus in some conditions and a budget deficit in others, perhaps extending to such matters as the rate of interest and the stimulation or restraint of capital investment; in any case deliberate State policy, which is thus assigned a positive role of key importance in the economic system. This takes us far from *laissez-faire*, a fact which most exponents of the views I am examining are eager to proclaim and to stress; for although eulogies of the price system and a free economy are again in fashion, the *laissez-faire* philosophy is not.

Without forgetting the qualifications mentioned earlier, we may therefore restate as follows the central prescription of price-system ideology: Let the State attend to the balance between aggregate demand and aggregate supply. Let it concentrate on that one all-important equation, and leave to the free play of impersonal economic forces all the detailed adjustments of the economic system. Let the State see to it that global equilibrium is established, and it need not worry about particular disequilibria. It can then leave the producer free to produce what he chooses as he chooses, in response to the inducements and deterrents of the price system; and it can restore a similar freedom of choice to the consumer, including the choice between home-produced and imported goods.

I have cast this restatement in a topical form in which it makes a wide and growing appeal, and to judge from recent publications is especially attractive to economists. From different angles and with important individual variations Professor Jewkes, Mr. Harrod, Professor Meade and many others in this country and abroad, can be observed converging on the formula: "Equate aggregate demand to aggregate supply and set the price system free." Nor is this formula propounded on purely practical grounds. It is suggested that it represents the fruits of the latest developments in abstract economic thought, the distillation of the genius of Lord Keynes, a profoundly thought-out synthesis of new facts and the wisdom of the ages, appropriate to the conditions of our time. We badly need such a synthesis, I agree; but for my part I cannot find it in this formula.

Up to a point, undoubtedly, it seems well adapted to our present practical requirements in Great Britain. In my opinion at any rate, it is vitally important to eliminate the excess of overall demand in our internal economy. Such as excess, if long-continued, depletes the stocks of finished commodities, raw materials, components and spare parts, which represent the indispensable lubricant of a smoothly working economic system. It increases the difficulty of making an adequate volume of goods available for export. It entails an inflationary trend of prices and wage rates, and a constant danger that the momentum of this trend may at any time become uncontrollable. I have no doubt, therefore, as to the paramount practical importance of eliminating the excess of aggregate demand as speedily as possible. It would be most rash, I would add, to relax our efforts towards this end, until we are quite sure that it has been achieved.

All this, however, leaves unanswered the pertinent questions why this excess of aggregate demand should have arisen and why it should be so very hard to get rid of it.

To continue the main argument, I hope and believe that the elimination of the general inflationary trend in our economy would carry with it the substantial elimination of many particular maladjustments, and would thus enable us to dispense with many of the controls that irk us today, and to simplify others. But would it enable us to remove them all? I do not believe it. On the contrary, I am convinced that controls, that is to say, direct, physical controls, working otherwise than through the price system, will remain indispensable in some important sections of our economy. I have in mind, in particular, the regulation of long-term capital expenditure, which I expect will be desirable for a fairly considerable time, and the regulation of imports which I am certain will be necessary for a much longer time.

My dissent from the ideology I am examining goes much deeper than a distaste for what I am sure all sensible well-informed persons would agree with me in regarding as its over-sweeping claims in matters of practical policy. Its logical foundations seem to me unsound. The main idea on which it rests is the concept of an equilibrium price to be brought about by the forces of supply and demand. In times of large-scale economic maladjustment, this concept of an equilibrium price is, I submit, ambiguous. The theory of value comprises two parts, a short-term part and a long-term part, though as Alfred Marshall was careful to warn us "of course, there is no hard and sharp line of division between long and short periods". In the short run, the supply in any market may be taken as a more or less fixed quantity; and the equilibrium price is that which will so curtail an excessive demand, or so stimulate a deficient one, as to match the immediately available supply. In the long run, the supply of most things can be radically altered; and the equilibrium price is that which will evoke a rate of supply sufficient to meet the demand which will be forthcoming at that price. For a particular commodity, accordingly, the long-run equilibrium price[1] corres-

[1] To avoid misunderstanding, it may be well to emphasize that by the phrase "long-term equilibrium price" I do not mean a forecast of what the price is likely to be in a distant future, but the price that is appropriate to current conditions on the basis of long-term equilibrium theory.

ponds to the cost of producing it, including in that term a fair profit margin.

Now in ordinary times, when the economic system has not been subjected to any recent large disturbance, the short-term and long-term equilibrium prices of most things are seldom far apart; and any small difference between them resulting from some small maladjustment between supply and demand serves as an effective and comparatively unobjectionable means of correcting that maladjustment. If, for example, the demand for some particular commodity or material expands so as to outrun the current rate of production, the price tends to rise, production becomes more than usually profitable, and the rate of production is increased until it becomes sufficient to meet the enlarged demand. For this purpose, a very moderate rise of price will usually suffice; and a very moderate rise is all that usually occurs when times are what I have called ordinary, though there may be important exceptions even then. These are the conditions in which the price mechanism in a free economy works efficiently.

The story is apt to be very different when the maladjustments to be corrected are very large. If it is a case of a large excess of demand over supply, the short-term equilibrium price may be very high indeed, much higher than is useful in stimulating additional production. For an exorbitant price does not stimulate production appreciably more than a good price; it frequently stimulates it less. Indeed it is a well-established paradox that an excessive price sometimes leads to a decline in output, because many classes of producers are disposed to work less hard when an accustomed income can be earned with less exertion. On the other hand, the disadvantages of an exorbitant price, or in more popular language, a profiteering price, may be very great.

Not that I wish to suggest that in the absence of controls a large excess of demand over supply will always lead to a price that is grossly in excess of costs of production. The actual price in such conditions will depend largely on the type of market in which the commodity is bought and sold. It will come near to the short-term equilibrium price for those things which are sold on organized exchanges, as are normally most staple agricultural commodities. But for goods which are produced to fulfil orders as are most industrial products, the prices at which the orders are placed usually represent some sort of compromise between those which might result from a free auction on the one hand and the costs of production on the other; a compromise in other words between the short-term and the long-term equilibrium prices. The character of the compromise varies from one type of commodity to another. It is useful to note in passing that the deviation of price from the norm set by costs of production is usually least when the price is fixed by the unilateral decision of the producer, as it is for branded goods, that is to say where competition is most imperfect. It is not monopoly but competition which forces up prices most in conditions of shortage.

It is a mistake, therefore, to suppose that in such conditions the theoretical short-term equilibrium price is either what we want, or what we normally get in a free economy; or that relative prices would be "right" if the State did not interfere with them by controls and subsidies. The paradox that the prices of second-hand motor cars are often a good deal higher than the prices of new cars of the same makes can be observed today in the United States, no less than in Great Britain. This matters little, but it illustrates the anomalies that are apt to occur in price relations when shortages are widespread. Some of these anomalies do matter; and it is important to limit their growth. Unless we are to go out of our way to force up the less volatile prices to profiteering heights, this means that we must keep down the more volatile by appropriate restraints. Prices fail, in these circumstances, to discharge the function of lopping-off excess demand; and problems of allocation must be dealt with by other means or left unsolved.

It is true that shortages or surpluses are apt to be most widespread, and the consequential anomalies most serious, when there is a large maladjustment between aggregate demand and aggregate supply. But it is not true that the former disequilibria are always a mere by-product of the latter. They may sometimes have a common origin, as in the great economic disturbance caused by a major war; they may sometimes arise independently; or the relation between cause and effect may be the other way round, for sometimes particular maladjustments may play a big part, as I believe they do now, in causing or maintaining a maladjustment between aggregate supply and aggregate demand. However this may be, particular maladjustments of large magnitude and crucial importance may remain, after global equilibrium has been restored. Wherever such maladjustments exist, the short-term equilibrium price may diverge widely from the long-term equilibrium price; and real difficulties and problems may arise, for which the ordinary price mechanism affords no adequate solution.

These are the generalities which seem to be relevant. I am conscious that they come very near to being platitudes which it should not be necessary to labour at such length. I have felt impelled to stress them by the fact that they are so completely, and sometimes it seems so perversely, ignored in current price-system ideology. I pass now to consider their bearing on the most formidable of all our national economic problems—the large and persistent deficit in our balance of international payments.

Is there really any reasonable prospect that the restoration of balance between aggregate demand and aggregate supply in our internal economy would enable us to entrust our external economy to the price mechanism, that is to say, to remove restrictions upon imports, including imports from dollar or other hard currency sources? Is this even conceivable, so long as the prices of the foodstuffs and raw materials which we have to import are as high as they are today? The question is one which we are in a fair position to judge; for though we have not yet eliminated the excess of aggregate demand in our internal economy, we are not, I hope, very far now from doing so. The progress we have made in this matter has not, however, brought us within sight of closing the deficit in our balance of external payments. Even the target laid down in the Economic Survey for 1948 went no further than a reduction of this deficit to £250 million in the present year; and in the light of what happened since, there is still chance that that target will be hit.

We are running a formidable deficit in this vital sector of our economy despite the fact that our total volume of imports is held down by means of an austere programme of import restrictions to about 80 per cent. of the pre-war level, and despite the fact that our commodity exports are considerably larger in volume than before the war, let us say by about one-quarter. Additional exports normally require additional imports of raw materials. Accordingly, the volume of imports available to satisfy the needs of our resident population is probably appreciably less than 80 per cent. of the pre-war volume, although this population is more numerous than it was. On the other hand, our consumption of goods and services as a whole, though its exact rate is a matter of some abstruse controversy, cannot reasonably be put much lower than before the war, at any rate when capital goods are included, as it is right to include them for the present argument. So we have the contrast: consumption of imported goods less than 80 per cent. of pre-war, total consumption about 100 per cent. of pre-war.

If the consuming public, together with manufacturers and traders, were free to choose between home-produced and imported goods, there is no reason to suppose that imported goods would represent a smaller fraction of their total purchases than formerly. It is true that in the absence of subsidies imported goods would have risen more in price. Against this, however, must be set the re-distribution of net income in favour of the lower income-groups, who spend a smaller part of their income than others on services, and a larger part on commodities from overseas. If, therefore, import restrictions were removed, it would seem only reasonable to expect that the volume of relevant imports would return from less than 80 per cent. to about 100 per cent. of the pre-war level, an increase of more than a quarter. At present prices, which might of course be increased by additional purchases, this would add over £400 million to our national import bill.

How would this result be affected by the definite removal of every vestige of inflation? This might serve to reduce our aggregate consumption somewhat, and the demand for imports correspondingly. Conceivably, our aggregate consumption may have to be reduced, failing a sufficient further increase in output. But no one, I imagine, would suggest, least of all the critics of austerity, that our aggregate consumption of goods and services may have to be reduced by 20 per cent. or more. This is the magnitude of the reduction that would be needed, if the removal of import restrictions were not to result in increased expenditure on imported goods.

It may be hoped that the elimination of excess demand will also help to increase our exports. That is one of the many reasons why it is so important to eliminate this excess. But we need a large increase in our export receipts in order to close the existing deficit in our balance of payments, which Marshall Aid is not enough to cover; and when Marshall Aid runs out we shall need in addition all the reduction in import prices for which we can fairly hope. In the meantime, we are in no position to contemplate a largely increased expenditure on imports. We have to keep our imports down and get our exports up as well. I cannot gainsay anyone who complains that once again I am labouring the obvious. I observe only that this disposes of the doctrine that if we re-establish global equilibrium we can leave the balance of payments to take care of itself.

The locker of price-system ideology contains, it is true, another shot. This is the idea that disequilibria in the balance of payments can always be corrected by variations in foreign-exchange rates, though opinions differ widely as to how this idea should be applied. Professor Jewkes, in his *Ordeal by Planning*, argues that the level of exchange rates should be left to the free play of supply and demand in foreign-exchange markets. Indeed, he seems to regard the fixing of even tentative exchange parities as constituting in itself an illegitimate interference with the price mechanism.[1]

In this, however, I think he is exceptional; and a more prevalent view is that exchange parities should be altered from time to time as a means of correcting balance of payments disequilibria. Those who hold this view are not all of one mind as to whether the pound sterling should be devalued in Great Britain at the present time. Some appear to advocate this course, or at any rate did so about a year ago; for on this matter minds not only differ but are apt to change. Professor Meade, in his inaugural lecture at the London School of Economics, expressly disclaims this proposition, and declares himself uncertain whether devaluation will eventually be needed. But he joins with the others in insisting that devaluation, in contradistinction to import restrictions, is the right remedy for our balance of payments difficulties, if they should prove obstinate.

[1] "What would have happened in the free economy? The State would have confined itself to its legitimate role of restricting the volume of money sufficiently to prevent domestic inflation. Exports would have been stimulated because that would have been the only outlet for goods. The cramping effect upon industry of physical controls would have been avoided. No export targets would have been fixed, exports would have been left to find their own level. The long-period exchange rate would have been left to determine itself. A deficit in the balance of payments would have been met by a fall in the exchange rate, thus increasing exports and reducing imports. If the nation was living at a level beyond its means, the fact would have been immediately signalled to all and the increase in domestic prices would have pressed down the standard of living to what was possible." Jewkes, *Ordeal by Planning*, p. 234.

On the other hand, Professor Hawtrey, whom I think it is fair to class as a price-system ideologue, though of a highly individual type, urges the opposite course, the raising of our exchange-rate with the dollar, on the ground that the pound is at present undervalued by reference to relative price-levels, and that this gives us bad terms of trade and acts as an inflationary force.

I cannot attempt in this address a full examination of these diverse views. But I point to their diversity to illustrate my central theme. The ardent advocacy of exchange depreciation in the abstract, in which most price-system ideologues indulge, is attributable to the pivotal role which they assign to the concept of equilibrium price. There *must* be, they believe, some equilibrium rate of exchange which would equate the supply of and the demand for dollars. I reply that when our import–export balance is so far from adjustment, there is a huge divergence between the theoretical short-term equilibrium rate and the theoretical long-term rate. The former is that at which the demand for foreign exchange would be in balance with the supply accruing from business transactions. The relevant long-term norm for the exchange rate between two currencies, corresponding to the cost of production as the long-term norm for the price of a commodity, is, to use the phrase coined in the last post-war period by Professor Cassel, their purchasing power parity; not, of course, that that is likely to remain constant in unstable times any more than the cost of producing a commodity remains constant.

It is to this norm that Professor Hawtrey appeals in maintaining that sterling is too low relatively to the dollar. I am not quite sure that he is right in maintaining this; subsidized prices and changes in relative productivity make the relevant price-level calculations a treacherous bog. But he may be right, or the trend of relative costs may soon make him right. If so, I infer that our exchange rate is about where it ought to be. For the price prescription which I offer for conditions of serious maladjustment is that the price should deviate from the long-term norm in the direction of the short-term equilibrium price, but only by a narrow angle.

It is important that the angle should be small. Just as an exorbitant price is seldom more effective than a good price in stimulating the output of a commodity, and may sometimes even lower it, so an exchange rate which is far below purchasing-power parity is seldom more effective than one which is only slightly below this norm in improving the balance of payments of a country in deficit, and may even worsen it. It would be foolish therefore, and possibly disastrous, to try to make actual rates of exchange correspond to the short-term equilibrium rates, when these would be far below current purchasing-power parities. This is not a matter of *a priori* dogmatism. It is the principal lesson which was taught, even if we have failed to learn it, by the runaway currency inflations on the Continent of Europe in the 1920s. A marked and almost invariable feature of these inflations was that exchange depreciation in the country concerned moved far ahead of the rise in internal prices, so that the deterrent to imports and the stimulus to exports were as strong as any price-system ideologue could possibly desire. Yet the balance of payments was normally worsened, because the effect on the terms of trade outweighed the effect on the relative volumes of imports and exports.

The inflationary process was therefore cumulative. The rise in internal prices, though never catching up with the external depreciation, at least until the final stages, was always hurrying after it. It proved difficult to balance budgets in such conditions; and the process continued until eventually it was ended, whether before or after it had culminated in a complete *dégringolade*, by applying what came to be recognized as the indispensable remedy. This was to hold the foreign-exchange rates firmly for a period by means of foreign credits or the free use of the country's own gold reserves at a level in the neighbourhood of the purchasing-power parity. So only could the breathing-space be secured in which any other measures that might be needed for stabilization could take effect.

These things happened in the days of unrestricted foreign-exchange markets, when individuals were free to put their money abroad. This freedom, by the way, was regarded then, and indeed right up to 1939, as an essential feature of a free economy. Now that capital movements are tightly controlled in most countries, it is unlikely that an inflationary movement would conform to the model of the 1920s in all respects. On the essential point, however, of the capacity of exchange depreciation to improve a country's balance of payments, this experience is extremely pertinent. If contemporary experience is preferred, the large and rapid increase in French prices which followed the devaluation of the franc in

January, 1948, is equally apposite. British economists, I suggest, would do better to heed these lessons than to bandy calculations in terms of elasticities conceived as quasi-constant ratios, capable of measurement. In effect, all such calculations beg the crucial questions at issue, taking for granted first that a country can push exchange depreciation to any degree desired without affecting its internal price-level, and second that the effect on the balance of payments, assuming this to be favourable, will increase without limit with the degree of the depreciation.

I submit, then, that for correcting a huge maladjustment in the balance of payments, such as still confronts Great Britain, counter-inflationary financial measures, though helpful, cannot suffice; and that exchange-rate variations might be harmful. It is essential to keep down the volume of our import purchases as effectively as we now do by means of import restrictions. And not only to keep down their total volume, but more particularly the part of them that comes from what we call hard-currency sources. The principle of non-discrimination does not fit a world in which the whole international balance of payments has been upset.

There remains another aspect of the problem to which I should refer. Might not the necessary limitation of our import expenditure be secured by means more conformable, as the phrase goes, to the price mechanism than quantitative import regulation; for example, by high tariffs or by the auctioning of import licences, as Professor Meade persistently suggests? My answer is, where we are free to choose, that that method should be chosen which will secure its object most simply and most effectively. For some commodities, duties are unquestionably the most appropriate form of import limitation, notably for tobacco where the objects are mixed, and the indirect saving of dollars through the raising of revenue may well predominate over the direct saving accruing from a cut in purchases. But many of our import restrictions are prohibitions, complete or nearly so, at least on imports from particular countries. Nothing would be gained, not even a saving of administrative costs, by replacing these prohibitions by duties designed to be prohibitive. Here the quantitative method is simpler, more straightforward and more certainly effective. For other commodities it may be important to avoid raising prices to the home consumer. Again, a large part of our imports is purchased at present directly by the State, and here manifestly it is impossible to evade the quantitative question, how much the State should buy.

The principle that I have suggested applies, of course, more widely. Wherever the need for effective regulation is made out, the question of the best method to employ should be settled on merits, in the light of the relevant circumstances, and not by ideological prepossessions, either for the price system or against it. Quantitative controls, allocation schemes and the like are crude and clumsy instruments, which it is absurd to idealize. My own experience confirms the lively account which Professor Jewkes gives of the lengthy administrative process of quite unscientific haggling by which allocation schemes are apt to be constructed. But it must not be supposed that there are no defects in the so-called financial controls which some prefer. When, for example, it is suggested that the need to ration scarce essential commodities might be averted by re-distributing purchasing-power by really drastic fiscal measures, it is well to remember that taxes have their disadvantages and sometimes arouse criticism, that their incidence is not always just or scientific, and that officials have to be employed to assess and to collect them.

The same scheme of analysis which I have applied to foreign-exchange rates and the balance of payments can be applied with appropriate modifications to the rate of interest and the balance between savings and investment. During the war, the production of capital goods for peacetime purposes was virtually suspended; consequently, the current demand for such goods is abnormally high. On the other hand, for various reasons the current rate of private saving is abnormally low. In these circumstances, an extremely high rate of interest might be needed to equate the rate of real investment to the rate of saving, if the demand for capital goods were uncontrolled. There is, therefore, a strong case for regulating this demand. The inter-relations of the capital market and the monetary system introduce many complications; and I cannot pursue this subject further in this address. It is worth noting, however, that modern economic thought, over-impressed as I think by these complications, is inclined on this matter to abandon the notion of an equilibrium price altogether. It has been suggested that there are no limits, set by underlying economic forces, to the power of governments and monetary authorities to manipulate interest rates.

This palpable exaggeration, as I have always thought it, served to encourage Mr. Dalton in the mistake which he undoubtedly made in carrying the cheap-money policy to excessive lengths. The mistake lay in trying to force interest rates down below the long-term norm.

I have concentrated in this address on what I may call the mechanics of the economic problem. My main theme can be summed up in two short propositions; first that, in conditions of large-scale maladjustment, the optimum price is to be found, as a rule, between the long-term norm and the short-term equilibrium price, but lies much nearer to the former; second, that in such conditions, regulation and deliberate direction may be useful and sometimes indispensable. To anyone concerned in a responsible capacity with the actual problems that arise, the latter proposition at least is obvious common sense. I deplore the fact that it is necessary to argue it among professional economists. A century ago economists were laughed at as the practitioners of the dismal science. They scarcely deserve that taunt, or should I say that compliment, today. I fear it must be recorded that during a period in which the British people have been faced with most formidable economic difficulties, to surmount which it is important above all else to appreciate the magnitude of the effort required, the most extravagant propagandists of go-easy illusions, the most pushing salesmen of enervating Fool's Paradises, have been found among economists of diverse schools of thought. We have now, I hope, done with the illusion that a much better time could be had quite easily by all if only industry were mobilized for national purposes, as it was to produce Fido, and Pluto and Mulberry. It would be no improvement to replace this by the illusion that our present austerities are unnecessary, and would vanish like the snow if the sun of the price system were allowed to shine.

8

THE CHANGING STRUCTURE OF THE BRITISH ECONOMY

AUSTIN ROBINSON

Oxford, September, 1954

THE dynamic development of the economy of any nation derives from a two-fold process of adjustment: it derives in part from a constantly continuing adjustment to technological progress; in part from adjustment to the changes in the quantities and distribution of resources of materials and skills possessed both by the particular nation and by other nations. There emerges from these adjustments superimposed upon its own past history the structure of that particular economy at that moment of time. The structure often reflects only imperfectly the needs of the moment, for economic structures change slowly, and it is only in a period of relatively slow change that the actual structure and the ideal structure are likely to be identical. It is the changes in the structure of the United Kingdom's economy during the past two or three centuries, and particularly during the past hundred years or so, that I wish here to review very briefly. For we live in a period when large and more than usually rapid structural adjustment is both needed and taking place. I believe that the problems that confront us today are more easily understood if we see them in the perspective of the changes of structure that have occurred in the past.

The essential features of any nation's economic structure are made up of the pattern of employment and activity, the pattern of export and import, and the pattern of consumption. These patterns are in their turns related to and derived from the available resources, both natural and, as in the case of skills, acquired and inherited from an industrial tradition.

It is normal to think of the economic structure of any one nation as greatly influenced by the abundance of certain resources and by deficiencies of others. At the beginning of the eighteenth century it was still true to say that the pattern of the British economy derived in large measure from our ability to export the indigenous products of which we had a surplus. Of the £3·6 million or thereabouts of exports of produce and manufactures of the United Kingdom, for the year 1688, about £2 million represented woollen manufactures, and most of the rest represented exports of coal, lead, tin and other indigenous products. It was quite late in the nineteenth century that there developed the complexities of our structure, whereby we import not only the materials required for our exporting industries, but also the greater part of the food needed to maintain our population.

May I begin, then, with the structure of 1688, when Gregory King, Lancaster Herald of Arms, made the study of *The State and Condition of England* which is the starting point for all modern macro-economic investigation? England, with a population which King puts at 5,500,000, had an income which, slightly adjusted to bring it into line with current definitions, may be put at about £50 million. Retained imports, which he estimates at £2·8 million, were approximately 5·5 per cent., therefore, of national income.

Of a total of personal expenditure which amounts to about £46 million, approximately 51 per cent. was estimated to be spent on food and 25 per cent. on clothing. Of the food consumed, a very small proportion, mainly composed of tropical produce and wines, would seem to have been imported. Down to about 1730, England was an exporter rather than importer of grain. The proportion of manpower resources devoted to agriculture cannot be estimated with any certainty from King's figures.[1] The proportion of gross national product estimated by him to be derived from agriculture is about 40 per cent., and the proportion of manpower employed in agriculture must clearly have been

[1] If one is prepared to regard his categories of "labouring people and out-servants" and "cottagers and paupers" as primarily agricultural the proportion would be as high as 75 per cent. If, as seems likely, the first of these categories is intended to include most of the unskilled labour in the towns (artisans and handicrafts are elsewhere included), and both of them a certain amount of domestic industry, the proportion might be nearer to 65 per cent.

at least of that order of magnitude, and probably considerably greater.[1]

Thus at the beginning of the eighteenth century we have a structure that is still predominantly self-sufficient, whose imports are primarily manufactures and the produce of other climates, whose exports are based on the utilization of plentiful indigenous resources, and whose manpower is primarily devoted to agriculture, and which provided a level of real consumption per head a little under half of that of 1925–34.

I wish that one could find an opportunity for comparisons in the middle of the eighteenth century. It is sad to have to say that the century of English economic history which is of greatest potential interest, in that it saw the largely unexplained acceleration from the slower processes of earlier centuries to the rapid cumulative progress of the past two hundred years, is also the century that is completely lacking in estimates of national income and of the other main bench-marks to which one can refer such other statistical information as we possess.[2]

The earliest date after 1688 at which we can again attempt to see the main features of our economic structure is around 1800–12. The various estimates of Beeke, Levi, Colquhoun, none of them individually wholly complete or internally consistent, none the less give us a sufficient basis from which to calculate rather imprecisely the essential elements of the contemporary structure. The national income of the United Kingdom was probably about £400 million at prices of 1812. Retained imports, affected by war, were fluctuating in the range at current prices of £40 million to £80

[1] In 1691 Sir William Petty commented, "There is much more to be gained by Manufacture than Husbandry; and by Merchandise than Manufacture" (quoted by C. Clark, *Conditions of Economic Progress*, 2nd Edition, p. 395).

[2] I believe that it is worth trying, even now, to see whether this deficiency cannot be remedied. We have greatly developed in the past twenty-five years the arts of establishing the orders of magnitude of the national incomes of backward countries by the ingenious use of many individual clues to establish the totals of incomes, production and expenditure and to permit estimates of each of these to be employed as a cross-check on the others. It is by no means clear that sufficient data do not exist to enable us to do much the same for the eighteenth and early nineteenth centuries, basing oneself in part in the latter case upon some of the rudimentary and internally inconsistent estimates made at the time. I am delighted that Miss Deane, of the Department of Applied Economics at Cambridge, is exploring these possibilities in connection with Dr. Simon Kuznets's big international project for the measurement of economic progress.

million,[1] with a mean at prices of 1812 of about £49 million. Thus the import ratio would appear to have become something of the order of 12 per cent. That is about the figure also for 1820, and it is from about 1820 that the data begin to accumulate from which one can see the main changes in the essential features of the structure in a peace-time economy.

In the years between 1820 and 1830, then, the structure of the United Kingdom had already begun to alter in many essentials. Exports were composed now only to the extent of about 50 per cent. of indigenous products of the United Kingdom and manufactures made from them; woollen manufactures accounted for a little under 12 per cent., and coal for about 1 per cent.; cotton manufactures accounted for about 48 per cent. of the whole, textile manufactures of all sorts to about 67 per cent. and manufactures of all kinds to about 90 per cent. On the other side of the account, in consequence, imports of materials were also about 60 per cent. of the whole, out of which textiles materials, mainly cotton, accounted for about 24 per cent. Retained imports of food, drink and tobacco were equal to about £20 million at actual values, and may be compared with a production of about £120 million in agriculture; thus foreign supplies of food represented something of the order of one-seventh of total supplies. The Census of 1821 gives us some limited help in seeing how the occupied population was employed: in England and Wales, about 34 per cent. (a figure close to that of France before the last war) are reported as employed in agriculture and fishing; about 46·5 per cent. were engaged in trade, manufactures and handicraft; the remaining 19·5 per cent. were accounted for by all other forms of services and employments. Thus the economy had already moved a long way from the pattern of 1688. It had no longer in anything like the same degree as then the features that we now associate with an "underdeveloped country": the relatively large proportion of population engaged in agriculture or engaged in the trading and handicrafts associated with it; the chief imports composed of manufactures and chief exports of primary products (that feature had largely disappeared before 1750). But the structure was still a long way from that which developed later in the century.

[1] As revalued from official values to current values by Professor A. H. Imlah, "Real Values in British Foreign Trade, 1798–1853", *Journal of Economic History*, November, 1948, pp. 148–49.

By 1850 we are beginning to see more clearly the features of what most of us were brought up to regard as the timeless characteristics of the British economy. The import ratio had now risen to about 18 per cent. Exports are composed to the extent of over 90 per cent. of manufactures; textiles still predominate and account for about 63 per cent. of total exports; woollens 14 per cent., cottons 40 per cent. and the rest mainly linen. Imports are still largely composed of raw materials for the textile industries, which account for 32 per cent. of the whole. Food imports are now increasing, and are about 34 per cent. of the whole, with grain imports up to 10 per cent. as against 4 per cent. in the 1820s. Exports are to a significantly smaller extent than in earlier years based on indigenous supplies. Of total exports of British products and manufactures, between 2 and 3 per cent. are accounted for by coal; wool from our own sheep provided now about 70 per cent. of total supplies, as against 95 per cent. half a century earlier, and we are beginning to be dependent on imported supplies of other materials also which had earlier been derived from home sources. The distribution of manpower reflects these and other changes. The proportion of occupied population engaged in agriculture has fallen to somewhere about 21 per cent.;[1] better Census classifications, introduced in 1841 and which persisted almost unchanged until 1911, enable one to see the employment of the rest of the occupied population in more detail; manufacturing in total employs just under 33 per cent. of the whole—a figure which was not exceeded until 1951—and of these over 22 per cent. are accounted for by textiles and clothing, a percentage very nearly three times as high as that of 1951.

Between 1850 and 1870 these features of high specialization, a high import ratio, great dependence on manufactured exports, and especially on textile exports, diminishing dependence on indigenous raw materials and diminishing dependence of home food supplies all took a much more pronounced form. Britain was very rapidly adjusting her economy to a world market, made accessible by new and improved forms of transport.

But it is important to remember how immensely different that

[1] There are considerable difficulties in interpreting the 1841 and 1851 Censuses in this respect, and particularly in judging from them the trend between those two years. See Charles Booth, "Occupations of the People of the United Kingdom, 1801–81", *Journal of the Royal Statistical Society*, Vol. XLIX, p. 325.

world was from the world of today. In 1850, so far as I can judge from some brave guessing to fill in gaps in the calculations of Mr. Colin Clark which cover the majority of the bigger countries, the real income of the world was between a fifth and a quarter of what it was in 1937. It has grown since 1850, partly as the result of unprecedented population growths, partly as the result of the great growth of productivity. But in the process of that growth it has come to be very differently distributed. Of the world income of 1937, about 29 per cent. was that of the North American countries and 4 per cent. that of Central and South America; Western Europe accounted for about 31 per cent. and Eastern Europe for about 11 per cent.; the Far East for only about 20 per cent.; all other areas, including Africa, Australasia, the Middle East, for about 5 per cent. Of the world income of 1850, the largest share almost certainly went to the Far East, which would appear to have enjoyed something over 40 per cent. of the whole; North America had a real income comparable with that of Africa today, and accounted for only about 10 per cent. of world income, with Central and South America representing about another 3 per cent.; Western Europe had a slightly smaller share than now, with about 29 per cent.; Eastern Europe was rather more important, with about 14 per cent.; the Middle East had about the same share as today; Australasia and Africa were almost completely negligible.

It was to the resources and requirements of that very different world that Britain was adjusting herself at the middle of the nineteenth century—a world in which the predominantly agricultural countries of new settlement were anxious to trade their primary products for manufactures; a world in which about 65 per cent. of the occupied population of the United States was still engaged in agriculture; a world in which Britain was probably responsible for over 40 per cent. of the world's total output of manufactures.

It was between 1850 and 1870 that the nineteenth-century structure reached its more complete form. By 1870 the ratio of retained imports to net national income at factor cost had risen to about 28 per cent.—a figure surpassed only for a short time in the 1880s, when it reached for a few years a level of about 33 per cent. The pattern of imports was changing. About 35 per cent. of all imports were now food, of which grain was 9 per cent., and about 50 per cent. raw materials; manufactures accounted for about 15 per cent. But the main sources of food were still in our own agriculture. For the year 1867, according to estimates by James Caird,[1] home agricultural produce accounted for about 82 per cent. of total supplies of the main staple foodstuffs, and probably about three-quarters of the whole when allowance is made for imports of sugar and other tropical produce. Exports of textiles accounted for about 56 per cent. of the whole; cotton now 35 per cent., wool 13 per cent. But exports of metals and metal manufactures were beginning to mount; they now represented 21 per cent. of the whole. At the same time the industrial distribution of the occupied population increasingly reflected this changing emphasis. Between 1851 and 1871 the proportion engaged in manufacturing of all kinds slightly declined, if one may trust the figures, from about 33 per cent. almost to 30 per cent.; but within the total metal manufactures rose from 6 per cent. to nearly 7·5 per cent. The proportion in agriculture fell heavily—from 21·5 per cent. to a little over 14 per cent., while the proportion engaged in transport and commerce rose from just under 11 per cent. to about 13·5 per cent.

Between 1870 and 1913 the overall ratio of retained imports to net national income remained relatively steady, rising from the 28 per cent. of 1870 up to a peak of 33 per cent. in the 1880s and then falling back to slightly lower figures in the 1890s. But in all else the change continued to be rapid. The redistribution of manpower continued. Agriculture, which had given employment to over 14 per cent. of the occupied population in 1870, was down to 8·5 per cent. at the turn of the century and to about 8 per cent. by 1913. The total of manufacturing retained its surprising stability around 29–30 per cent. of the whole, but within this total the redistribution continued, away from textiles, which fell from about 18 per cent. in 1870 to about 13·5 per cent. by 1913, and towards metals and engineering, which rose over the same period from about 7·5 per cent. to about 10 per cent. of the total. And the trend towards transport, commerce and distribution continued; this group rose from 13·5 per cent. in 1870 to about 20 per cent. in 1913.

Parallel with this redistribution, and springing from the same

[1] See James Caird, "On the Agricultural Statistics of the United Kingdom", *Journal of the Royal Statistical Society*, Vol. XXXI, pp. 127–45. The estimates are concerned only with such basic foodstuffs as grain, beef and mutton, butter and cheese, potatoes, and take no account of tropical imports, fruit, tea, coffee and the like.

causes, was a change in the pattern of imports. At 1850 and again at 1870 food imports had been close to 35 per cent. of the whole; they rose to about 42 per cent. of the whole at the turn of the century, and for the first time were larger than raw-material imports; the share of the latter increased again by 1913, but it remained nearer to 40 per cent. than to the 50 per cent. of 1870 or the 60 per cent. of 1850.

It is not easy to measure precisely the degree of dependence on imported food at the culmination of the nineteenth-century development, much as one would like to do so. As regards grain of all types, we imported about 50 per cent. of our total supplies at the turn of the century[1] and 55 per cent. in 1913, as compared with about 70 per cent. in 1936–38. As regards meat, we imported about 40 per cent. in 1900, and again in 1913, rising to just under 60 per cent. in 1936–38. Overall, and including products in which we were much nearer to self-sufficiency, I would guess (and it can be no more than a guess) that home agriculture provided about 50 per cent. of our food in 1900, about 45 per cent. in 1913,[2] about 35 per cent. in 1936–38, with a return to about 50 per cent. in the last few years.

Thus by 1913 the structure based on a high specialization in manufacture, on imported materials and on imported food had reached its fulfilment. At the 1911 Census agriculture accounted for only 8·1 per cent. of the occupied population, as compared with 21·6 per cent. seventy years earlier. Manufacturing in total gave employment to just about the same proportion of the whole. The proportion of the occupied population engaged in transport, commerce and distribution had grown by about as much as that in agriculture had declined.

It was a specialization no longer based on indigenous resources. Coal, it is true, still accounted for 10 per cent. of our exports, and woollens for 6 per cent. But the woollens were increasingly produced from imported wool; it had formed 50 per cent. of the available

[1] See R. F. Crawford, "Notes on the Food Supply of the United Kingdom, Belgium, France and Germany", *Journal of the Royal Statistical Society*, Vol. LXII, pp. 597–629.

[2] See estimate for 1911 by Sir Henry Rew, "The Nation's Food Supply", *Journal of the Royal Statistical Society*, Vol. LXXVI, pp. 98–105. The proportion in terms of value, provided by home production was about 52 per cent. if tea, coffee, cocoa and sugar (of which there was then no home production) are excluded.

supply[1] in 1857–63; it now formed about 84 per cent. It was a specialization still based predominantly on textiles. And new textile industries were beginning to grow all over the world—not only in North America, but also in Japan, India, China, and later in South America. Thus the structure became insecure almost at the moment that it was completed. The British share of the world total of production of manufactures inevitably declined as new industries grew up in other countries; it is almost a tautology to say so. Whereas the British share had been probably appreciably above 40 per cent. in 1850, it was down to about 32 per cent. in 1870, about 20 per cent. at the turn of the century and about 14 per cent. in 1913.[2]

The structure of 1913 was one of very considerable immediate advantage to Britain, but it was inherently fragile. No one country could possibly hope to retain indefinitely, however great its technical leadership, the share of world manufacturing that fell to us in the middle of the nineteenth century, or the share of world trade in manufactures that went with it. The share of that trade held by Britain fell from about 40 per cent. in 1870 to about 30 per cent. at the turn of the century and 27 per cent. in 1913. It was a declining share, however, in a rapidly growing total. Thus the problem of paying for imports was never acute before 1913; normal imports had never been increased to the full capacity to pay for them, and invisible earnings left a handsome investable surplus in most years. But what I wish, nevertheless, to emphasize is that, quite apart from wars, our 1913 structure was based on an advantage which was temporary and not permanent: that the incentives to shift resources to industry and reduce primary production were already in operation in many countries on which we depended, and might have been expected in the course of time to push us back from the position of extreme specialization that suited us so admirably for the moment.

It was, moreover—and I do not think this is generally realized—a structure that was not based, or not in its extreme form, on a system of comparative advantages. It is not true to say that British productivity in manufacturing was higher in relation to British productivity in agriculture than that of many of the countries from which we were increasing our imports. The ratio of the value of

[1] See C. T. Saunders, "Consumption of Raw Materials in the United Kingdom, 1851–1950", *Journal of the Royal Statistical Society*, Vol. CXV, pp. 336–38.

[2] See *Industrialisation and Foreign Trade*, League of Nations, 1945, p. 13.

production per head in industry to the value of production per head in agriculture has been more favourable to industry and less favourable to agriculture in the United States than in the United Kingdom certainly since 1870. The same is also true of Canada, if one may make plausible assumptions regarding Canadian productivity per head in agriculture for which contemporary estimates do not exist for the earlier years. It was only in Australasia and in South America that the comparative advantage lay throughout heavily on the side of agriculture.

The gain that we secured by specialization derived from the terms of trade subsisting everywhere between manufactures and primary products. Over the greater part of the last eighty years there has been an advantage to any economy anywhere (with exceptions in Australasia and South America) which moved resources out of agriculture into industry and which exported manufactures and imported primary products. We in Britain could benefit through the fact that our technical lead, our financial resources and our geographical setting put us in the position to move more quickly than others.

The structure was inherently fragile in a second sense. Growing population to be nourished with food, growing industries to be nourished with materials, meant increasingly that marginal supplies must be derived from abroad. Food supplies by 1913 came, as I have said, to the extent of about 55 per cent. from abroad. At the same time we were coming to depend ever more and more on raw-material imports, not only because of increased needs but also because of exhaustion of supplies. In 1857–63 we could supply all our needs of lead, 88 per cent. of our needs of tin and 71 per cent. of our needs of copper. By 1907–13 we supplied only 11 per cent. of our lead, 21 per cent. of our tin and 1 per cent. of our copper. In 1857–63 we could depend on our own wool supplies for 58 per cent. of our needs; in 1907–13 the figure was down to 22 per cent., and similarly for flax.[1]

The years from 1919 to 1939 saw the working out of some of these forces that already existed before 1913. But to those already existing forces was added a new and more powerful force: the emergence of the United States during the First World War to a position of leadership in manufacture. Her share of world production of manu-

[1] See C. T. Saunders, loc. cit.

factures had first exceeded our own in the 1880s; it was about two and a half times our own by 1913, and remained about four times our own through most of the inter-war years. But the United States share in foreign trade in manufactures was by no means proportionate to her production, and remained between a quarter and a third of our own down to 1913. It increased to well above a half of our own in the years immediately following 1918, and rose to about four-fifths of our own during the later inter-war years. That dramatic growth of competition in our markets, and the subsequent and comparable growth of that of Japan, together with the loss of foreign assets during 1914–18, meant that the structure of 1913 required to be changed far more rapidly and more extensively than would otherwise have been necessary. I would in retrospect regard many of the travails of the 1930s as part of the inevitable and painful process of world adjustment and of our own adjustment to the growth of the United States and Japan.

The immediate effects were, however, obscured and their severity diminished by the favourable turn of the terms of trade in the 1930s,[1] partly, it is true, the consequence of the lower prices of primary products relatively to manufactures to be expected in depression, but chiefly to be ascribed to the great revolutions in agriculture: mechanization, new fertilizers, better strains, better transport. This favourable turn permitted us to survive the 1930s with appreciably less structural change than would otherwise have been required.

What were the chief changes in our structure during these years? First, and largely a consequence of the change in the terms of trade, the ratio of the value of retained imports to net national income fell back from the 28 per cent. of 1913 to 20 per cent. in 1938. But with the aid of these improved terms of trade, and in the face of increasing difficulties, we retained the other main features of the 1913 structure. Manpower in agriculture continued to fall; it was down to about 5·7 per cent. of the occupied population[2] by 1931; the proportion in manufacturing remained about constant; that in commerce, finance and distribution continued to grow. But the main feature of these years was the decline of the textile industries and the growth

[1] The volume of imports which would have cost 100 units of exports in 1913 could be bought by an average of 70 units during the years 1931–39.

[2] On the classification of the period 1841–1911; the classification was slightly changed in 1921.

of the metal industries. In 1851 there were 22 per cent. of the occupied population in the textile industries; by 1911 the figure was about 13·5 per cent.; in 1931 it was below 11 per cent. and in 1951 under 8 per cent. The metal industries employed 6 per cent. in 1851; they had reached nearly 10 per cent. in 1911, about 12 per cent. in 1931 and 17·5 per cent. in 1951.

This change was naturally associated with the change in the character of our exports. Textiles had provided 63 per cent. in 1850 and 34 per cent. in 1913; by 1937 the figure was down to 24 per cent. and by 1951 to 19 per cent. Metals and engineering products provided 18 per cent. in 1850; they were 27 per cent. in 1913; they were up to 35 per cent. by 1937 and to 49 per cent. by 1951.

Despite the strains of the 1930s, we continued to increase our dependence on imported food. For our raw-material supplies, with the possible exception of iron ores, we also became increasingly dependent on imports. Home supplies of wool and flax and of non-ferrous metals declined further.

This structure was, however, proving increasingly difficult to maintain. Despite exceptionally favourable terms of trade, we were failing to pay our way on current account and balancing our payments with the help of drafts on our past foreign accumulations. Thus we entered the war with a structure very imperfectly adjusted to our current circumstances. The consequences of the war and, far more than those, the consequences of a reversal of the terms of trade left us with a structure very ill-adjusted to the world in which we now live.

May I look back for a moment on the century as a whole? In 1820 and right down to the 1870s we were scarcely as yet in any full sense a nation of shopkeepers. We were a nation of linen drapers—of John Gilpins rather than of William Whiteleys. We built our nineteenth-century economic structure and we multiplied the population of 1750 six-fold on the basis of our ability to sell cotton and woollens. We created by 1913 a nation which depended for about seven-eighths of its raw material supplies, apart from coal, and for over half of its food supplies on its continued ability to sell some kind of export into a world which was becoming less dependent on its textiles. Since the 1870s we had expanded metal and engineering exports, and by 1913 they were a quarter of the total. But it is mainly in the period between the wars that we changed to being a nation dependent primarily on our ability to sell engineering goods, and in that field we have never enjoyed the sort of predominance we had for over a hundred years in textiles.

Before I go on to consider the forces that may during the next decade require further adjustment of our structure, may I pause to contrast the structure that has emerged from our history during the past two centuries with that which has emerged from the very different history of Western Germany.[1] Western Germany has a population very similar to our own—49·0 millions, as against 50·8 for the United Kingdom. The total areas of the two countries are almost identical. The agricultural areas are not widely different: Western Germany had 8·5 million hectares of arable in 1948–52 as against 7·4 million in the United Kingdom; the United Kingdom had 12·1 million hectares of permanent grass against Germany's 5·5 million; Germany had 7·0 million hectares of forest as against our 1·5 million In normal peacetime conditions the real incomes per head have not been widely different; the United Kingdom probably had an advantage of some 15 per cent. as compared with the average of all Germany before the war, but the advantage over the more industrialized Western Germany was almost certainly less; recent calculations have shown a wider discrepancy for 1952, possibly as great as 20–25 per cent., a discrepancy not unexpected and largely explicable in terms of the different consequences of the war.

In all else the structures of the two countries are radically different. In 1953 the import ratio for the United Kingdom was about 26 per cent., that for Germany about 16 per cent. It is not possible to carry back the German ratio in terms of anything like the present area. In 1937–38, when the United Kingdom ratio was about 20–22 per cent., that for pre-war Germany as a whole, very much larger and more self-sufficient, was about 7–8 per cent. But the discrepancy had been much less in earlier years. In 1913, when the United Kingdom ratio was 28 per cent., that for the contemporary area of Germany was about 24 per cent.

The lower ratio and the lower income per head taken together mean that in 1953 German retained imports were about two-fifths British imports. Western Germany supports at present an industrial

[1] See, *inter alia*, *Economic Survey of Europe since the War*, United Nations, Geneva, 1953, pp. 97–99.

production about two-thirds of that of the United Kingdom, with imports of raw materials about one-third of the United Kingdom. She succeeds in doing this partly because of a much smaller activity in the textile industries, partly because of her almost complete dependence on her own timber resources; these two sources of savings of imports accounted for two-thirds of the difference.

In food, the United Kingdom is now dependent on imports for about half her foodstuffs; Western Germany for about one-fifth. But, with the imported food, the United Kingdom real consumption per head was in 1952 some 15–20 per cent higher than that of Germany.[1] The agricultural output of Western Germany is almost half as great again as that of the United Kingdom. She has achieved this by devoting to agriculture about 16 per cent. of her occupied male population, as against 6 per cent. for the United Kingdom.

I do not wish to hold up the Western German economy as a model that we ought to copy. Both countries have much that they might learn from each other. The higher standard of life that we have enjoyed has in the past, I am convinced, derived in considerable measure from our greater specialization and trade. I believe that Germany will be found as the years go by to be progressively moving again towards higher imports and higher exports, and in consequence becoming more directly competitive with the United Kingdom. But I do believe that one may learn both from the history of our own past and from a comparison with Germany that economic structures are not unchangeable and permanent for all time, but capable of great variation, and from time to time requiring great variation.

In what directions can we expect our own structure to change under the stimulus of the market forces and the economic pressures of a changing world? My own view—and I claim for it no special authority—is that the structure which we created to such profit in the second half of the nineteenth century was fundamentally based on two factors. First, it was based on the possession by us of a leadership in manufacturing and a corresponding share of world trade in manufactures which have been diminishing progressively. I do not think that it is within our power, whatsoever energy and skill we may develop, to recapture anything comparable with that leadership. It was based on a concentration of discovery, of scientific

[1] See *An International Comparison of National Production and the Purchasing Power of Currencies*, by Milton Gilbert and Irving B. Kravis, Table 12.

knowledge and of practical expertise within a single country such as we can hardly imagine to be capable of repetition by any country. It was based on a slowness of the dispersal of knowledge and a lack of the technical background required for receptivity such as can hardly be re-created once it has disappeared. The degree of technical leadership of the United States today is in no sense comparable with that of the United Kingdom in the middle of the nineteenth century. And to that we must add the continuing improvements in means of transport, and particularly in land transport. I think the degree of difference in comparative productivity in different industries, apart from advantages of access to very advantageous raw-material supplies, is diminishing as compared with the nineteenth-century differences, and to an increasing extent the country in which manpower is four-fifths as productive as that in another in one industry is apt to be four-fifths as efficient in a very wide range of industries. Thus the opportunities for one country to secure and hold a large export trade by leadership and the advantages of specialization seem to me to be less than they were.

Secondly, it was based on a relation between primary production and industry which in its extreme form I believe to have been temporary. There are signs that the forces which enabled us to benefit from the favourable terms of trade between manufacturing and primary production are working themselves out. The shift of resources from primary production in North America has been on on such a scale that United States agriculture has fallen from a share of 65 per cent. of the occupied population in 1850 to 29 per cent. in 1920 and to 16 per cent. in 1950. In North-western Europe as a whole the proportion in agriculture has fallen from 26 per cent. in 1920 to 19 per cent. in 1950. In Asia and in South America also there has been a very marked increase in industrial activity. Thus it is not only the high levels of activity and consequent demand for primary products in recent years which, despite the continuance of the rapid upward trend of productivity in primary production, have reversed the trend of the terms of trade. The movement out of primary production and into industry consequent upon the powerful incentives of the 1930s has also, I think, contributed largely and more permanently. The ratio of the value of production per head in agriculture to the value of production per head in industry is now almost everywhere much more favourable to agriculture than it has been for a generation. The prosperity of British agriculture in the past few years has been not solely, or even predominantly, the result of subsidies and other political favours; they have shared in the general recent prosperity of all primary producers everywhere.

For these reasons I believe that we are progressively moving into a world in which the advantages of our nineteenth-century structure in its extreme form will be less than in the past. I believe that by degrees, and under the pressures of the ordinary market forces, we must expect and be prepared to adjust ourselves to an import ratio a little nearer to that of Germany than that of today, and to the adjustment of the pattern of activity that may go with it. I have no desire to accelerate any necessary transition beyond the pace that changing world conditions may require; least of all have I any desire to lead the United Kingdom into uneconomic autarky.

But I am anxious lest an undue conservatism may regard the structure of fifty years ago as not only the ideal of that period but also the ideal for the present, and so resist structural change at the pace at which it may be necessary. For, as I see it, conservatism in these things may lead us to seek to preserve an unsuitable structure by taking measures to secure a balance of payments on current account of which the short-term effect is to reduce imports by reducing activity. By such measures we may well forfeit through reduced activity, and through reduced capital formation and reduced growth of productivity, considerably more than we gain at the margin by better international division of labour.

After such dramatic changes as have occurred as the result of the two wars of this century it is inevitable that our economy should require greater and more rapid change than if events had moved more smoothly and continuously. What we know least of all in the whole field of economics is the limits of practicable rates of change. We know how fast—or rather how slowly—the pattern has in fact changed over the past century. But we do not know just how fast it can be made to change by normal price incentives. These incentives will work in two ways; modifying the pattern of consumption through the change of relative prices, and modifying the pattern of production through the change of incentives. But there can be no question that large structural change requires considerable time. It requires a change in the pattern of our fixed capital, of our skills and of the geographical and industrial distribution of the working population. In some cases the required structural change can be facilitated by a change in the pattern of imports and their ratio to national income as different types of resources but relatively more or less scarce. But any large scale resort to this solution requires the expansion of exports, and that may well be the critical factor in all our problems.

In wartime, when very rapid structural change is essential, we have been accustomed both to accelerate the change and to diminish its immediate necessity by the twin operations of controlling the use of resources and rationing forms of final consumption involving resources which are temporarily scarce. My own fear is that events may continue to require us to make changes faster than a free and smoothly working economy can easily carry them through. It is for a willingness to face the necessities and implications of change when they come, and to foresee them and to be prepared for them before they come, that I would plead.

TABLE I

The Dependence of the British Economy on Imports

Year	Population of United Kingdom[1] (million)	Approximate ratio of retained imports to net national income at factor cost[2] (°/₀)
1688	7·4	5·5
1820	20·9	12
1850	27·4	18
1870	31·5	28
1880	34·9	33
1900	41·5	26
1913	45·8	28
1937	47·3	21
1951	50·2	32
1953	50·4	26

[1] For 1688 I have taken Gregory King's estimate, since I am using his national income and import estimates. For England (meaning, as is made clear, England and Wales) he estimates 5·5 million; he says that, "Scotland and Ireland are . . . not two-fifths of England in number of people." He goes on to say that, "England, Scotland and Ireland together contain . . . somewhat more than 7 million of people." I have taken the mean between 7·0 million and 7·7 million. All other figures down to 1900 from the Census of the following year. Figures for isolated years since 1900 are mid-year estimates. The figures for 1937, 1951 and 1953 refer, as does the national-income estimate, to the area now defined as the United Kingdom, i.e. excluding Eire; the figures for earlier years include what is now Eire.

[2] Estimates of Net National Income at Factor Cost from A. R. Prest, "National Income of the United Kingdom 1870–1946", *Economic Journal*, March, 1948, pp. 31–62, continued with help of official estimates. Earlier estimates of national income based on material from Colin Clark, *Conditions of Economic Progress*, and A. L. Bowley, *British Overseas Trade, 1700–1930*. Retained imports as revalued for earlier years by A. H. Imlah, loc. cit.

TABLE II

Percentage Distribution of the Occupied Population of England and Wales

	1821	1831	1951
Agriculture and Fishing	34·0	28·6	5
Trade, Manufactures and Handicraft	46·5	42·2	60
Others, not employed in above	19·5	29·2	35
	100	100	100

Note: The figures for 1951 represent only a rough guess of the orders of magnitude of the similar categories today.

TABLE III

Percentage Distribution of the Occupied Population of England and Wales, 1841–1951

	1841	1851	1861	1871	1881	1891	1901	1911	1911	1921	1931	1951
Agriculture and Fishing	21·6	21·4	18·2	14·2	12·4	10·3	8·5	8·1	7·8	6·8	5·6	4·7
Manufacturing	28·9	32·9	32·6	30·2	29·9	29·6	29·1	29·0	29·9	31·2	30·0	34·1
of which:												
Textiles and Clothing	19·0	22·2	20·6	18·1	17·2	16·4	14·1	13·4	13·7	11·4	10·7	7·7
Metals, Machinery, etc.	5·5	6·1	7·2	7·3	7·7	7·8	9·1	9·7	9·8	12·8	11·6	17·5
Other Manufacturing	4·3	4·6	4·7	4·8	5·0	5·4	5·9	6·0	6·4	7·1	7·7	8·9
Manufacture of Food, Drink and Tobacco	1·5	1·7	1·6	1·6	1·7	1·9	2·2	2·4	2·9	3·1	3·3	3·3
Mining and Quarrying	3·3	3·9	4·2	4·2	4·6	5·0	5·5	6·3	6·9	7·5	6·4	4·4
Building, Decorating, Contracting	5·4	5·0	5·3	5·7	6·3	5·7	7·1	5·8	5·3	4·4	5·6	6·2
General Labourers	5·8	4·1	3·4	4·9	5·0	4·7	2·9	1·8	1·5	—	—	—
Transport and Communications	3·0	5·4	6·2	6·6	7·6	8·4	9·7	9·5	6·9	7·0	6·8	7·7
Commerce, Finance and Distribution	4·8	5·3	6·0	6·8	7·2	7·9	9·0	10·5	13·2	13·2	15·5	13·8
Personal Service	19·2	14·6	15·6	16·6	16·1	16·3	14·6	14·1	15·1	11·8	12·8	7·5
Central and Local Government Employment	1·3	1·5	2·0	1·9	1·9	2·1	2·6	3·1	4·4	6·5	6·6	8·2
Residual	5·2	4·1	4·9	7·3	7·3	8·2	8·9	9·3	6·0	8·4	7·5	10·2

Source: 1841–1931: Census of Population, Occupation Tables; 1951: 1 per cent Sample Tables.

Figures for years prior to 1911 should be compared with those in the *first* column for the year 1911, and those in the *second* column of the year 1911 should be used for comparison with 1921–51. This break is rendered necessary by a changed method of classification introduced in 1911. Prior to that year the classification had been a mixed industrial and occupational one. In 1911, in addition to the main tables on the old mixed classification, there appeared tables on an industrial classification. But it was not until 1921 that there appeared a complete separation of the classification into an industrial one and an occupational one. The 1921 General Report commented that this involved a very substantial change. For this reason no significance should be attributed to small changes between 1911 and 1921.

From 1911 onwards the industrial classification has been used. This is not only more useful from an economic standpoint, but is also to be preferred from the point of view of comparability. The 1921 General Report commented that although the classification prior to 1911 was a mixed one, yet it was largely industrial in nature, with only a few general occupational headings. This was so even after 1881 when certain occupations, such as clerks or porters, which should formerly have been classed to the separate manufacture or trade with which their work was connected, were collected together under general headings. That this change probably did not destroy the comparability of the figures before and after 1881 is apparent when the numbers in these affected occupations in 1871, 1881 and 1891 are compared.

Table III is based in the first instance on a comparative table for 1881–1921 reprinted in the 1921 General Report and originally prepared at the request of the Balfour Committee. This table has been extended forwards and backwards by adjusting the classification in other censuses to conform with that on the table. The odd general occupational groups which exist prior to 1911 are where possible allocated to their most appropriate industrial group, i.e. carmen are put in transport. Where this is not possible, as in the case of clerks, they are omitted and included in the residual group.

The separation of distribution from manufacturing was not effectively carried out until 1911, though in 1901 it was nearly complete. The censuses prior to 1901 do permit, however, a high degree of separation. For most manufacturing groups the proportion of those engaged in wholesale and retail distribution in 1911 for which separate figures are available in earlier censuses is in the region of 90 per cent. The principal exception is the group concerned with distributing the products of the textile and clothing industries. In this case separate figures exist in earlier censuses for only about three-quarters of those engaged in distributing these products in 1911. This incomplete separation of manufacture and distribution prior to 1901, sizeable only in the case of textiles and clothing, affects the comparison of figures before and after 1901. Prior to 1901, particularly in the case of textiles, the manufacturing figures will be a little higher than they should be and the distribution figure rather lower.

The residual in the table is composed principally of those engaged in professions (by far the most important), public utilities, entertainments and sport.

Down to 1911 the Census authorities were improving their classification in minor respects, and by degrees indefinite classes, such as general labourers, were absorbed into their appropriate classifications without substantial change of the character of activity. This will somewhat affect the comparability of such groups as building.

The preparation of this Table, in addition much other assistance throughout the article, I owe to Mr. G. D. Garton of the Department of Applied Economics, Cambridge University.

Table IV

Composition of the United Kingdom Exports

Year	Manufactured exports as percentage of total exports	Textile exports as percentage of total exports	Metal and engineering exports as percentage of total exports	Coal exports as percentage of total exports
1830	91	67	11	1
1850	93	63	18	2
1870	91	56	21	3
1890	86	43	25	7
1913	79	34	27	10
1937	78	24	35	7
1951	88	19	49	1

Note: Manufactured exports correspond to Class III: Textile exports are broadly III, I, J, K, L, and part of III, U (1951 classification); i.e. they exclude clothing. Metal and engineering exports are broadly III, C, D, E, F, G, S, and part of III, U. Coal exports are II, A. Prior to 1913 the alphabetical list has been put on a classification as close as possible to that of 1913–51.

Table V

Composition of United Kingdom Imports

	1820	1850	1870	1900	1913	1929	1933
Food and Livestock	31	34	35	42	37	40·5	46
Of which: Grain	4	10	9	9	9	7	8
Raw Materials	60	59	50	39	43	39·5	41
Of which: Textile Materials	24	32	28	16	17	11	13
Finished Manufactured Goods	9	7	15	19	20	20	13
Total	100	100	100	100	100	100	100

Note: The analysis given above is derived from the work of Werner Schlote, *British Overseas Trade from 1700 to the 1930s* (translation by W. H. Chaloner and W. O. Henderson, Blackwell, 1952). He has attempted to distribute the recorded imports according to the Brussels international classification, and has revalued the imports for the purpose of calculating volumes and the prices of a series of base years and has then linked the separate series. While the latter process is irrelevant to my immediate problem, I have used his material, since it gives a convenient and constant set of classifications and enables me to go back to 1820. But a reader should be warned that the relative values of different products underlying this table are those that emerge from Schlote's work (*vide* op. cit., pp. 27–30), and which Schlote calls "quantities at base year prices". Since Schlote's analysis ends at 1933, the comparison cannot be extended into the post-war period.

Table VI

Ratio of Productivity in Agriculture to Productivity in Industry

	1870	1900	1913	1937
United Kingdom	1·07	0·93	0·80	0·60
United States	0·52	0·44	0·39	0·39
Canada	0·96	0·63	0·43	0·27
Australia	—	—	1·39	1·41
New Zealand	—	—	1·38	1·09
Argentine	—	—	—	2·12
Germany	—	—	0·60	0·48
France	2·0	—	0·77	0·59
Denmark	—	—	—	0·49

Note: The above table is derived from estimates made by Mr. Colin Clark in *The Conditions of Economic Progress*. The underlying figures are calculated by him in his "international units", and are therefore at the relative prices of 1925–34 and not at current relative prices. The output of agriculture is valued at world prices, and does not reflect the special advantages or protection available to domestic agricultural producers. The ratios are—it should be emphasized—the result of comparing *average* productivity in industry with *average* productivity in agriculture; the ratios of the *marginal* productivities may be appreciably different.

9

ECONOMIC FOUNDATIONS OF WAGE POLICY

J. R. HICKS

Bristol, September, 1955

TWENTY-SIX years ago, when the British Association was meeting at Cape Town, the President of Section F was Henry Clay, and he took as his subject "The Public Regulation of Wages in Great Britain."[1] I remember, from that time, how great a stimulus that paper was to my own thinking, and I have not changed my opinion of it. Of the problem of wages, as it then stood, Clay gave what I still believe to have been a substantially correct analysis. But a tide of events, which set in almost as he spoke, was to bring about a great transformation. The revolutions which have occurred in the realm of fact, quite as much as those which have occurred in the realm of ideas, have presented us with a wages question which looks very different from the wages question of 1929. Nevertheless, underlying the differences, some of them real differences, some of them seeming, there is a certain continuity. I propose, in this paper, to survey some aspects of the developments which have occurred, and to attempt an estimation of their significance. I believe that the time has come when it is desirable to make an effort to bring the whole matter back into focus.

The first thing on which Clay had to remark, from the standpoint of 1929, was the spread of collective bargaining (and other forms of *public regulation*) from the mere fraction of the wage-earning population (perhaps a quarter) which had been covered some twenty years previously, to a point where (as he said) "we may safely conclude that there are few important gaps left in the provision for the settlement of wages by collective bargaining in Great Britain". But then went on:[2]

[1] *Economic Journal*, Vol. XXXIX, p. 323.
[2] Ibid., p. 324.

"The precise nature of this change is worth some consideration. It was not the introduction for the first time of standardized rates of pay in time-work occupations. Even if we leave out of account the considerable part of the field covered by Trade Unionism at the beginning of the century, it is probable that in most districts, in which an occupation was followed by considerable numbers, there were customary rates commonly recognized, which the majority of employers observed. These rates were not so definite and secure as they became when they were embodied in a collective agreement; but outside the so-called 'sweated trades', they were a limitation on the freedom of the individual employer to vary rates. Immediately, wages were fixed for him rather than by him, although ultimately they had to conform to the demand for labour, of which he was the channel. Nor was the change a universal substitution of collective for individual bargaining about rates. In piece-work industries after the change, as before, the vast majority of rates were settled by an individual bargain between the workman and the employer's representative. . . . The significant and essential change was the change in procedure. Wage-rates in any case have to be adjusted to changes in the demands for different kinds of labour, changes in the purchasing power of money, changes in the general prosperity and activity of industry. Before the war, outside the organized industries, the adjustment was made by the individual action of the employers, who first felt the need; today the process of general wage-changes has, we may say, been constitutionalized."

I have quoted this passage from Clay's paper because it seems to me to describe, with considerable precision, just what it was that had happened. It has never been the general rule that wage-rates have been determined simply and solely by supply and demand. Even on pure grounds of efficiency, it is desirable that the wage which is offered should be acceptable, acceptable both to the worker himself and to those with whom he is to work. There has in consequence always been room for wages to be influenced by non-economic forces—whether by custom (which, economically speaking, means supply and demand of the day before yesterday), or by any other principle which affects what the parties to the wage-bargain think to be *just* or *right*. Economic forces do affect wages, but only when they are strong enough to overcome these *social* forces. Now what happened, as a result of the spread of public regulation, was that the social forces grew in strength. As Clay put it:

"The mere fact of publicity, or organized discussion, invites appeal to social and ethical standards of 'fair' and 'living' wages, to pseudo-principles such as the sanctity of pre-war *real* wages, to the unpopularity of reducing the rates of wages of the lower paid workers, none of which have any bearing on the capacity of industry to pay wages and provide employment."

The main thing is that the new procedure insulated the wage structure from its old exposure to economic pressures, so that it could move—to a considerable extent—on a course of its own.

But the economic forces were not abolished by the increased resistance which could be offered to them; if they were not allowed to influence the determination of wages, they would express themselves in other ways. If the actual wage-level drew too far away from the "equilibrium" wage-level, being (as in fact it would be) above the equilibrium wage-level, the discrepancy would express itself in a growth of unemployment. And though the "social" wage-structure could stand up to a certain amount of unemployment, there must (so Clay thought) be a limit beyond which it must give. Then, after much pain and grief, there would be a return to something nearer to an "equilibrium wage".

That is what Clay expected to happen; but, as we know, it is not what did happen. Unemployment did increase, as he expected; but though the wage-structure yielded a little, on the whole it did not give way. What did give was another link in the chain—the Gold Standard.

In the new world which began after 1931 the problem of wages is bound to have a distinctly different character from that which it had in the older time. Since 1931, wages questions have been closely associated with monetary questions; it is even true that the *general* level of wages has become a monetary question. So long as wages were being determined within a *given* monetary framework, there was some sense in saying that there was an "equilibrium wage", a wage that was in line with the monetary conditions that were laid down from outside. But the world we now live in is one in which the monetary system has become relatively elastic, so that it can accommodate itself to changes in wages, rather than the other way about. Instead of actual wages having to adjust themselves to an equilibrium level, monetary policy adjusts the equilibrium level of money wages so as to make it conform to the actual level.[1] It is hardly an exaggeration to say that instead of being on a Gold Standard, we are on a Labour Standard.

I should like to make it quite clear, before going further, that I myself regard the Labour Standard as an unquestionable benefit. So long as we retain it, we are protected against the unemployment that arises from a discrepancy between the actual wage-level and the "equilibrium wage-level"; and though there are other causes of unemployment than this, it has been one of the main causes of unemployment in the past, and it is a great gain that this cause of unemployment has been removed. It is not a gain which anyone should desire to give up; it is nevertheless not a simple matter to find ways by which we can be sure of preserving it.

For the Labour Standard, in our twenty years' experience of it, has been shown to possess a number of defects, of which some are decidedly dangerous. The first set of defects, which merit attention, though they fall rather outside my present subject, relate to the international consequences of the new arrangements. If the value of the pound is fixed in terms of British labour, and the value of the mark is fixed in terms of German labour, the pound–mark exchange will not remain steady unless the value of British labour in terms of German labour remains steady. But this last is a matter of the real economic progress and economic policies of the two countries; it requires something more than a monetary arrangement to control it. While the Gold Standard was an international standard, the Labour Standard is a national standard; even at its best, it is bound to be a source of difficulty in the sphere of international currency relations. But these difficulties are very familiar; I need do no more than allude to them in this place.

Already, in the first years of the Labour Standard, these international repercussions were a grave preoccupation; indeed, at that time they were the only consequence of the change which aroused much anxiety. But as time has gone on another weakness has been revealed, which (at least for the time being) has pushed the international weakness into the background. Whereas, under the Gold

[1] I do not want to suggest that it does this perfectly; but this is what it is trying to do. The problems which arise when demand is extended too far, or not far enough, to maintain the desired general level of employment, are of major importance; but they lie outside the scope of this paper.

Standard, the value of the national money in terms of the Standard was fixed by the State (and the maintenance, or in a few cases the regulation, of this gold value was recognized as a major responsibility of the State), under the Labour Standard the value of money in terms of labour undergoes no deliberate determination. It is a mere by-product of the process of wage-fixing; wage-fixing being sectional, the value of money in terms of the standard comes to be determined by impersonal forces, and those forces seem to have a strong tendency to pull it one way.

It is not surprising that this danger took some time to declare itself. In the last days of the old system, when the new (fortified) wage structure was resisting the monetary pressures that were being exerted upon it, successful resistance expressed itself in the form of rigidity. Economic forces were pressing wages downwards; social forces held them up. The net effect was that the level of money wages held firm. It was very natural for Clay, in 1929, to think in terms of rigid wages. Over the years 1924–28 (the only "normal" years which were available to him as a basis for generalization) the Bowley index of weekly wage-rates in Great Britain had been rock-like—it had never moved by as much as a point. Under the impact of the Depression, there was indeed a marked *fall* in wages (though much less than the fall in the cost of living); but it was some time before the relief of that pressure led to a rise which went beyond the previous level. As late as 1937, the wage-index was within 1 per cent. of its 1924–28 figure. Thus the Labour Standard started operations with the very natural assumption that the level of wages (or the value of money in terms of labour) could, at least in Britain, be taken as given. With rigid wages, the problem of the new standard was one of external stability; internal stability did not seem to be a problem.

During the war years the position was, of course, very different; but war inflation is no new experience, and the significance of war inflation for the future of the Labour Standard did not reveal itself at once. It is only in the years since 1945, which have been marked by a continual rise in the wage-index, rarely falling short of 4 per cent. per annum, that the existence of a special problem of the Labour Standard has become apparent. Must we conclude, from the experience of the last ten years, that the Labour Standard has an inherent inflationary bias? If so, is it much more dangerous than the similar biases which have been detected in other monetary systems? These are the main questions which I want to discuss in the rest of this paper.

One further point must be cleared out of the way before I can begin. It is possible to argue that the main evil of monetary instability, as it was known in past times, was the unemployment which periodically accompanied it; if we have to expect an age of monetary instability, but are guaranteed against the accompanying unemployment, the expectation can be borne with equanimity. There is something in this argument, but the optimism which it engenders can be carried too far. A rapid rate of wage-inflation must surely be an evil, if only because of the diversion of effort into fixing and re-fixing of wages and hitherto stable prices, effort which might otherwise be used for more productive purposes. A very rapid rate of wage-inflation could threaten the continuance of the Labour Standard altogether. I would, however, admit that there is some rate of wage-inflation which, if it can be prevented from accelerating, is by no means intolerable; the question is what means exist for keeping it within tolerable limits.

Let us, then, go back to the labour market, and look at it more closely. Granted the labour standard, can we lay down any general principles about the ways in which wages are likely to be determined? What are the factors making for inflation, and what (if any) are those by which the inflation may be held in check? These are questions which can, I believe, be answered if we tackle them in the spirit of Clay's analysis, though we get no sensible answers to them if we persist in treating them as pure problems of economics, in a narrow sense.

The purely economic analysis of collective bargaining, in terms of the theory of bilateral monopoly, used to conceive of wage-rates being fixed, on a balance of bargaining advantage, between a trade union which sought to push wages as high as possible without causing intolerable unemployment, and an employers' association which sought to press wages as low as possible without causing a shortage of labour. If one thinks in those terms the prospects of anything like stable wages, under a Labour Standard, do indeed look bleak. For the labour market then becomes a pure case of unstable equilibrium. It is not necessary to suppose that each trade union is completely safeguarded against the danger of unemployment in its own trade. If it is laid down that a rise in wages in the A-industry is not to produce any general increase in unemployment, that is enough. For effective demand (for goods in general) will then have to be expanded somewhat when A-wages rise.[1] But that will increase the bargaining power of the workers in other industries, so that if wages in these other industries are determined on the same bilateral monopoly principle, they will rise too. But that, under the assumptions we are making, will call forth a further increase in effective demand, which provides an opportunity for a further rise in the A-industry. The only thing which would slow down the general rise in wages would be the time taken to negotiate wage-changes; and that, if it was to people's interest to speed it up, could presumably be speeded up.

Now I would quite admit that there are some occasions on which the actual process of wage-fixing takes a form which is not far away from that implied in this model; but I find it hard to believe that it has any general validity. We are now learning that the pure theory of monopoly has a very limited application to the behaviour of businessmen on the markets on which they sell their products; it is even less likely that it has much application to the labour market—on either side. We get a better clue to actual behaviour if we think of wages as being determined by an interplay between social and economic factors, instead of being based on economic factors—and crude economic factors at that—alone. As we have seen, this was true to a considerable extent under the old conditions. It is still more likely to be true under the Labour Standard, when everyone is bound to have some realization that the number of shillings in the pay packet are not the thing that really matters. Money wages are not demanded for their own sake, but as a means towards something else.

The only exception to this rule which I can think of, and it is a very partial exception, is that a wage claim may sometimes be made on the basis of comparison with what the wage of that class of labour has been in the past. It certainly was true, in the old days, that a

[1] How far this rise in demand comes about *naturally* (if monetary and fiscal policy does not prevent it), or how far deliberate intervention is needed to procure it, is a question that I do not have to raise in this paper. It will be simpler to talk as if "steps have to be taken" to procure the increase in demand; but by using such expressions I do not mean to prejudge the question whether these steps are of a positive or negative character.

wage-cut would be followed, at the first opportunity, by a demand for a restoration of the wage to its former level. But with the increased strength of the unions, under the Labour Standard, all that is left of this point is the general resistance to any cuts in previously agreed wage-rates, which is one of the principles on which the new wage-system seems to proceed. It is true that if wages can go up, but cannot go down, that is enough in itself to give the system an inflationary bias; it does not, however, follow that the bias will be so strong as to be unmanageable.

Otherwise, if we think of the grounds on which cases are made for a rise in the wages of any section of labour, the mere money value of the wages received has nothing to do with them. Wage disputes are not concerned with money wages; they are concerned with the relations of money wages to the money values of other things. But the things with which comparison is made differ from one wage-dispute to another; it will be useful to classify them under three heads. Of course, it may often happen that more than one sort of comparison is playing a part in some particular claim; nevertheless, the distinction between them is readily recognizable in practice. And the economic significance of claims on one ground or another is decidedly different.[1]

The three things with which comparison is most naturally made are: (1) the prices of the things labour buys—the cost of living; (2) the wages of other workers—differentials; (3) the profits earned by the employer. I propose to discuss these three comparisons rather separately, but in each case from a double point of view. On the one hand, I want to ask about the conditions in which wage-claims on the basis of each comparison are most likely to be pressed—a question which, if we can answer it, may throw some light upon the probable extent of wage-inflation in the future; on the other hand, I want to say something about the attitude which other members of society should take towards wage-claims made on one

[1] I should like to emphasize that the classification I am making does not merely refer to the grounds on which claims are put forward by the Unions; the same motives play a part in determining the attitude taken by employers to the claims which the Unions make. Doubtless it is true that supply-and-demand considerations have more influence on employers than they have on the Unions; but it is impossible to make sense of what happens unless one admits that the same general principles of equity in wage-determination are accepted, in a large measure, by both sides.

basis or another, with special reference to the economic arguments by which that attitude may be (or perhaps I may dare to say should be) affected.

The first of my three heads is the cost of living. The ratio of wages to the cost of living is what the economist calls real wages; the desirability of having real wages as high as possible, consistently with high employment, is a social objective which he is inclined to take for granted. Nevertheless, it is clear that wage-claims are not ordinarily made on the mere ground that the workers would like to have higher real wages; rises in real wages do for the most part come about in fact as a consequence of rises in productivity (either at home or abroad) without wage policy playing, at bottom, any more than a passive part in the process. When the cost-of-living motive does become important, in relation to wage-claims, is when extraneous factors are tending to produce a rise in the cost of living relatively to wages—or what comes to the same thing, a fall in real wages. It is in such circumstances that the cost-of-living motive takes the lead, and becomes, under the Labour Standard, an independent force making for inflation.

But in a modern economy, what has normally to be expected is rising productivity; and rising productivity, combined with constant money wages, means falling prices. So long as this tendency remains dominant, there is no need for there to be any pressure for rising money wages on account of the cost of living. The cost of living appears as an independent cause of wage inflation only at times when the normal course of economic progress is interrupted; its appearance is a symptom that something more fundamental is going, or has gone, wrong. Thus it is, of course, a major issue in war-time; it is also important whenever the march of rising real wages suffers a setback, due (for instance) to some change, adverse to this country, in our economic relations with the world outside. The novelty of the Labour Standard is that in the latter case, as well as the former, the cost-of-living motive becomes a source of inflationary pressure. In this respect the lessons of the Korean episode were perhaps more significant than those of the war with Hitler.

The only anti-inflationary measures which are available, under the Labour Standard, to deal with such situations are price-control and, if necessary, rationing; it is one of the costs of the Labour

Standard that these measures required to be introduced in order to deal with slighter and more temporary falls in real wages than would previously have required such drastic treatment. Further, though this is the only way out, it is difficult to make it wholly effective; if it is not wholly effective, it brings other troubles with it.

Suppose, for instance, that some external event (say an adverse movement of the terms of trade) makes it necessary to reduce consumption by a small percentage. If the reduction could take place by a rise in prices, without wages rising, prices would fall again when the shortage was over, and consumption would recover without further action. Alternatively, if the rise in wages could be wholly prevented by control over prices, the reduction in consumption (which cannot be avoided) would be brought about by an excess of demand over supply; supplies would recover when the shortage was over, and the controls could be lifted forthwith. But if the controls do not wholly prevent the rise in wages, or are introduced too late to have that effect, there may be an *apparent* rise in real wages amid the shortage; though consumption has to be diminished, the ratio of the money wage to the controlled price-level rises. In this case a mere recovery of supplies to their old level will not immediately enable the controls to be lifted without a renewal of inflation. For though the old real wage could be re-established, the apparent real wage (in the sense of the ratio of wages to prices) cannot be made effective on a free market until productivity has risen further. I think one can detect an element of this story in our own recent experience. It is one of the drawbacks of using controls to meet a temporary emergency that a "phoney" relation of wages to prices can be established under the shelter of the controls, a relation which does not truly measure the real gains of labour; yet it is this "phoney" relation which is sought to be maintained, in place of a maintenance of the real standard of living, when the controls are removed.

I turn to my second heading—relative wages in the narrower sense, the relation of one wage to another. If we have to take it for granted that it is hardly possible, under the Labour Standard, for the money wages of any group of workers to be *reduced*, it follows that troubles about wage differentials can themselves be a cause of inflation. In the simplest possible terms, if A-workers think that their wages should be 10 per cent. higher than those of B-workers, while B-workers think that their wages should be equal to those of A-workers, the satisfaction of the claims of one party must necessarily give rise to claims by the other. If both sets of workers are employed in the same industry, a series of concessions to such claims may push the costs of this industry right out of line with those of other industries; then, even under a Labour Standard, the industry will find itself in difficulties. But if troubles about differentials become widespread, this brake on the wage-rise may disappear. The increase in effective demand, which has to be induced in order to prevent the first wage-rise from causing unemployment, facilitates wage-increases elsewhere. The industries which have been left behind in the advance then become sensitive in their turn, both because of the inter-industry differentials which have come into existence through the sectional advance and because of the rising cost of living. It accordingly appears, without going further, that though wage-differentials can give rise to a certain amount of soreness without causing more than localized trouble, they must, on the whole, be moderately acceptable if they are not, under a Labour Standard, to be themselves a source of inflation.

But how can wage-differentials be acceptable? To those who feel the ethical urge to equality as a guiding impulse, the clearest thing about wage-differentials is that they ought always if possible to be reduced. Such sentiments have lately been expressed with cogency by Mrs. Wootton, the title of whose book[1] I have deliberately echoed in the title of this paper. Nevertheless, one can appeal to Mrs. Wootton herself for a demonstration that these sentiments, though they are without doubt *one* of the "social" forces at work on the wage-structure, are in practice overlaid by other "social" forces which work in the opposite direction. In practice, differentials do tend to be acceptable if they have custom behind them—if they are in accordance with what the people who suffer from them, as well as those who gain from them, have come to expect. Thus in conditions when the level of money wages is, broadly speaking, stationary, the purely egalitarian urge to raise the wages of the lower-paid workers relatively to others is not often in practice very strong. It is true that egalitarian sentiments have more power when wages are changing. Especially if the impetus to a wage-rise is

[1] *The Social Foundations of Wage Policy.*

derived from the cost-of-living motive, it is recognized that a fall in real wages is a more serious matter for the lower-wage than for the higher-wage groups; the former have a stronger case for a cost-of-living bonus than the latter. In such circumstances wage-differentials do tend to narrow: sometimes actually in money terms, but more often by giving both groups the *same* rise in money terms, in spite of the difference in the wages from which they began. This has in fact the effect of diminishing the real advantage of the better paid, in view of the higher price-level.

Thus, if one looks entirely at these "social" forces, custom is the static and equality the dynamic element; time, especially when aided by inflation, might be expected to iron all differentials flat. Certainly there is a tendency in that direction; but how far it can go depends upon the economic obstacles which may lie in its path. There are economic factors to be taken into account, though the precise way in which they can operate under a Labour Standard needs some consideration.

Let us begin from a state of all-round full employment of labour, in which there is yet no "over-employment"; the demand for labour equals the supply in all trades. Now suppose that wage-rates, in some particular trade, are raised to such an extent as would cause a substantial reduction in employment in that trade, if there were no expansion of demand in general. If, however, demand is expanded, the appearance of unemployment may be prevented. But the expansion of demand will have to take a particular form (involving special protection for the high-wage industry) if its difficulties are thereby to be overcome. Otherwise, though the demand for its products will indeed be expanded (so that employment of the high-wage labour will fall less than it would have fallen if the expansion had not occurred), the demand for other products will be expanded at the same time. Among the labour producing these products we have assumed that there is no unemployment. A moderate increase in demand will accordingly produce a situation which there is some fall in employment in the A-trade (as we may call it) combined with an excess of demand over supply (involving unfilled vacancies) in other (B) trades. There are now two cases, according as the workers who are unable to get employment in the A-trade can, or cannot, step into the vacancies which have appeared elsewhere. If they can, there will be no net unemployment as a result of the change in relative wages; all that will have happened is a transfer of labour from A to B. But if there are difficulties in the way of the transfer, it may be necessary to create a severe shortage of labour in the B-trades before the labour displaced from the A-trade can be absorbed. The maintenance of full employment then implies the creation of severe labour shortages.

But let us take the milder case first. It is highly probable that the situation implied in this case is no novelty. If the workers in skilled trades, by the use of bargaining power, push their wages to an unnecessarily high level, they limit the scope for employment in those trades, but they do not necessarily cause any labour to be unemployed; all that happens is that some people, who might have got employment in those trades, have to seek it elsewhere. This sort of thing could occur under the old conditions, and it can still occur under a Labour Standard. Differentials which owe their origin to no better cause than this can last a long time, and become hallowed by custom. And differentials which did once have an economic function, but are maintained by custom after they have lost it, fall from the economic point of view into a similar category.

It is obviously probable that the wage-structure, at any particular time, will contain many "unnecessary" or "uneconomic" differentials of this type; but their identification can never be a simple matter. The test which the economist would be inclined to use, whether or not a reduction in wages would increase employment and output in the trade affected, is not easy to use, nor is it in all cases quite conclusive. It is true, if this test is satisfied, that the additional employment is a clear gain to the workers who move (for they need not move unless they think it is to their advantage to do so); while the consequential increase in output is a clear gain to the consumers who take the additional units (for they need not take them unless they conceive themselves to gain by so doing). It is true that these shifts are clear gains, while the loss to the workers who were previously employed (and whose wages are reduced) is in some sense "balanced" by a reduction in cost which is a gain to other parties. But though these principles may be accepted, some weight can nevertheless be given to the counter-contention that the lowering of (relative) wages may lower standards of skill and craftsmanship, in such a way as to wipe out in the longer run much or all of the short-run gain. Those concerned have a strong interest to make as much as they can of this counter-argument; we can recognize that, and still admit that there are cases in which it does have a certain validity.

It does nevertheless seem clear, in the light of this analysis, that actual differentials are always, to a considerable extent, historically determined; their correspondence with those which would ensure maximum efficiency in the distribution of labour cannot be expected to be very close. It follows that the "squeezing" of differentials (which we have seen to be a feature of cost-of-living inflation) has some economic as well as social function. It squeezes out differentials which have become fossilized; in doing so, it serves the cause of efficiency as well as that of distributive justice.

All the same, the fact that it does so is really no more than an accident. Since it is not itself impelled by any motive of economic efficiency, it can easily go too far. If it overshoots the mark, and reduces differentials below the amounts which are economically justified, we get a new problem, which is in fact a problem of the second case which I left over a little while back, and to which I must now turn.

If the differential between skilled and less skilled is fixed too low, so that it is the relatively low-wage labour which is overvalued, an intensity of demand which is sufficient to maintain full employment among skilled workers will be insufficient for the full employment of the less skilled; an intensity which is sufficient to employ the less skilled will cause a shortage of labour in the skilled trades. An intensity which is between these two limits will leave some unemployment among the less skilled, and some unfilled vacancies among the skilled; but the less skilled will *not* be able to move over to fill these vacancies. Those who are unemployed are unlikely to be suitable to fill the vacancies, even if they are trained; while those who would be suitable will not move, because the incentive is insufficient. It is accordingly impossible, if differentials are too narrow, to maintain full employment without creating a scarcity of skilled labour.

Such a scarcity need not be inflationary, but it is only too likely to work out in such a way that it will be. For it is necessary, at this point, to distinguish between those trades in which the collectively agreed rates have a close correspondence with actual earnings, and those in which the agreed rates are minima, so that actual earnings can easily move out of line with what has been collectively fixed.[1] If the skilled trades, whose wages had become relatively depressed, were all of the first class, then (so far as I can see) the shortage of skilled labour would create inefficiencies, but would not lead to any general movement in wages. If, at the other extreme, they were all of the second class, it would be impossible to reduce *earnings* differentials below the amount which was economically justified. Any attempt to do so would merely cause the earnings of the higher-wage group to rise above their minima; the market for their labour, under the conditions of scarcity, would become a competitive market. In fact, however, we have neither of these extreme cases; the actual situation is a mixture of the two, some skilled trades belonging to one type, some to the other. The effect of labour scarcity must then be a rise in earnings in the "free-wage" trades; but this creates a disparity (which is felt to be a disparity) between them and the other skilled trades in which wages are "fixed". Conditions thus become favourable for a rise in wages in the "fixed-wage" skilled trades; and such a rise, in the circumstances supposed, is not without economic justification. But these "fixed" wages are a part of the regular structure of agreed wages; a rise in any part of it tends to produce a general tendency to an upward movement, working through the "social" links which tie the various parts of the structure together. This is the way in which an attachment to "wrong" relative wages can be an inflationary element; its inflationary influence cannot be removed (consistently with full employment) until people become prepared to accept economically reasonable differentials—differentials which are sufficient, that is, to ensure that lasting shortages of important classes of skilled labour are avoided.

I would emphasize the word "lasting". It does not follow from my analysis that a temporary scarcity of some particular kind of skilled labour, even if it leads to a sharp increase in the earnings of that trade, out of line with those of other comparable trades, need have very far-reaching effects on the wage-structure in general.

[1] The importance of this point was brought home to me by the studies of Mr. Kenneth Knowles, which have appeared in the *Bulletin* of the Oxford Institute of Statistics from 1951 onwards. (See in particular his "Structure of Engineering Earnings", *Bulletin*, September, 1954.) But this is not the only place in which my reflections have been stimulated by a consideration of the facts which Mr. Knowles has so ably brought together.

Since it takes time, often a considerable time, to select and train additional workers for any specialized trade or occupation, it must be expected that the wage (or earnings) which will equate supply and demand in the short run, after a rise in demand has taken place, will be higher than that which would induce a sufficient supply in the long period. This is indeed one of the common ways in which unnecessarily high differentials come into existence; wages are pushed up at a time of initial scarcity, and they fail to come down at the later stage when there has been time for the supply of labour to become more ample. Ideally, what should happen in such cases is that the agreed minimum should be kept in relation with the long-run supply-price of labour, while the incentive to move (only temporarily required) should be given by a temporary rise in wages above the minimum. For sufficiently temporary scarcities, one can perhaps detect a tendency for the wage-system to be operated in something like this manner. It is indeed more in accordance with trade-union principles that negotiated wages should reflect what can be maintained as a regular thing over a period than that they should fluctuate up (and, at least relatively, down) with every fluctuation of demand and supply on the labour market.

This brings me to my last heading, profits—on which I shall have to be brief, and must therefore do much less than justice to the subject. It is obvious that when businesses are earning high profits they can be more easily brought to concede claims for higher wages; it follows for this reason alone that it is in conditions of high profits that claims for higher wages are most likely to be made. But under the Labour Standard we have the complication that profits in general are not compressed by a rise in wages in general; thus if it should be the case that the level of profits necessary to induce full employment was itself so high as to call forth wage claims automatically, indefinite wage-inflation would be inevitable from this cause alone. But though it is easy to make our flesh creep with this argument, the assumptions on which it is based are not really very convincing. If wages were centrally negotiated, between a Grand National Trade Union and a National Employers' Association, inflation might indeed proceed in this manner for a time; but the futility of the proceeding would rapidly become apparent, so that the wage-bargain would have to be merged in a treaty which would cover far more than the determination of wages. But as things are, both the structure of the trade-union movement and the variety of the systems of wage-payment that are practised (on the whole for good reasons) in different trades make such centralization exceedingly unlikely. So long as wage-bargaining remains sectional, the profit comparison, though it must always be an element in the determination of wages, can hardly become so dominant as it has been assumed to be in the argument to which I have just been alluding.

Though wage-claims on other grounds are more likely to be pressed in conditions of high profits, a direct claim for higher wages on the grounds of the profits that are being made by employers is a dangerous claim to make. It can so easily be turned the other way up. If it is laid down as a rule that wages should go up when profits are high, the consequence, that they should not go up (or should even go down) when profits are low, cannot easily be resisted. This is a lesson which trade unions have had much opportunity to learn in the past; and on the whole their history would suggest that it is a lesson which they have learned. Even in conditions of full employment, there remain enough industries with relatively low profits to ensure that the lesson will not quickly be forgotten. The principle that it is wiser to put forward wage-claims on other bases than the profits of the employer is one which may be reckoned, for British trade unions at least, as a permanent acquisition. It is an acquisition for which (I believe) the economist has every reason to be thankful. Not only does it diminish the danger of inflation; it has also some effect in diminishing the danger of business monopolies defending themselves by a *de facto* collaboration with labour monopolies—handing over to their employees a share in their monopoly profits, in order to have the help of their employees in defending themselves against potential competition.

In its relation to the present situation of this country, the argument of this paper has been intended to be rather optimistic. For it is implied in what has been said that the continual rise in money wages since 1945 is not a necessary consequence of Full Employment (or of the Labour Standard); it is sufficiently explicable in terms of factors that are peculiar to the time through which we have been passing. Especially over the last four years, the main factors pushing up wages have been: (1) the dismantling of the controls, with its somewhat "phoney" effect on the cost of living, and (2) the difficulty that has been experienced in the establishment of a new pattern of relative rates after the war-time disturbance. But these are difficulties which, in the absence of external shocks, we can expect to overcome. A condition in which the wage-level has again become relatively stable, so that movements in basic rates are exceptional rather than normal, should be coming into reach. Even if this expectation is too optimistic, I would still contend that it is for this condition that we must strive, and for which we should do our planning. For it can hardly be doubted that any serious disturbance to our rate of progress would itself push the level of money wages, under conditions of full employment, in an upward direction. If this push is superimposed upon a wage-level that is otherwise stable, then (within broad limits) it can be borne; but if it is superimposed upon a wage-level that is already rising as fast as is tolerable, the additional strain of a more rapid rise must be very dangerous.

Note

What is said about differentials in the body of this paper can be filled out a bit with the aid of a diagram. This diagram is of the conventional supply-and-demand type, but in order that it should give satisfactory results it must be interpreted in a somewhat special manner. In the first place, the wage-level which is measured on the vertical axis is the wage-level in the particular (skilled) trade under consideration, deflated by an index of wages in comparable occupations; what it shows is the relative wage, in this sense, in the occupation we are considering. In the second place, the quantity of labour supplied is taken to be measured by the number of workers, having at least a certain prescribed efficiency in that trade, who are available for employment in it in the circumstances we are going to examine. Thirdly, when we speak of the labour supplied at a given wage, we imply that the given wage (the relative wage) is expected, so far as such things are expected, to be permanent; the effects of purely temporary differentials, which are felt to be abnormal, would require a different treatment.

With these understandings, a supply curve of labour to our trade can be constructed, but the form of the curve will still depend upon the time allowed for adjustment. We may speak of a short-period curve and a long-period curve; but it is better to think of a family of curves, varying continuously in form as more time is allowed. The shortest of the short-period curves will be sharply kinked at the actual number (ON_1) who happen to have the required capacity just at the moment; it will accordingly follow the course HVS_1 where the stretch VS_1 is vertical and the stretch HV may be nearly horizontal or rise quite gradually—the successive ordinates along HV measuring the wages at which successive existing employees would leave the trade, in order to seek less skilled but more remunerative employment elsewhere.

A rather less short-period curve would take the form $HTPS_2$. A wage which is between VN_1 and PN_1 will keep existing workers attached to the trade, but the supply of labour will nevertheless diminish by normal wastage, a wage at this level being insufficient to attract enough labour to fill the gaps. Above PN_1 there will be sufficient recruitment to fill the gaps, both from new entrants into employment and (at a suitable level) by transfer from occupations with neighbouring skills. On the whole, one would expect this recruitment to be more rapid, the higher the wage offered; but bottlenecks in training facilities will sometimes set a limit on the rate at which new labour can be absorbed. The curve HPS_2 may therefore become vertical after a certain point.

As more time is allowed, T will move to the left, S_2 to the right, so that the ultimate shape of the curve (in the *very long period*) will approach $H'PS_3$. In general, it would seem right to suppose that this long-period curve is upward-sloping, like the rest; but if the skill in question is such that almost anyone can acquire it if he is willing to undergo the necessary training, the upward slope will be very slight. If, on the other hand, the skill cannot be successfully acquired unless one possesses the capacity to acquire it, even the long-period curve may slope upwards quite steeply. For it is then not merely necessary to offer a sufficient wage to induce a sufficient number of suitably gifted persons to enter the trade, as against the competition of other uses of these same gifts; it has also to be remembered that such a person will not know that he can acquire the skill successfully until he has endeavoured to acquire it, so that enough must be offered to make him willing to bear the risk of lack of success. Different people are bound to vary in the importance which they set upon such risks, so that this also is a factor making the long-period curve slope upwards.

Let us now start from a position in which the actual supply of qualified labour is ON_1, and the longer-run supply curves are as

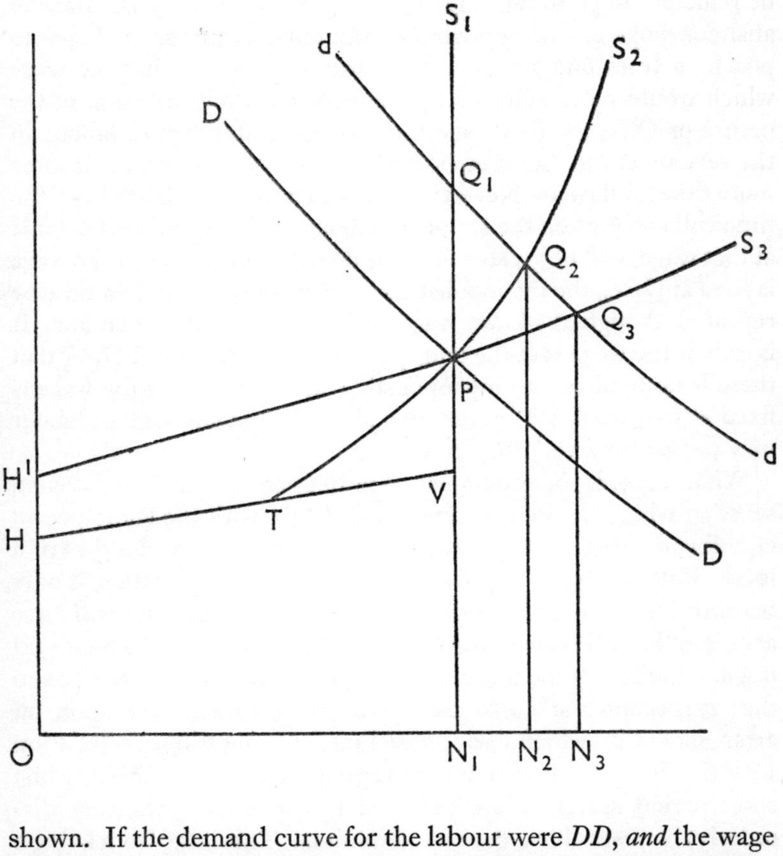

shown. If the demand curve for the labour were *DD*, *and* the wage were at PN_1, the existing labour would be fully employed, and there would be no tendency for supply to vary. If, while demand remained at *DD*, the wage were pushed above PN_1, some of the existing labour would be unable to get employment in this trade; and while the wage itself would attract more labour, the attraction would be offset by the difficulty of getting employment. Again, if the demand curve were at *dd*, the wage (of the existing labour) could be pushed up to Q_1N_1 without causing unemployment; if the labour is unionized, and the Union pursues an aggressively monopolistic policy, this is presumably the wage which it will try to fix. But neither of these is the case which I want primarily to consider. If wages are raised by competition among employers, they may well be reluctant to go so far as Q_1N_1, a wage at which they will have to abandon hope of drawing labour from outside, but are reduced to poaching from one another. I accordingly suggest that the wage which would be established by competition would be more in the nature of Q_2N_2; at this wage there is still a shortage of labour in the very short run, but it is a shortage that will be overcome if some more time is allowed. Nevertheless, even if the wage is at Q_2N_2, the time will come when the supply of labour, which could be available at that wage, will be greater than the demand for it; thus if the wage is *fixed* at Q_2N_2, the monopolistic situation (of Q_1N_1) will in time be repeated, though at a lower wage and a higher supply of labour. It is only if the wage is at the long-period equilibrium level Q_3N_3 that there is no tendency to monopolistic restriction; but if the wage is fixed at that level, and never rises above it, the shortage of labour may persist for a very long time.

What, then, is the economist to recommend? There is a certain sense in which the ideal solution is to begin with the short-period equilibrium wage and gradually to reduce it to the long-period level. But this would be bound to cause trouble in practice, if only because it means cheating the expectations of those who will have acquired the skill because the wage was at the higher level, and would not have done so if the wage had been lower. It does, however, seem that the economist could look with some satisfaction upon an arrangement by which basic agreed rates are kept in some relation with the differentials that are appropriate in the long period, while short-period scarcities are reflected in (no doubt relatively disorderly) bonuses above the agreed minima. This is far from being a perfect solution, but the problem is in its nature very difficult; it does not look as if it can admit of any simple way out. If relative wage-rates are to exercise their full influence upon the supply of labour, they ought to be steady and reliable; but steady differentials will not exercise a proper effect if demands (and supplies) are changing, as they must often be expected to change.

In an opening page of my *Theory of Wages* (1932) I committed myself to the foolish remark that these problems (of the distribution of labour among occupations) are "one of the easiest parts of wage theory". For this I was most properly rebuked by Gerald Shove, in his admirable review of my book in the *Economic Journal*. On this, as on several other matters where he corrected me, I have come to know better.

10

MONETARY THOUGHT AND MONETARY POLICY IN ENGLAND

R. S. SAYERS

Cardiff, September, 1960

THE purpose of this paper is to review certain basic notions that have underlain English monetary policy during the nineteenth and twentieth centuries. I shall contend that the theoretical approach to the problems of policy needs redirecting in the light of changes in the institutional and political environment. I have nothing revolutionary to say and, restricting myself to the more elementary aspects, I shall throughout emphasize theory rather than the course of events.

In some of the more lively phases of monetary controversy during the last 160 years the front of the stage has been occupied by questions of the foreign exchanges and the balance of payments, but even in these phases discussions of practical policy have more or less explicitly assumed certain views on internal policy; indeed, the classical contribution of English thought was the insistence on the connection between the internal and external objectives of monetary policy. At other times, when attention has been focused on troubles common to many countries rather than disturbances in the monetary relations between countries, considerations most relevant to a closed system have naturally come to the forefront. It is with these internal aspects that I am directly concerned—remembering always, however, the sound tradition that we separate the internal from the external at our peril.

Throughout the period—we can date it from the Bullion Report of 1810—the broad approach of every generation has been a Quantity Theory approach. I take this in the most general sense of a belief that the value of money is dependent, to an important extent, on its quantity, and that therefore some control of the supply of money is an essential prerequisite of any sensible monetary policy. The Quantity Theory, in all its simplicity, has great attraction. It is a supply-and-demand analysis, with a demand schedule whose peculiarity derives directly from the concept of money not as an object of exchange but as the medium of exchange. That this is only a small part of the truth is acknowledged even by those economists who rate it most highly, and I should be guilty of travesty if I were to accuse authoritative writers of allowing the Quantity Theory to monopolize their thoughts on monetary action. But I am going to suggest that we should all have a clearer view if we went back to the starting-point and looked afresh at the basic concepts. We must go back to the nature of money and the demand for it.

The word "money" is used in two senses. Money is the standard by which we measure the exchange values of things and in which debts are denominated. This is the abstract sense in which we use the term; we know what pounds, shillings and pence are, in the sense that we know they are the units in which debts and prices are stated. We run into difficulties—the familiar index-number problem, on which I shall not comment—when we begin to generalize about "the value of money", still using the word "money" in this abstract sense, but at least there is no doubt about what is the "money". When we say that our economic system has acquired its present shape on the basis of a general assumption that the value of money is reasonably stable, it is of this abstract sense that we are thinking. Yet when we say that, in order to achieve this stability in the value of money, we must control the supply of money, we have switched away from the abstract sense of money to its other, concrete sense. For by "control of the supply of money" we mean control of the availability of certain assets which are used as media of exchange and stores of value. We have switched from an unambiguous abstraction to a class of marketable objects whose boundary has neither sharpness nor certainty or permanence. And we have arrived at one of the perennial questions of controversy: the question of what assets are, and what are not, included in the "money" category. I suspect that, because money in the abstract sense is an unambiguous concept, people have subconsciously believed that there must also be a simple answer to the question of what is money in the concrete sense. They have been looking for a sharp line of distinction where only Marshallian shading has reality. This pursuit of a will-o'-the-wisp has had its effects on discussions of policy, for people have been too ready to believe that there is an identifiable quantity the control of which is all-important.

The difficulty of identification has derived from the twofold nature of money (we are now speaking only of the concrete sense) as a medium of exhange and as a store of value. Money is both these. An asset which entirely ceases to be a store of value ceases to be used as a medium of exchange, as has been seen when a money is rejected in the final stage of hyper-inflation. There are articles which are stores of value but are clearly not money because they are *never* used as media of exchange. But are we to label as money all other stores of value, that is to say all those which are ever brought into use, whether commonly or occasionally or only rarely, as media of exchange? The usual answer is that we should include as money only those assets which are commonly used as media of exchange. Resort to the adverb "commonly" at once emphasizes the absence of any sharp line of distinction. Are balances in a clearing bank to be labelled money while deposits in the Post Office Savings Bank are not? I find it impossible, on the evidence of recent practice, to find any watertight reasons for so distinguishing. It is sometimes supposed that the distinction can be made to turn on the simplicity of the procedure for transferring the asset. When I take a coin or a note out of my pocket, and hand it across the counter, I am using money to make a payment. When I draw a cheque on a current account at a bank, economists would certainly say that I am using money to make a payment. But if this act of writing an instruction to a bank is a use of money, why not also written instruction to the Post Office Savings Bank or a Building Society? And what could be more simple than the showing of a consumer's credit card? Nor is it altogether satisfactory to retreat to the fact that many Post Office and Building Society balances lie for long periods undisturbed, for this is also true of many balances in the Clearing Banks. Especially this is liable to be true of deposit account balances, yet most economists would regard them as money, equally with current account balances, and the procedure for paying them over to other people is scarcely less simple than drawing a cheque on a current account.

Nor is there conviction in the notion that the line can be drawn by reference to whether interest is earned. Present English practice is that interest is not paid on current accounts, but this has not always been so, nor does it universally apply in other countries where banking competition is more free. Even in present English conditions, large sums are held in current accounts as minimum balances, ordinarily undisturbed, as inducement to the banks to operate accounts without charge: interest is thus virtually paid and offset by turnover charges. Whether the question of what is money is made to turn upon what has been common usage among economists, or on whether the asset is commonly used as a medium of exchange, or on whether it yields interest, it is not possible to give an unambiguous answer.

A similar attempt to escape from the difficulties of identification of money is to be found in the distinction sometimes drawn between "active money" and "idle money". The actual division of bank deposits into demand deposits and time deposits is often thought of as a statistically convenient approximation to an economically significant division into active money and idle money. But this distinction is at best misleading. No asset is in action as a medium of exchange except in the very moment of being transferred from one ownership to another, in settlement of some transaction, and no class of asset used in this way can logically be excluded from the class of active money. Between transactions all money is idle. Yet if activity is held to cover the state of being held in readiness against possible use in exchange, then all monetary assets are active all the time. It is not merely that we cannot easily earmark for statistical assessment the quantity that is active: there is no such quantity, except in the all-embracing sense of all those goods or claims regarded by their owners as potentially useful for settling market commitments. It is this wide concept of liquid assets that we must put, in the place conventionally occupied by "the supply of money", as the monetary quantity influencing total effective demand for goods and services. And we must interpret it widely enough to include credit that can be brought into existence concurrently with a decision to exercise demand.

When all the assets included in this class are reviewed in detail we find that they include not only the deposit liabilities of banks but also the readily callable liabilities of a large and widening range of other financial intermediaries. The ease with which these intermediaries enlarge their balance-sheet totals is as relevant to the monetary situation as is the behaviour of those financial intermediaries we call "banks". Nor should we limit the range to firms ordinarily regarded as financial intermediaries. Among firms whose main activity is manufacturing or trading, most do a great deal of lending and borrowing: they extend "trade credit" to their customers, and they take "trade credit" from their suppliers. Many are active on both sides of the account, and nearly all are involved in credit transactions on one side or the other. The distinction between banks as creators of credit and other firms as users or intermediaries in the monetary field is if not completely false at least misleading. From the point of view of the pressure of effective demand, the crucial step is that which increases the power to acquire goods and services, on the part of people inclined to exercise it immediately; and banks are by no means the only firms to place this power in the hands of others.

That trade credit, in the sense of credit granted by firms whose primary business is non-financial, is an effective element in the supply of purchasing power, is a view sometimes conceded but with the odd qualification that it is only "net" credit that counts in this way. If, for example, a statistical measure is sought, it is supposed that only the excess of a firm's claims over its debts to others should be counted.[1] This is a position that cannot be sustained. We are thinking of the power to exercise demand for goods and services, and for this purpose the gross total of trade credit is relevant. An entire closed circle of firms in manufacturing industry may begin giving credit more freely, and all of them proceed to place large orders with each other; there is no doubt about the increase in effective demand, although the increase in credit granted by all the firms together is balanced by the increase in credit taken by all the firms together. No one would seriously suggest that bank credit should be "netted out" by deducting the debts people owe to the

[1] Cf. J. Viner, *Studies in the Theory of International Trade* (1937). In the course of his review of the writings of the Banking School and the Currency School, Viner says (p. 247) that "J. S. Mill went too far" in including trade credit in the stock of purchasing power. But Viner concedes the substantial point later in the same paragraph.

banks, although one of the tables in the Radcliffe Report curiously errs in this way.[1]

We should pause here to notice that a distinction between "credit" and "capital" is no more helpful in monetary analysis than is the distinction between banks and other creators of credit. This distinction between credit and capital was vigorously argued in the nineteenth-century literature of the subject, and there are echoes of it in those contemporary views that draw a distinction between the "money market" (or "credit market") where the central bank has its business and, on the other hand, the "capital market", upon which the influence of the monetary authorities can only be indirect. It is better that we should think of a single market, or at least a single group of markets, in which immediate purchasing power is traded against claims whose variety, in maturity and in other respects, is infinite. In some countries this is a more imperfect, in others a less imperfect market; but the important likeness that links all parts of the market is the trading of more immediately for less immediately available purchasing power. All participants in the market are so trading; all are trading in capital in the sense of purchasing power, and none is trading in capital in the sense of goods. Each part of the market is as fundamentally a money market as any other, and each part of the market is just as much a capital market as any other. All are adding to the supply of credit when the claims against themselves are more immediately useful than the other claims which are the trading counterpart. This supply of credit, which can be immediately used for exercising demand, is no monopoly of the banks; the power of the banks to create credit (and it is credit, not money, that is relevant here) thus provides no justification for control of the banks while other credit agencies are left uncontrolled.

A presumption in favour of discriminatory control of the banks can, however, be established if it can be shown that there is a sufficiently firm proportionality between the volume of bank credit and the volume of other credit. If, when bank lending is curtailed, other lending must necessarily be curtailed in equal proportion, the

[1] Cmnd. 827 (1959), Table 22 (on p. 171). That in twelve months no one should, to my knowledge, have drawn attention to the oddity of column (1) in this table, is a sad commentary on the extent to which the arguments used in the Report have been understood.

control of banks becomes a useful technique, on the administrative principle that their heads are the easiest to hit. If every firm dealing in credit always held absolutely stable the proportionate distributions of its assets and its liabilities—that is to say, if balance sheets always had exactly the same structures—this proportionality of the supply of effective purchasing power to the supply of bank credit could be taken as the basis of policy. In fact, there are two important reasons why this strict proportionality cannot be assumed. The first is that in course of time people devise new financial intermediaries; the efficiency of the financial system increases, and this process tends to accelerate in a prolonged spell of business prosperity. The second—and in the short period relevant for most purposes of policy, this is the more weighty—the reliability of non-bank debtors varies according to the general trade prospect. This is, of course, our old friend "the inherent instability of credit"; but it is important to recognize that in its modern form it refers not so much to bank credit as to the relation between bank credit and non-bank credit. At a time when, as an anti-inflation measure, the authorities are enforcing a restriction of bank credit, the apparently favourable position of other debtors makes the extension of non-bank credit peculiarly easy, as we saw in England in the middle 1950s.[1] The important practical question is how easily one source of credit can replace another, and whether such a disturbance sets up any corrective process which will act quickly enough to be useful for purposes of policy.

Before I turn to this fundamental question, I must refer to the use of another concept, deeply embedded in the literature of our subject. This is the velocity of circulation. I have hitherto been formulating monetary phenomena by referring to the supply of and the demand for various assets and liabilities; but many writers have thought it more convenient to refer to variations in demand as

[1] No comprehensive statistics of trade credit exist, even for joint-stock companies. For companies quoted on the Stock Exchange and engaged in manufacturing, building and distribution, however, some figures can be extracted from the investigations made by the National Institute of Economic and Social Research. For these companies, the balance sheets relating to late 1956 showed trade creditors £2,050 million, as compared with £444 million bank loans, and trade debtors £2,609 million, as compared with £649 million cash and bank balances. The swings in these figures for trade credit, from one year to another, also dwarf changes in the bank credit and bank balances employed by such companies (*v.* Radcliffe Report, Cmnd. 827, paragraphs 297–311).

variations in the velocity of circulation of money. They think of people not as wanting more or less intensely to hold money but as being less or more quick to pass on money in exchange for goods and services. Put like this, the one concept is simply the reciprocal of the other, and it does not matter which we use. I myself prefer to think in terms of the demand for money balances, because the term "velocity of circulation" implies closer analogy with a physical process than I can find in the working of the monetary system, and I notice that when economists seek to explain changes in the velocity of circulation they at once begin to talk about the intensity of the demand for money. Like houses and other assets, money is not going round steadily all the time. Instead—again like houses and other assets—it is always resting in the ownership of one person or another, save for the isolated moments when it changes ownership. What people mean when they say that the velocity of circulation has increased is that the volume of transactions has increased relatively to the stock of money (in some sense), or that the national income has increased relatively to the stock of money (the ratio more specifically referred to as the "income velocity of circulation"). As a label for the purely statistical phenomenon of the ratio of one quantity to another, the term velocity of circulation is harmless enough, and so well established in the literature that it would be foolish to refuse the convenience of using it. The trouble begins when we jump to the conclusion that a rise in the ratio of payments to bank deposits means only that firms have decided to put their bank deposits to faster use, whereas much of what has happened is that firms have decided to give more credit and people have shifted some of their savings into the hands of more nimble intermediaries. The artificiality of the concept lies, in short, in its reliance on a distinct and identifiable category of money; and one danger in using it lies in its encouraging us to overlook the relevance, to the pressure of total demand, of sources of credit outside this defined category. A further danger is that the definition normally used being either bank deposits or bank deposits plus notes, which (particularly the notes) come fully into action only late in productive processes, a rise in the velocity of circulation is a phenomenon that lags behind a rise in the disposition to spend. The existence of this lag should warn us against undue reliance on any corrective mechanism set up by "a rise in the velocity of circulation".

The basis of such a corrective mechanism is sometimes represented as the anchorage of the velocity of circulation in the peculiar demand for the medium of exchange. Our examination of the nature of money and of the demand for it has, however, warned us that there is no single asset or group of assets that uniquely possesses a uniform monetary quality that is totally absent from all other assets. Except for purely didactic purposes, it does not help to talk about a normal velocity of circulation any more than it helps to say (which is the same thing) that the elasticity of demand for money is unity. On the other hand, convenience in settling transactions is *an* important quality in a monetary asset; various monetary assets have this quality in varying degrees. If money income rises, or if the supply of some of these assets falls, people will feel some lack of this convenience in relation to the contingent needs against which they hold such assets, and this is the substance to which economists refer when they assume a certain normality in the velocity of circulation. But we must remember that many assets have the monetary quality in varying degrees; if, as the supply of some of them falls relatively to income or turnover, others can easily be increased, the sense of inconvenience is minimized, and we have to ask ourselves whether it remains effective enough to be interesting. We are in fact back at our major question of the relation between supplies of different classes of monetary assets, having merely reformulated, with the help of the concept of the velocity of circulation, the problems we had already traversed.

In our own time most attention has been given to a comparatively late link in the chain of argument: the question of how, as the supply of monetary assets becomes less adequate, increasing inconvenience manifest in rising interest rates provokes a fall in total demand. Although this part of the argument has always had some attention, the almost exclusive concentration upon it is something of a post-1920 novelty. In the great controversies of the nineteenth century the prior question of the relation between varied monetary assets was always well to the fore. In the early part of the nineteenth century one of the major questions related to the connection between the Bank of England's note issue and the issues of the country banks. Thornton, in his *Paper Credit* (1802), had developed the view that the issues by the country banks were substantially governed by the Bank of England's issue.[1] He may have been wrong in this opinion, but he certainly regarded it as important, because he regarded both kinds of notes as money, the supply of which was relevant to the price level. When the Bullion Committee (of which Thornton was a member) in 1810 investigated the depreciation of the pound they adopted this view in one of the more emphatic statements in their Report,[2] but only two pages later they carefully explained the power of country bank-notes permanently to displace Bank of England notes.[3] They also noted the importance of increasingly effective use of bank deposits in circumscribing the real demand for bank-notes. In the controversy which raged round the Report, and more especially in the controversies of the next three decades, the relation between country notes and Bank of England notes continued to be hotly debated. There were no indisputable statistics that could be used to help settle the argument, just as in our own day there are not yet statistics to enable us to convince each other on the question whether or not the liabilities of the clearing banks are absolutely crucial to the behaviour of the wider structure of credit.

In the next generation the most hotly debated question was the regulation of the issue of bank-notes. In this phase—the Currency School and Banking School controversy—those who argued for strict regulation of the issue of Bank of England notes were no longer prepared to rely upon any automatic dependence of country issues upon Bank of England issues. They argued for—and obtained—strict and direct limitation of the country issues. But this relation of country to London issues of notes now scarcely held the centre of the stage. The main dispute now raged round the position of other claims—bank deposits, bills of exchange and trade credit generally. The Currency School argued for strict regulation of the issue of bank-notes. The Banking School, more diffuse in their remedies for economic instability, were united only in their negative view that the Currency School remedy was invalidated by the fact that bank-notes formed neither the only nor the governing part of the supply of purchasing power. The use of bank deposits, bills of

[1] H. Thornton, *An Enquiry into the Nature and Effects of the Paper Credit of Great Britain*, pp. 211–41.

[2] In the opening of their Section IV.

[3] Cf. Thornton's Chapter IX, where qualifications are as abundant as in any modern survey.

exchange and other forms of credit as substitutes for bank-notes had long been acknowledged in the literature; on the historical order of events as we know them, it might rather have been argued that bank-notes were a substitute for bills of exchange. But now that a strong case was being made for strict control of the supply of money, the question which was money and which was not money became of high practical importance; moreover, the spectacular growth of banking was emphasizing the weight of bank deposits in the total circulation.

The simplest Currency School view was that only gold and notes were money, and that therefore the circulation of gold and notes together should be made to reflect the changes in the gold supply; this is the essence of the 1844 Bank Act. But this is doing the Currency School less than justice. Its protagonists did acknowledge the relevance of banking and other credit, but some took the line that while notes should be strictly controlled, deposit banking should be kept in order by some other measures; others argued that the velocity of circulation of banking and other instruments was comparatively so low that these were unimportant parts of the money supply; again others argued that, since gold or notes could be demanded in all final payments, the pressure of purchasing and economic activity could never for long get out of line with the supply of the basic monetary instruments. It was this last view that was destined to dominate many decades; it prevailed against the Banking School view that the components of the money supply were so many and varied, and such effective substitutes for each other, that any attempt to control their quantity was doomed to failure, and would probably aggravate economic crises.

The prevailing doctrine—which gave Britain its basic monetary laws for seventy years—depended on the fact that gold or Bank of England notes could be demanded in all final payments. This derived not merely from the law of 1833: it was deeply rooted in the country's practice for a long time before that. This singular quality of gold and notes became directly important as soon as a general breakdown of credit developed; at other times bank deposits and bills of exchange were generally good enough, but in a crisis a businessman had to be able to put his hands on notes or gold, or he risked bankruptcy. As long, therefore, as a financial crisis was thought a possibility, bankers and other granters of credit paid some regard, in the conduct of their lending business, to the state of the Bank of England's reserve. And just in these decades Bank Rate movements were beginning to be employed by the Bank of England as the method of protecting the Reserve. A rise in Bank Rate became all important as an index—a warning that a breakdown of credit, followed by a disastrous spell of depressed markets, might be just round the corner.[1] The Banking School were right in emphasizing the variety and the importance of sources of credit, but the Currency School were right in arguing that the superstructure of credit could not for very long get out of line with the supply of the basic money, the gold and bank-notes. In this situation the broad line of argument developed in the first part of this paper was not important. But the economy was distressingly unstable.

It was also one in which some of the most relevant circumstances were changing. If it was right to assume that the superstructure of credit could not for very long get out of line with the supply of the basic money, experience very quickly showed that the possible time-lag could be of devastating importance. Partly because the Bank of England was not using its warning signal promptly enough, and partly because the underlying causes of instability were very strong, crises of the first order of magnitude recurred in 1847, 1857 and 1866. This experience led the authorities to modify the Currency School policy to the extent of admitting that the Bank of England must act as lender of last resort to prevent breakdown of the system. The crisis of 1866 was the last of the old kind, and Bagehot's writings ensured the respectability of the new policy. Nevertheless, Bank Rate continued to retain something of its power as a warning signal internally; this was partly because memories of the old-fashioned crises lingered on, and partly because, although it ceased to portend a breakdown of credit, a high Bank Rate was still apt to portend a spell of trade depression. Not until the effective adoption of Full Employment policies was the warning power of Bank Rate reduced to a ghost of its old self.

The scene was also changing in that the internal effects of Bank Rate were becoming relatively unimportant. In the second half of

[1] This interpretation of the *modus operandi* of Bank Rate at this time is convincingly argued by A. B. Cramp in his article, "Horsley Palmer on Bank Rate" (*Economica*, November, 1959), and in his unpublished Ph.D. thesis (London), *Opinion on the Operation of Bank Rate, 1822–60*.

the nineteenth century London's power as an international financial centre grew fast, and the Bank of England was enabled to perform its duty of keeping the pound on gold by operating principally on the international capital position.[1] (This had always been an element in the *modus operandi* of Bank Rate, but in the period 1860–1914 it became the principal element.) Some of its direct influence as a signal for businessmen remained, as I have suggested above; more importantly, the disturbance of the international capital situation disturbed investment in the developing countries overseas, with severe repercussions on the trade of the home country. Just how much monetary conditions really affected the trade cycle it is impossible to say; if we are looking only at the last few decades before 1914 I find myself much in sympathy with Rostow's view of "an essentially negative element",[2] for the rise in interest rates often waited until the boom was already cracking, and merely ensured that the depression should be severe. However, without going so far as this we must still admit that the quick power of Bank Rate on the international capital position was the dominant feature, and this change of emphasis was duly reflected in the dwindling literature on monetary questions. Bank Rate as the controller of international gold movements came to occupy a leading place in expositions of the monetary system; the Quantity Theory and the 1844 Act remained alongside the discussion of Bank Rate, but the old and the new were in this phase never really integrated. It was the literature of this phase that was more or less my introduction to the subject, and I well remember my first impression of confusion, whether a rise in Bank Rate increased the quantity of money (which seemed to be the result of attracting gold) or decreased the quantity of money (which seemed to be a necessary part of the deflation a rising Bank Rate was supposed to provoke). My teachers soon put this right, but when I look back at the pre-1920 literature I am not surprised at my early difficulties.

The main development of monetary thought in the course of the 1920s was the integration of these various elements into a single coherent body of theory. The development originated mainly, I

[1] For a contemporary exposition, see, e.g. G. Clare, *A Money Market Primer* (2nd Edition, 1905), especially pp. 103–7 (on effects on international movements) and p. 36 (for attitude that no disturbance of the internal economy is sought).

[2] W. W. Rostow, *British Economy of the Nineteenth Century*, p. 57.

believe, in the pre-1914 academic activity in the study of the trade cycle, though there was also powerful stimulus from the international monetary strains of the 'twenties themselves. Having regard to what we know Marshall to have been thinking at the turn of the century, it is not surprising that the reshaping of monetary thought in the next generation was largely the work of Marshall's successors, especially Lavington, Keynes and Robertson; and we must not forget that English economists were beginning to notice the work of Wicksell and his followers on the Continent.

As a survey of this kind must necessarily concertina many intricate episodes in the history of thought, I will summarize these developments of the 1920s simply by reference to the form in which they emerged, at the end of the decade, in Keynes's *Treatise on Money*. The *Treatise* has between its four covers many strands of thought, as those who were students in those days will remember too well; but for our present purpose we may confine our attention to two of them. The first is that the demand for money was refashioned by looking at money primarily as one among other stores of value, the preference for the peculiar convenience money possesses being weighted in the manner traditional in the ordinary theory of value, against the interest that could be obtained on the other stores of value. The second idea we must notice was, along Wicksellian lines, that the rate of interest influenced the balance between the demand for capital and the willingness to lend, thus providing a mechanism whereby the supply of money (and the demand for it) was linked with the pressure of total demand, and so with movements in the general level of prices.

The first of these developments—the liquidity preference theory of interest—represented a clean break from the Quantity Theory, in that money, ceasing to be a pure medium of exchange, ceased to have that freakish unit elasticity of demand and became something whose value was determined in a way we need not feel strange when we had just been learning a more universal Theory of Value.[1] But in his formulation Keynes preserved his links with tradition by notionally dividing money into "active money"[1], whose elasticity of demand was unity, and "idle money", the utility of which behaved in the more ordinary way and had to be balanced against the

[1] Cf. J. R. Hicks, "A Suggestion for Simplifying the Theory of Money", *Economica*, February, 1935, p. 3.

interest that could be earned by holding bonds. For the purpose of establishing his main propositions Keynes need not have made this bow to his ancestors, but he did, and I suspect that life would be easier if we forgot about it; I have already noted the artificiality of the distinction. However, its use did facilitate demonstration of an equilibrating mechanism in the system. A rise in prices increased the amount of active money needed, the money available for idleness was thus reduced, the demand for bonds therefore fell, the rate of interest rose, demand for capital goods was checked—and so the rise in prices was stopped. This is the Keynesian system of 1930 in baldest form, and the précis omits many sources of friction continually emphasized by Keynes. In terms of practical policy, the analysis did point advantage in control of the supply of money; to Keynes this meant control of the supply of bank deposits, and his attention to such subjects as the cash ratio in banks and central bank operations is always related to this. He emphasized throughout—and this is a big step beyond the Currency School position—that there is a dangerously long time-lag between movements in "bank-money" (i.e. bank deposits) and the corresponding movement in notes, "so that a control over the volume of notes operates too late—after the evil has been done by a change in the volume of bank-money which may have taken place some months earlier".[1] He went further and, emphasizing the crucial position of the rate of interest in the equilibrating mechanism, urged central bankers to think more directly in terms of forcing the rate of interest to behave in the required way.[2]

This was, of course, not the end of the Keynes story, and in the *General Theory* (1936) Keynes developed ideas that drastically modified any notion of the economic system as a self-stabilizing system. Particularly, he argued certain consequences of the shortcomings of the rate of interest as part of the equilibrating mechanism: the liquidity trap and the notion of an under-employment equilibrium came in. Like the *Treatise* before it, the *General Theory* bristled with ideas, many of which were hotly disputed; but both in his 1930 emphasis on the rate of interest as a crucial cog in the mechanism and in his subsequent relative loss of faith in its efficacy

[1] Vol. II, p. 264.

[2] Ibid., pp. 369–74; cf. Report of the Committee on Finance and Industry ("Macmillan Report"), Cmnd. 3897, 1931, paragraph 359.

Keynes had wide following. In such investigations as they were able to make the Radcliffe Committee found a good deal of support for the later Keynesian view. In this sense the scepticism of Radcliffe is Keynesian, but in certain other respects—and here I am thinking of parts of the *Treatise* that Keynes did not revise—the Radcliffe view of the economic system is quite unlike that of Keynes.

The break from the Keynesian exposition may perhaps best be seen by exaggerating it, imputing to Keynes a simplicity that was never his. Keynes was thoroughly traditional in drawing a sharp line between money and other assets. To him money had changed from being coin and notes to being notes and bank deposits, notes being the small change of "bank money". In his model there are four major classes of assets: cash, bank money, bonds and others; there are central banks (whose liabilities are cash), there are banks (whose liabilities are bank money and who are holders of cash and bonds as well as other assets) and there are non-banks (i.e. corporations and individuals who are holders of cash, bank money, bonds and other assets, and who are also much concerned with spending on "real" assets). A distinction between money and bonds is that the former is useful for payments and the latter are not; another distinction between them is that bonds do and money does not carry interest. With this classification and some reliance upon the interest rate as a balancer of savings and investment, we can make a coherent working model, useful for explaining how policy should be shaped.

But the world in which we live lacks these sharp distinctions. And, remembering that for purposes of policy we must get as close as we can to the points of business decision, the more we try to eliminate dangerous time-lags, the more blurred the distinctions become. There is no clear line between purchasing power that carries no interest and interest-earning assets that have no influence on purchasing power. "Commercial banks" shade into industrial banks, savings banks and building societies, and these into a host of other financial intermediaries; the liabilities of these are close substitutes for each other, so that a clamping down on one group will not create such an abrupt scarcity of liquidity as will have a worthwhile impact on the pressure of total demand. This is, of course, the kind of argument that was being used by the Banking School a hundred years ago, when J. S. Mill and others pointed out that the substitutability of bank deposits for notes was high, whence they argued that a control of notes alone would be merely a nuisance. Time's answer to the Banking School was the recognition that bank deposits were as good as notes, coupled with institutional arrangements for making good a Currency School contention that the supply of bank deposits was proportional to the supply of notes. Having got so far, we then got into the habit of saying that bank deposits were the important quantity, that our central banks should regulate the bank deposits and that notes could be left to take care of themselves.

Can we now, as a latter-day Currency School, argue that, although other financial claims are good substitutes for money, we can rely upon the constancy of their ratio to the bank deposits we have learned to control? I doubt it. Or can we now, following those who taught us all about central banking, force the non-bank lenders into a pattern by imposing on them liquidity rules analogous to those whereby the clearing banks are controlled? The Radcliffe Committee looked at the question, and shuddered. Or can we try to check the development of financial institutions, by proclaiming that none but the clearing banks may create money? This is not just an idle fancy: our ancestors did something like this when they strangled the country note issue—but they did not stop the private creation of money. They could not stop it, because money is the creation of the public that chooses to impute certain qualities to certain claims.

I have referred repeatedly to the Currency School and Banking School controversy because I believe that the arguments of the last few years have very close parallels with that earlier controversy. The Currency School case depended on sharp lines of distinction and rigid proportionalities. The case was accepted as the basis for practical policy; we muddled through the next hundred years partly by modifying the policy, partly by imposing proportionalities and partly enduring disadvantages we no longer find tolerable. In modification of the policy, we developed central banking to dull the terror of financial crises, and now we have gone much further by insisting that there shall be no trade depression. The age-old tendency of financial institutions to become more numerous, more varied and more efficient flourishes in an economy that avoids major breakdowns; the process is accelerated, and a policy that depends on a stable relationship between institutions become less and less realistic.

This is a negative conclusion, and it is because they took this view of the nature of money and the monetary processes that the Radcliffe Committee's conclusions appeared to give such little positive guidance. But even negative conclusions have their importance: we sometimes need to search around for something quite different which will get results. And the conclusions to which our general discussion points do, after all, have highly practical implications. To take a major point, restriction of the supply of bank deposits, if long continued, can be expected to become increasingly ineffective as a curb on total demand, because the demand for liquidity can be so well satisfied from other sources. Worse than this, restriction of the banks will increase the opportunities for alternative lenders, so that the banks will lose ground to their competitors and the heads the Government can hit will become progressively less influential in the behaviour of the economy. Or to take another point, on which the Radcliffe Committee's recommendation was grossly misrepresented in some quarters, consider the channels for local-authority borrowing. The fact that Treasury bills are, and local authority mortages are not, "liquid assets" to the clearing banks has some very short-period relevance, in that the banks are outstandingly efficient lenders, but if the market for credit is fundamentally a single market, an addition of short government paper has much the same effect on the monetary situation wherever it is injected. Banks are not the only lenders sensitive to liquidity.

Our analysis has its uses for bankers as well as for policy-makers. The English clearing banks, acting as a cartel, fix the rate they pay on time deposits, and have only one class of such deposits: at seven days' notice. They are sometimes urged to compete for deposits now going to building societies or hire-purchase finance houses by offering higher rates for longer periods. Against this proposal, it has been argued that the total of deposits in the clearing banks is fixed by the supply of "liquid assets", and that therefore the banks could get no more deposits by offering higher rates but would simply reduce their own profits. This over-simple argument can be made true only if we make certain assumptions about strictly rigid proportionality in the balance sheets of all sorts of firms and households, and insist that for one size of the national debt and one size of the national income there is only one possible size for the total of bank deposits. This is a particular manifestation of the old idea that there is only one kind of money (in this case bank deposits) and that the demand for it is rigidly related to the national income. But once we admit that the liabilities of other institutions may be quite good substitutes for the liabilities of the clearing banks, and that business attracted by non-bank intermediaries affects the non-bank demand for national debt, the consequences of non-competition by the clearing banks become expensive to them. By refusing to compete, they stand to lose a larger and larger proportion of the total lending business in the country. To put the point in an extreme way, if the banks always ignored competition on the principle to which I have referred, their place as creators of the chief monetary assets would gradually be lost to other more aggressive financial intermediaries. And no doubt there would be quantity theorists a century hence to point out that the then predominant money (claims on the aggressive intermediaries) had increased roughly in proportion to the national income: they might even find that clearing bank deposits had become the small change of the monetary system!

Or are we perhaps already there? If the crucial decisions to place orders for production depend "upon the composition of the spender's assets and on his borrowing power and . . . upon the methods, moods and resources of financial institutions and other firms which are prepared (on terms) to finance other people's spending",[1] then in an important sense bank deposits have already become the small change of the system. This is no fad of a theorist's exposition, for its implications are surely lessons of the first importance to practical policy. For it means that there is no dependable monetary ceiling against which a boom will bump its head. As the boom rises, the sources of liquidity broaden, and the rising demand for the means of payment comes too late and is too easily satisfied. It follows that a policy of stabilizing bank deposits and waiting for the expanding volume of payments to force interest rates upwards, while intuitive central bankers try to be nimble in "following the market", is not enough; action would always be too late, as it was when strain on the note-issue was expected to set the corrective mechanism in motion. If monetary policy is to be used at all, we must make it operate on as broad a front as possible; action on the

[1] Radcliffe Report (Cmnd. 827), paragraph 389.

supply of bank money must be thought of as purely incidental to a positive, aggressive and far-reaching interest-rate policy. How far we can depend on this is, as the Radcliffe Committee emphasized,[1] a matter on which much more systematic investigation is required. If we want to catch up with events and accept the implications of the Full Employment policy we must urgently investigate the efficacy of a far more vigorous interest-rate policy than any we have yet seen, and, lest this should (as I expect) prove a non-starter, we must think again on how the flexibility of fiscal policy might be increased.

[1] Ibid., paragraph 474.

11

IS INFLATION INEVITABLE?

E. VICTOR MORGAN

Cambridge, September, 1965

TWICE during the past fifteen years this section has been addressed by its president on inflation; in 1953 Professor Paish talked about the then very topical problem of open versus repressed inflation, and five years later Professor A. J. Brown reviewed the effect of inflation on the performance of the British economy. Since then, however, much has happened and much has been written, so I hope I may be forgiven for returning to the subject, especially as I wish to concentrate on a rather different aspect of it from those chosen by my predecessors. There is a formal sense in which the answer to my question, "Is inflation inevitable?" is simply "No." I am sure that any one of us, given unlimited powers and a mandate to stop inflation at any cost, could easily devise policies which would do so; whether the cost would be one which our fellow citizens would be willing to pay is another matter. I intend, therefore, that my question should be taken in the context of present-day Britain, and I shall be asking whether the avoidance of inflation is consistent with a level of employment and a pace of economic growth that are politically acceptable.

The attempt to answer this question requires an excursion into some recent theoretical developments. The study of inflation is certainly a growth industry; the manpower engaged in it has been expanding rapidly, and productivity, if measured in words per man year, is remarkably high. The situation is less satisfactory, however, if we measure productivity in terms of the output of theoretical propositions that are logically consistent, that stand up to empirical testing and that are useful for prediction and policy-making.

Bronfenbrenner and Holzman, in their "Survey of Inflation Theory", remark that:

> "Since 1945, the geographical extent and the temporal stubbornness of 'The Great Inflation' have shaken many economists' faith in the orthodoxies of preceding generations. Neo-orthodoxies, including restatements, are only dimly in evidence. Our survey is accordingly more of a guide through chaos than a history of received doctrine or a systematic critique of a few rival positions."[1]

There are many important questions on which distinguished economists take diametrically opposite views. Some examples are: Whether inflation is or is not a major social evil; whether it is caused by excess demand, or by the excessive bargaining power of sectional interests; whether it is an impediment to growth or a necessary condition for it; whether it should be cured by curtailing demand, or by running the economy "flat out" in the hope that productivity will rise so fast that all competing claims can be met without pushing up costs and prices; and whether an incomes policy is essential to stability or whether it is dangerous nonsense.

You may think that this state of affairs reflects little credit on our profession, but there are reasons, if not excuses, for it. Inflation raises problems which give unusually wide scope to economic rationalization of political prejudice. Even more important, however, the difficulties in the way of empirical work are more than usually formidable. The evidence is nearly all in the form of statistical time series, not all of them very accurate, and some of them available only at inconveniently long intervals; moreover, many of the variables which we want to study, such as output, employment, prices and profits, move very closely in step with one another. In these circumstances it is very difficult to distinguish between cause and effect, or to devise tests that have real power against any one of a number of widely differing hypotheses.

At this point I had better confess that anyone who hopes that I may shed a new and revealing light upon this darkness will be sadly disappointed. My aim is the much more modest one of reviewing some of the theoretical achievements to my colleagues, selecting a

[1] M. Bronfenbrenner and F. D. Holzman, "Survey of Inflation Theory", *American Economic Review*, 1963, p. 594.

few propositions on which some measure of agreement appears to be emerging, and considering their relevance to our practical problems.

There is no unanimity even about the definition of inflation and, indeed, many writers have preferred to avoid tying themselves down to any definition at all. Time forbids a discussion of definitions, but in this paper inflation will be defined as "a situation in which either the national money income is growing faster than the national real income or there is a growing backlog of unfilled orders".

II

The form in which the modern theory of demand inflation has come down to us has been largely influenced by Keynes (especially in his *How to Pay for the War*),[1] but it is a logical extension of earlier monetary theories. In its simplest version the theory assumes that all prices are flexible and are adjusted to changes in supply or demand in a manner which clears the market. If, then, total planned expenditure rises above the value of the current output of goods and services, and if this output cannot be significantly increased, prices must rise and go on rising until this excess demand has been eliminated. The initial rise in aggregate spending may be due to one of several causes, including deficit spending by the Government, an increase in the opportunities for profitable investment or an increase in the money supply; similarly, expectations, income redistribution or the growing difficulty of financing rising money expenditure with a fixed stock of the means of payment may all play their part in restoring equilibrium.

Even when refined to take account of these alternatives the theory just outlined is an over-simplification in at least two important respects. First, the rise in prices is likely to provoke demands for higher money incomes from trade unions who see their members' real income reduced by rising prices. Secondly, by no means all prices are, in fact, adjusted within a short period of time so as to clear the market; on the contrary, some remain constant over long periods and, when they do change, appear to do so in response to changes in cost rather than changes in demand. Where prices behave in this way, the first symptom of excess demand will be

[1] J. M. Keynes, *How to Pay for the War* (London, 1940), especially Chapter IX.

unfilled orders. Firms may try to reduce their backlog of orders by hiring more labour, and the increased demand for labour may raise costs by pushing up wages. Alternatively, rising prices in sectors which are sensitive to increased demand may increase the cost of living and give rise to demands for higher wages. In either case prices which are "cost determined" would rise only after the rise in wages, and the situation would look very like a cost inflation instead of a demand inflation.

A satisfactory theory of inflation must, therefore, explain the mechanism by which both money wages and money prices are fixed in circumstances in which they are not automatically adjusted so as to clear the market.

The problem of wage fixing has been studied both by econometricians constructing and testing macro-economic models, and by labour economists looking at individual wage bargains. The former group have focused attention mainly on five variables—the demand for labour, the cost of living, profits, productivity and the "pushfulness" of trade unions.

Statistical indicators of the demand for labour may be found in figures of employment or unemployment or in the relationship between unemployment and unfilled vacancies. Phillips took the view that a very high proportion of the changes in wage-rates in Britain between 1861 and 1957 could be explained by a combination of the level of unemployment and the rate of change of unemployment.[1] Lipsey, treating the same material by rather different methods, maintains that the cost of living is more important (especially since 1919) than it was believed to be by Phillips, and that the influence of unemployment has been declining.[2] However, he still finds that the demand for labour is among the significant determinants of wage rates, and the conclusion is supported by other British studies including those of Clark,[3] Klein and Ball,[4] and Dicks-

[1] A. W. Phillips, "The Relation Between Unemployment and the Rate of Change in Money Wage Rates in the U.K., 1861–1957", *Economica*, 1958, pp. 283–99.

[2] R. G. Lipsey, "The Relationship Between Unemployment and the Rate of Change of Money Wage Rates in the U.K., 1862–1957", *Economica*, 1960, pp. 1–31.

[3] C. Clark, "An International Comparison of 'Over-Employment' Trends in Money Wages", *Oxford Economic Papers*, 1957, pp, 178–89.

[4] L. R. Klein and R. J. Ball, "Some Econometrics of the Determination of Absolute Prices and Wages", *Economic Journal*, 1959, pp. 465–82

Mireaux and Dow.[1] By contrast, Bhatia found only a very weak relationship between unemployment and the rate of change of earnings in the United States between 1948 and 1958.[2] Another interesting point is that, for Britain, the relationship between wages and the demand for labour appears to be less close for individual industries than it is for the economy as a whole. Dicks-Mireaux and Dow, applying their model to seven industries as well as to the whole economy, found that in only one case did special factors affecting the industry appear to be as important as demand conditions in the economy as a whole.[3] Phelps-Brown and Browne, using a much finer breakdown of no less than 132 industrial groups, found little association between changes in earnings and unemployment and also between changes in earnings and in the size of the labour force except in a few cases where the latter was very large.[4]

These results cast some doubt on just how the demand for labour affects the wage bargain. If it were simply a matter of employers offering more when they wished to increase their labour force we should expect to find evidence of this in the figures for individual industries. An alternative hypothesis is that a strong demand for labour in the economy as a whole is a sign of a strong demand for goods and also an indication that wages in other industries are likely to be rising. For both these reasons it may cause employers to feel confident that they will be able to pass on higher labour costs in higher prices, and so lessen their resistance to claims by the unions.

The cost-of-living figures so prominently in wage claims that it would be surprising indeed if there were not a close connection between current wage increases and the price increases of the recent past, and such a relationship has been found by all those who have have econometric studies.

It was suggested by Kaldor[5] that the main stimulus to wage increases was high profits, and that Phillips obtained his close correlation between changes in wage-rates and unemployment only because

[1] L. A. Dicks-Mireaux and J. C. R. Dow, "The Determination of Wage Inflation", *Journal of the Royal Statistical Society*, 1959, pp. 145–74.

[2] R. J. Bhatia, "Unemployment and the Rate of Change of Money Earnings in the U.S.A., 1900–58", *Economica*, 1961, pp. 286–96.

[3] Dicks-Mireaux and Dow, op. cit.

[4] E. H. Phelps-Brown and M. H. Browne, "Earnings in Industries of the U.K., 1948–59", *Economic Journal*, 1962, pp. 517–49.

[5] N. Kaldor, "Economic Growth and the Problem of Inflation", *Economica*, 1959, pp. 287–98.

periods of low unemployment were also periods of high profits, and vice versa. This hypothesis was tested by Lipsey and Steuer,[1] who found that profits had virtually no explanatory power before the First World War, but that they came out better than unemployment during the inter-war period. For 1946–58 profits were of about the same explanatory power as unemployment in the test of the whole economy, but very weak in individual industries. In a similar study of post-war United States data, Bhatia found a very much closer relationship; indeed, no less than 80 per cent. of changes in United States earnings could be explained in terms of the rate of profit on equity capital and changes in that rate. It is worth noting that a high rate of profit in the economy as a whole is a symptom of a strong demand for goods and an encouragement to employers to believe that they will be able to pass on increases in labour costs.[2]

Productivity is often discussed in connection with wage claims, but there is very little evidence in the statistics of any relationship between productivity changes and changes in either rates or earnings. Both Dicks-Mireaux[3] and Klein and Ball[4] in their aggregate models and Phelps-Brown and Browne[5] in their studies of separate industries found no general relationship, though Phelps-Brown did find big increases in productivity associated with large increases in earnings in a few very capital-intensive industries. Again it is significant that employers' resistance to wage demands is likely to be weak in capital–intensive industries with rapidly rising productivity. Apart from these special cases, however, it seems that workers whose productivity has been growing only slowly have fared as well as those whose productivity has been growing more rapidly, and this may be an important part of the mechanism that has generated rising prices.

Finally, there is some evidence that the degree of aggressiveness of trade unions has an influence on the size of negotiated increases and, through them, on earnings. Dicks-Mireaux and Dow conclude

[1] R. G. Lipsey and M. D. Steuer, "The Relation Between Profits and Wage Rates", *Economica*, 1961, pp. 137–55.

[2] R. J. Bhatia, "Profits and the Rate of Change of Money Earnings in the U.S. 1955–59", *Economica*, 1962, pp. 255–62.

[3] L. A. Dicks-Mireaux, "The Interrelationship Between Wage and Price Changes, 1946–1959", *Oxford Economic Papers*, 1962, pp. 267–92.

[4] L. R. Klein and R. J. Ball, op. cit.

[5] E. H. Phelps-Brown and M. H. Browne, op. cit.

that "pushfulness" of unions is a significant influence; rates certainly rose by less during the period of "wage-restraint" from 1948 to 1950 than they did subsequently; and the equations of a number of econometric models contain a constant term representing an "independent" rate of increase not explained by any of the other variables. These impressions are confirmed by the qualitative judgements of labour economists based on their experience of actual negotiations.[1]

Labour economists have also drawn attention to factors which may influence the behaviour of unions but which do not lend themselves to incorporation in aggregate models. Perhaps the most important of these are relationships between different occupations. Both trade unionists and arbitrators are imbued with a strong sense of what is a "fair" relationship between wages for different types of job, so that an increase given to one group soon provokes demands from others so as to maintain the generally accepted relative position. The fact that both differences in the rate of growth of productivity and in the demand for labour appear to have had so little effect on relative wages in different industries is an indication of how successful the unions have been in maintaining this objective.

To sum up, this evidence is by no means sufficient for a complete theory of money wage determination, but it takes us a little way along the road. In the nineteenth century, it seems clear that money wages were demand determined; a very high proportion of changes in wage-rates can be explained by changes in unemployment, and no other observed variable has any great explanatory power. The past fifty years have changed this situation greatly. The demand for labour still shows up in statistical analyses as an important influence, but its explanatory power has been considerably reduced, and there is some reason to believe that it works indirectly, through employers' confidence of being able to pass on increases in labour costs, rather than directly. Changes in the cost of living have become more important, partly no doubt because they have been very much larger than they were in the nineteenth century. And trade-union bargaining power has shown itself both as an influence on the rate of increase of money wages as a whole and in the maintenance of

[1] For example, D. J. Robertson, "The Inadequacy of Recent Wage Policies in Britain" and A. Flanders "Can Britain Have a Wage Policy?" *Scottish Journal of Political Economy*, 1958, pp. 99–113 and 114–25.

accepted relationships between the wages of different groups in face of divergences both in demand and productivity. It may not be a grave over-simplification to say that, in present conditions, the two main determinants of changes in wages are changes in the cost of living in the recent past and the relative toughness in bargaining of unions and employers' associations, with the prospect of passing on higher labour costs as an important element in the latter. Incidentally, this is consistent with the observations of Bhatia and Lipsey about the explanatory power of unemployment and profits. With the higher level of unemployment in the United States, changes in the profitability of business may be a better guide than changes in unemployment to the general buoyancy or otherwise of demand, and so to the prospect of passing on higher costs.

The distinction between different methods of price fixing goes back to the very early post-war discussions of inflation, but again there is considerable disagreement about its precise form. Prices which adjust to changes in demand quickly, and so as to clear the market, have been called "demand determined", "competitive" or merely "flexible". The essence of the matter is that no individual seller can charge a price significantly different from that of his competitors. Hence a change in demand affects the price charged by all sellers, causes a change in the profitability of operations and so evokes a change in supply. A change in costs, on the other hand, cannot directly affect the price charged by any seller; its direct effect is on the profitability of operations, and it is only as this evokes a change in supply that prices move so as to restore normal levels of profit. When, however, firms can charge prices which differ significantly from those of their competitors they can, if they choose, pass on increases in costs directly in higher prices, though they may risk the loss of a certain amount of business. In this case, we need a theory of how prices are fixed and what causes them to be changed, and again there are a bewildering variety of alternatives.

The simplest and least satisfactory explanation is that firms simply take their direct costs and add a purely conventional "mark-up". More sophisticated theories attempt to explain the size of the mark-up by reference to a number of factors, including firms' judgements of the likely reactions of their rivals; their fear that "too large" profits may lead to a loss of goodwill, to claims for higher wages or to government intervention; their desire to secure a "target" rate of return on capital when operating at the proportion of capacity regarded as normal; and their desire to assure themselves of finance for expansion to meet an anticipated long-run growth of demand either by ploughing back profits or by paying dividends generous enough to make their shares attractive in the market. An exhaustive study of inflation theory would obviously need an evaluation of all these and other possibilities. For our present purposes, however, we need only note a few points on which there is a large measure of agreement. In important sectors of the economy prices tend, for one or other of the reasons mentioned above, to be fixed at a level below that which would maximize short-run profits; they are changed only at fairly infrequent intervals; they do not appear to be sensitive to short-run changes in demand unless these are very large; and they do appear to respond fairly quickly to changes in costs, even when these are quite small.

III

Our present problem is to explain the genesis of inflation in an economy in which wages are fixed in the way we have described; in which some prices (including most imported foodstuffs and raw materials) are demand determined and some "administered" and which is operating very near to the limit of its physical capacity. For the moment we also assume that there are no effective monetary or fiscal restraints on the growth of money income.

In such circumstances it is clear that if demand grows faster than productive capacity this will raise "demand-determined" prices directly, and others indirectly through rising wages. There have been periods in the past twenty years when all the signs indicated that this was happening, and when economists have shown a rare measure of agreement that excess demand was the main, if not the whole, trouble. Unfortunately, most countries have also experienced periods when output has been static or even falling, when there has been an appreciable amount of idle capacity, but where prices have still risen. These periods have usually been short, if only because governments anxious to maintain "full employment" have set in hand inflationary monetary and fiscal policies. It is possible, therefore, to explain the continued price rise in terms of the lagged effect of past excess demand. Many economists, however, have not been satisfied with these explanations, and so have evolved alternative "cost-push" and "structuralist" theories.

In its purest form a "cost-push" theory would assert that rising costs can be passed on in higher prices and that, in the process, there will be generated enough additional purchasing power to buy up the former level of output at higher prices, so that no one need price himself out of the market, and the inflationary process will not be arrested by the emergence of unemployment or excess capacity. It has been suggested that the initial "push" could come from one of three sources: wage claims by the unions; imports; or an enhanced "target" rate of return on capital set by employers. The three, however, are distinctly different in their method of operation.

Suppose that one industry, which we will call *A*, concedes a wage increase and attempts to pass on its enhanced costs by an appropriate increase in price. Further, let us assume that management believe that the increase in price will not have any significant effect on their sales, so that they continue to employ the same labour force and produce the same rate of output as before. The additional wage payment will have created additional purchasing power equal to the enhanced costs of the *A* product. However, only a small part of this will go on good *A*; most of it will spill over into other goods and services. Moreover, the rise in the price of good *A* will reduce its sales to other sectors of the economy. Hence if the *A* industry were alone in raising wages and prices, employers' expectation of being able to maintain their sales would be disappointed; output would have to be cut back and unemployment would ensue. As one American writer put it, "If the wage bargain is to be inflationary, the steel corporation must be able to increase steel prices without impairing production; it cannot do so simply because steel workers with a wage increase might be able to buy more pork chops."[1] However, if this process is not confined to one industry, but is going on more or less simultaneously everywhere, no one industry will for long be at a great disadvantage in relative prices, and all will benefit from purchasing power "spilling over" from wage increases elsewhere. The resulting changes in demand will roughly balance one another; there will be many minor variations, but no section of the

[1] C. L. Christenson, "Variations in the Inflationary Force of Bargaining" in "Big Unions and Inflation", *American Economic Review*, 1954, pp. 347–62.

economy is likely to suffer a large and prolonged fall in demand, with its associated excess capacity and unemployment. The only circumstance in which this would be likely to occur would be if some sectors did not share the general confidence of being able to pass on wage increases, and so lagged behind the rest in raising wages and prices. Even in this case, however, the Government (if it interpreted its full-employment commitment as Governments have done in the past twenty years) would soon come to the rescue with inflationary monetary or fiscal measures. I conclude, therefore, that in circumstances such as those of modern Britain it is quite possible for trade-union pressure to exert an independent upward push on the price level.

If the initial push comes from rising import prices the situation is different. Higher import prices give more spending power to overseas suppliers, but (except in so far as this is spent on our exports) they put no extra purchasing power into the domestic economy. Hence, the passing on of these costs in higher domestic prices must result in a deficiency of demand and in unemployment, unless it is accompanied either by falling prices in other sectors or by expansionist monetary or fiscal policies.

The same argument could be applied to profits push, unless it is assumed that enhanced profits are either distributed to shareholders and spent by them or spent by the companies earning them within a short time. There is, however, a quite different difficulty in supposing that profits are an independent cause of inflation in the way that we have shown wages may be. Some writers have blamed rising "target" rates of return on capital for rising prices, but without showing any good reason why these targets should rise. Monopoly prices will be higher than competitive prices, but with given demand and cost conditions they will not show a continuing tendency to rise.[1] I do not believe, therefore, that the desire to raise monopoly profits is an independent element in the inflationary process.

The so-called "structuralist" theories of inflation have their origin in South America[2] and owe their application to industrial

[1] G. Haberler in *Inflation*, ed. D. C. Hague (London, 1962), pp. 27–29.

[2] D. Seers, "A Theory of Inflation and Growth in Underdeveloped Countries", *Oxford Economic Papers*, 1962, pp. 173–95, gives an account of the work of South American economists.

economies largely to the work of Schultze.[1] The basic assumptions are:

(1) that wages and prices rise when demand increases but do not fall when demand declines, at least until the decline is so large as to produce an unacceptable amount of unemployment;

(2) that at any one time there are considerable inequalities between different sectors or different regions in the balance between demand and resources; and

(3) that, over time, changes in taste, in the availability of factors and of technology are continually changing this balance.

In such conditions it is possible to have excess demand in some sectors at the same time as there are considerable idle resources in others. Excess demand, where it exists, operates on prices and wages as in an ordinary demand inflation. If the products concerned are used in other industries costs in those industries will be increased, while increases in wages in booming industries may provoke claims, based on fairness, elsewhere. In this way the rise in prices spreads even to sectors where there are considerable idle resources. It is, of course, possible to develop an exactly similar argument in respect of regional differences in economic activity. The last stage of this process does not seem to me entirely plausible, but I believe that there are at least two important points that emerge from the structuralist thesis. First, once we escape from the simplicity of aggregate models, excess demand can exert an upward pull on prices in some sectors, even though the economy as a whole is by no means fully employed. Secondly, the process of economic change requires frequent changes in relative prices; if absolute prices are insensitive, as they often are, to small falls in demand, then the necessary relative changes must impart an upward bias to the general price level.

Finally, there is the possibility that price increases may be generated by the way in which the system reacts to differing rates of productivity growth. Suppose that, where productivity is increasing at a more than average rate, the gain is taken out in higher incomes rather than being passed on in lower prices. Ordinary market forces would, of course, tend to produce an upward pull on wages elsewhere, but this is likely to be greatly accelerated by collective

[1] C. L. Schultze, "Recent Inflation in the United States", *U.S. Congress Joint Economic Committee, Study Paper No. 1* (Washington, 1959).

bargaining and arbitration. The lack of any statistical relationship between changes in productivity and earnings is a testimony to the speed with which this process normally takes place. However, higher wages in occupations where there is little change in productivity can be paid only out of higher prices, so that, once again, an upward bias is imparted to the price level as a whole. If this bias is to be avoided, and that mentioned a moment ago is to be counteracted, then a large part of the benefit from increases in productivity needs to be passed on in the form of lower prices.[1]

IV

The purpose of analysing the causes of inflation is, of course, to discover the most appropriate remedies. We need to distinguish between at least three groups of situations:

(i) those in which a general contraction of demand brought about by monetary or fiscal measures will halt inflation without any significant adverse effects on employment or growth;
(ii) those which call for selective cuts in demand combined with action to promote the mobility of resources; and
(iii) those which require an attack on the mechanisms by which increases in costs are generated and passed on.

Those who have argued as between cost inflation and demand inflation have usually been concerned with the distinction between categories (i) and (iii).

Unfortunately, however, none of the statistical indicators is wholly suitable. A comparison of the timing of wage and price changes raises the problem of choosing a starting-point when each follows the other at short intervals. Even if we could start from a period of stability, however, this test would fail to distinguish between a demand inflation and a cost inflation if a large number of prices were "administered". A similar criticism applies to comparisons between the growth of incomes and that of either productivity or real output, both of which have been used to a surprising extent. However, money incomes can grow faster than both

[1] For a detailed analysis of this problem, see K. Lancaster, "Wage Policies, Productivity Geared", *Economica*, 1958, pp. 199–212, and "Productivity Geared Wage Policies, Further Note", *Economica*, 1959, pp. 156–7.

productivity and output in a pure demand inflation if unions have enough defensive strength to prevent wages lagging too far behind the rise in prices. In such circumstances it is formally true to say, as Harrod has done,[1] that the excess of the rise in incomes over that of output is a measure of the rise in costs, but this gives no clue at all to the true cause or the appropriate cure.

It is also argued that excess demand will encourage employers to pay for overtime and also to offer payment in excess of ordinary negotiated rates in order to maintain and expand their labour force. In that case an increase in "wage drift"—the gap between wages and earnings—should be a sign of demand inflation. There is certainly a tendency for wage drift, measured by the difference between the rise in the official index of earnings and that of wage-rates, to be large at times of strong demand, but wage drift is a complex phenomenon, and we still know too little about the full range of forces that affect it.[2]

Another possible guide is the change in the relative shares of wages and profits in the national income. If a rise in prices is accompanied by a rise in the share of profits this would be strong evidence of demand inflation, but the converse is not necessarily true. If prices over a large part of the economy are "administered", and are raised only after an increase in demand has raised costs, there might be no shift to profit recorded in the statistics. A constant, or even falling, share of profits does not therefore rule out demand inflation.

In such a situation, however, we should expect to find falling unemployment and a growing number of unfilled vacancies, and also an increasing backlog of unfilled orders. The unemployment figures can provide a useful pointer, though there appears to be a rather long time lag between changes in output and in unemployment. Unfilled orders can be a very useful indication both of the general state of demand and its distribution between industries, and there is a strong case for extending the collection of these figures over a much wider field.

No single indicator can distinguish infallibly between different

[1] Sir Roy Harrod, *The British Economy* (New York, 1963), pp. 154–60.

[2] For a sceptical view of the relationship between "wage drift" and demand see H. A. Turner, "Wages, Productivity and the Level of Employment: More on the Wage Drift", *Manchester School*, 1960, pp. 89–123.

types of inflation, but we may hope to make progress by a judicious use of several. However, much needs to be done in the analysis of the logical relationship between different series, in the actual collection of information and in empirical study of the time lags and other difficulties that arise in its use.

V

Finally, let me turn briefly to the controversies over policy against inflation. Again there are many differences of detail, but most of the protagonists fall into two broad groups. In one are those who believe that the main inflationary danger comes from the side of costs and that any check to demand is likely to enhance costs by causing a fall in productivity, while wages continue to rise. They therefore advocate running the economy extremely near to the limit of its physical capacity, in the hope that this will give high productivity and rapid growth, while relying on an incomes policy, supplemented if necessary by government controls, to ensure that costs and prices do not get out of hand. In the other, are those who believe that excess demand is the main danger. They would have the monetary and fiscal authorities promote a steady growth of demand at a pace within the limits set by technological progress and starting from a point which would leave a little more excess capacity than we have been accustomed to in the past few years. So far from these resources being wasted, it is believed that they would give a big return in greater flexibility, more vigorous competition and enhanced efficiency. Economists of this persuasion believe, of course, that with a little spare capacity the working of the competitive market would both keep down costs and prices and stimulate growth. Those who share my own distrust of government intervention tend to fall into the second group.

There are several reasons why I believe that policies of the first kind are unlikely to succeed, even if they include a large number of direct controls. First, they may well not succeed in attaining the desired growth rate—a study of different countries over the past twenty years shows no systematic connection between the average level of capacity use and the average growth rate, while our own experience shows that operating very near the limit of capacity creates rigidities which, if continued for long, could seriously hamper growth. Secondly, if the economy as a whole is, almost literally, fully employed there are bound to be some sectors in which there is strong excess demand; if this is checked by controls resources will be hindered from moving in the directions that afford the greatest opportunities for growth; if it is not checked, however, this excess demand must inevitably raise prices.

Whatever may be thought of incomes policies in other conditions, it is hard to see how they can help when there is a strong excess demand for labour. Unless there was a general and effective system of price controls, there would be almost universal expectation that higher costs could be passed on. Moreover, even if rates negotiated in national agreements could be kept within tolerable limits, their effect would be in danger of being nullified by an increase in wage drift.

Perhaps most important of all, the attempt to run the economy even nearer to absolute capacity than in the recent past would place an intolerable strain on our not very adequate regulators. A quite small unforeseen expansion of demand could create a threat to the balance of payments. Such a threat could develop very quickly, yet all the usual correctives involve substantial time lags—there are lags between the occurrence of an event and its becoming apparent in the statistics, lags while the statistical evidence is being evaluated and turned into policy decisions, and yet further lags before a change in monetary or fiscal policy induces changes in expenditure and in economic activity. A policy change which is mistimed can, of course, accentuate a recession instead of curbing a boom.[1] There are strong reasons for believing that the deflationary measures of 1952, 1957 and 1961 did just this, and those of 1965 may well do so again. The attempt to drive the economy even harder would very likely frustrate itself by leading to "stop–go" policies, in which the stops were even more jarring than they have been in the past.

My own sympathies lie with those of my colleagues who believe that we should benefit from having—on average—a little, though not very much, more spare capacity than we have had in the past few years. I am impressed by the argument that a little more spare capacity would make for more effective competition, greater flexibility and, in the long run, a better growth potential. Also, if we

[1] A. W. Phillips, "Stabilisation Policy in a Closed Economy", *Economic Journal*, June, 1954, pp. 290–323.

were prepared to tolerate (if necessary) slightly wider swings as well, there would be less need for frequent changes of monetary and fiscal policy; intervention, when it did prove necessary, would have more time; and there would be less chance of making matters worse by errors of timing. This might even produce the paradoxical result that the willingness to accept somewhat larger fluctuations might result in our having actually to suffer smaller ones.

This does not, however, imply the complete rejection of an incomes policy. I have given my reasons for believing that, in the conditions of present-day Britain, wage push can exert an independent influence on prices. Obviously this depends on at least a permissive attitude by the monetary and fiscal authorities. It could not persist for long in face of either a strict control of the money supply or fiscal policies which effectively restrained the growth of money income. In such circumstances, however, present collective bargaining and arbitration procedures would produce unemployment, which would increase until unions were weakened and employer resistance toughened sufficiently to keep wage increases within the bounds which could be paid without raising prices. No one knows how much unemployment would be necessary; Phillips believes it might be less than 2·5 per cent.,[1] but other estimates have been much more pessimistic. Doubtless we could find out by experiment, but I see no reason for conducting so hazardous and unpleasant a social experiment (even if it were politically possible) if it can be avoided.

An incomes policy cannot have any real value when there is a strong excess demand for labour, and there is one real danger in the policy as expressed in the recent White Paper.[2] There is no mention of changes in demand either in the criteria regarded as justifying a price increase or in those under which "enterprises will be expected to reduce their prices". If these criteria were strictly adhered to, all prices would be "administered" and would change only with changes in costs; demand could have no direct effect, and would affect prices only in so far as it affected costs. This would introduce a most unhealthy rigidity; and it is not a danger that can easily be avoided. The introduction of demand into the price-fixing criteria

[1] A. W. Phillips, "Unemployment and the Rate of Change of Money Wage Rates in the U.K., 1861–1957", *Economica*, 1958, p. 299.

[2] *Prices and Incomes Policy*, Cmnd. 2639, April, 1965.

would have implications for profits which cannot be analysed here, but which would probably be unacceptable to many trade unionists. Subject to these qualifications, however, it seems to me highly desirable that organized labour and organized employers should jointly recognize the economic realities that are the necessary conditions of an efficient, acceptable and non-inflationary incomes structure. Such co-operation might also be very useful in ensuring that price increases made necessary by a deterioration in the terms of trade were not made the basis for further wage claims.

If our earlier diagnosis was right it is important to break down the expectation that increases in cost can be passed on. This expectation has been nurtured for twenty years, both by the way in which the full-employment commitment has been expressed and by the eagerness with which governments have rushed in with inflationary measures as soon as a little unemployment appears. To break it down now may need not only tough words from the authorities, but tough action in restraining the overall growth of demand and in allowing firms which try to pass on wage increases to price themselves out of the market. It should not, however, need a chronically high level of excess capacity to convince businessmen that they cannot automatically recoup higher costs in higher prices without reducing sales.

May I conclude by giving my own personal answer to the question posed in my title. I do not regard inflation as a necessary concomitant to a high level of employment or a rapid rate of growth. If we are to avoid inflation, however, I believe that we shall have to give price stability a high priority in the framing of policies as well as in the writing of speeches; that we need to accept a rather higher average level of spare capacity and possibly a rather wider range of fluctuations than we have in the recent past; that we must break down the expectation that higher wages can be passed on in higher prices without loss of sales, and that we must ensure that a much larger share of the gains from technological progress are passed on in lower prices rather than higher incomes. Some of these things, especially the last, will not be easy. On the brighter side is the large influence which past price changes appear to exert on current wage claims. This should mean that each success in reducing the rate of inflation will make further reductions easier. If an incomes policy brought such an initial check this in itself could be of great value.

It is even possible that such a breakthrough might have been achieved in 1948–50 had it not been for the Korean War. Co-operation between organized employers and unions could reduce the inflationary effect of future rises in import prices, and the more the two sides can agree on the distribution of income, the higher the level of employment that is likely to be compatible with price stability.

12

ECONOMIC MODEL BUILDING FOR CONTROL

R. J. BALL

Lister Lecture,[1] Nottingham, September, 1966

Introduction

FIVE years ago Dr. (now Professor) R. G. Lipsey delivered the Lister Lecture to this Association on the subject of the theory of wages. He was particularly concerned to examine the view that "economics can be a discipline that deals *in a scientific manner* with human behaviour".[2] In particular he dealt with the case of wage determination. The modern scientist is very much aware of the pace of technological change in all accepted fields of science, but is unlikely to think of economics as a field in which change has been equally rapid. In this paper I propose to illustrate how modern economics has advanced in its ambitions to treat not only individual problems in a more scientific way, but also to encompass the analysis and behaviour of economic systems.

In his earlier paper Professor Lipsey remarked that "as a practitioner in the field of economic science I search for stable patterns of human behaviour in the economic sphere"[3]. This is only one function of the economist, his function in developing what we describe as "positive" economics. Positive economics is concerned with establishing such patterns in order to predict and control events. Thus we want to know how firms will react to the Corporation Tax or households to changes in hire purchase conditions fixed

[[1] Lister Lectureships were established by the British Association in 1958. They are designed to give young research scientists an opportunity of reporting on the nature and significance of their work.]

[2] R. G. Lipsey, "Can there be a Valid Theory of Wages?" *Advancement of Science*, Vol. 19, July, 1962 [included in this volume].

[3] Loc. cit., p. 105.

by the Government. To achieve this aim we must relate the behaviour of decision making units to changes in the environment as represented by the variables that enter into their decision making processes which are beyond their control. Historically, however, the economist has been concerned also with the general problem of the allocation of resources amongst competing uses, or the development of "normative" economics. Normative economics is concerned with establishing the existence of conditions that determine optimal situations, e.g. what distribution of resources will maximize the welfare of consumers or what combination of inputs of factors of productions will minimize the costs of producing a given output. Positive economics is concerned with establishing what people *actually* do; normative economics with what they *ought* to do to realize specified economic objectives.

There are of course important links between both these concepts of what economists do. In order to decide what ought to be done it is generally necessary to establish the behavioural patterns of decision makers, the technical nature of relations in production, and the institutional character of the environment within which decision makers operate. But on the methodological side the most important link is that to become operational, positive and normative economic concepts must be quantifiable. To establish stable behavioural patterns one needs to apply statistical techniques to economic data, while in the field of normative economics the subject has been made increasingly operational through the development of linear, non-linear and dynamic programming.

The major development in the field of economics in the last 20 years has been the growing use of quantitative methods. In the past, the economist has failed to relate what has often been a valuable conceptual framework, to the mass of observable economic phenomena. In a sense, while scientists have sought to explain and understand phenomena, and developed theories to help them which have been tested against the facts, economists have all too frequently constructed theories related to a phenomenal world of their own creation. In the event it was not surprising that great difficulties arose in translating their contributions into operational terms. At some levels this was not entirely their fault. With regard to the economy as a whole, data about aggregate behaviour was sadly lacking. Only in the last 11 years, for example, have we had available data on the Gross Domestic Product of our economy for each quarter of the year. At the level of the individual enterprise however, much data has been available within firms themselves. But here we find the accountant rather than the economist sitting in the seat of judgement on pricing, costing and the decision to invest capital resources. This has in large part resulted from the failure of economics on the quantitative side, which has led to the accountant, closely tied to the facts and figures of the day, achieving the major control positions by default. It is significant that in the past Chancellors of the Exchequer have been more prone to listen to economists than Managing Directors. This picture is being transformed. Even in the last five years since Professor Lipsey addressed this Association, considerable strides forward have been made in introducing quantitative methods into economic curricula. One would not claim that the use of such methods means that we are on the verge of transforming our ability to handle economic problems. It simply means that the subject is pressing forward in an increasingly scientific manner to reduce its region of ignorance.

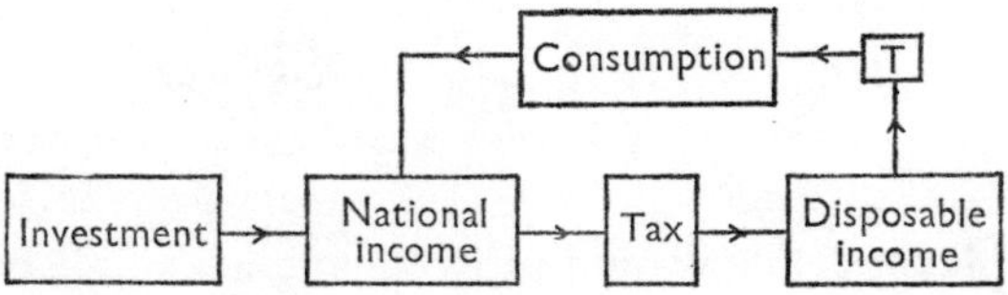

FIGURE 1

The positive economist, as Professor Lipsey pointed out, seeks for stable patterns of economic behaviour. For example, we may wish to study the way in which changes in costs affect prices in order to predict what will happen when wages rise. The study of this problem involves establishing a relationship between price, the dependent variable of the analysis and the independent or cost variables. Thus schematically we have a situation as in Fig. 1. This figure shows the data on two cost elements feeding into a transforming function that converts the basic information into a price figure. Thus the T-box could stand for the operation of multiplying each of the cost values by a co-efficient and adding them together to give the price. In this particular case Fig. 1 illustrates the fact that price is a linear combination of the different costs that affect price.

The figure is an illustration of a simple economic model. For present purposes an economic model can be described as a relationship or set of relationships between economic variables, which can usually be represented in mathematical form. The basic characteristic of economic models is that they entail systems of logical relationships and as such can usually be expressed in mathematical form. They can also be expressed in physical form by the use of analogue models relating stocks and flows together. Generally speaking, however, it is more convenient to turn them into a set of mathematical equations, which means that the models can then be converted into digital form and simulated or experimented with on an electronic computer.

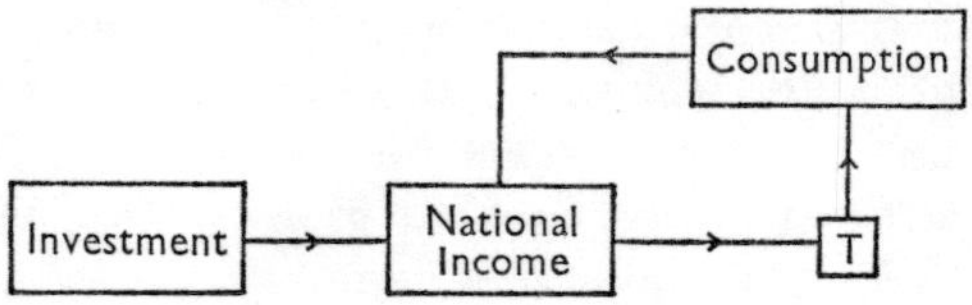

$$Y = C + I$$
$$C = \alpha + \beta Y$$

FIGURE 2

The simple model depicted in Fig. 1, entails a single relationship between an economic variable and those variables that it depends on. Generally speaking, however, economic models consist of a number of such relationships, which reflect the existence of what an electrical engineer would call "feed back" between different parts of the system. To illustrate the point, it is useful to consider the following model. Suppose that we have an economy in which level of national income consists of the sum of expenditures on consumption and expenditures on investment. Suppose further that the level of investment is determined outside the system—in the jargon it is an exogenous variable. Let the level of consumption C, depend on the level of income Y, i.e. income effectively determines the decision to spend on consumption goods. This model may be represented as in Fig. 2. The level of investment (I) is assumed to be given. The two arrows feeding from investment and consumption into the national income box imply that they are added together to give national income. There is only one "behavioural" relationship in the system indicated by the T-box that shows that national income is "transformed" into consumption. A particular mathematical form of this model is given by the side of the schematic presentations. In this model a change in investment leads to a change in income which is then fed back into a change in consumption with a consequent further change in income, and so forth.

The basic principle of this model is of course capable of unlimited extension. The national income characteristically is the sum of a whole variety of consumer and investment expenditures—by the private sector, of Government expenditure, and of expenditures on exports by foreigners, less the value of goods imported that are already included in figures of domestic expenditure. Furthermore changes in the values of expenditure can be decomposed into changes in the real quantities of goods produced, that affect the level of resources engaged, and changes in the prices of goods sold. For many purposes it is important to separate these two effects, so that a useful model of the economy as a whole would normally be expected to provide information as to the determination of many price levels, wage levels and interest rates that both determine and are determined by economic activity.

At the national level, the management of the economy as a whole focuses on a variety of objectives related to the problems of inflation, the balance of payments, the level of employment and the rate of growth of output. Broad objectives such as stable prices or a satisfactory balance of payments can be translated into a set of specific objectives relating to certain measurable characteristics of economic performance such as the numbers unemployed, the level of national income, the rate of investment, the level of wages and the volume of output exported. The purpose of model building of the kind illustrated is to provide a framework of logical relations that shows how these variables are related to each other. But prior to the model building exercise it is necessary to separate the variables with which one is concerned into two classes, the dependent and independent, or as the jargon goes, the endogenous and exogenous variables. The dependent variables are those that are explained or determined by the model. The independent variables affect other variables in the model but are not themselves determined by it. To illustrate the point, let us return to the model of Fig. 2, and suppose that the authorities in our hypothetical economy decide to collect a constant amount in income tax irrespective of the level of income. Consumers would be expected to decide their expenditure on the basis of their income after tax, or disposable income. A revised version of this model might then appear as in Fig. 3. In this model, given the rate of investment, the income flow will be affected by the amount drawn out of the system in tax. Here we have two independent variables, the rate of investment and the level of tax. In

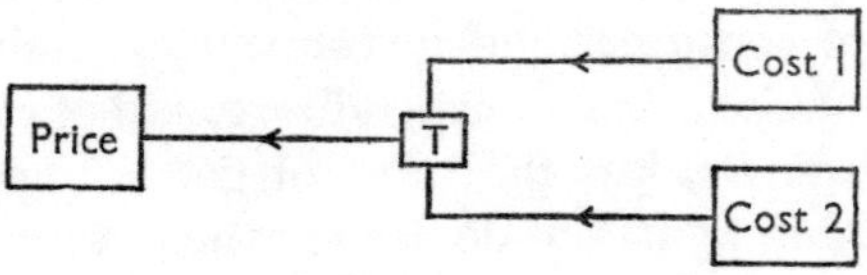

FIGURE 3

more realistic models, the flow of investment will of course be a dependent variable in the system, and the tax system will be infinitely more complicated. But tax variables such as tax rates and allowances will generally remain exogenous, for one of the functions of the models is to enable us to examine the effects on variables such as income, exports and employment of changes in such rates and allowances.

Widening the logic further, we may conceive of an economic model of this kind as "transforming" the independent into the dependent variables of the analysis by the use of a system of equations or structural relationships. The independent variables at any period of time will generally include past or lagged values of some of the dependent variables. This characteristic of such models makes them dynamic and subject to change over time because of their own internal structure. Thus there are "feed back" effects in the solution of the models due to simultaneity, and "feed back" in the sense that values generated yesterday enter into today's calculations. The existence of lags in the relationships of such systems also means that the effects of changes in the independent variables are generally speaking distributed over time.

Given a set of equations of a particular form, the structure of a model is determined by the co-efficients that enter into the particular relationships of which it is composed. These co-efficients may be estimated from available data of time series of the variables that appear in the model or in some cases with the additional help of cross-section data from surveys of firms or households. Whatever the precise statistical method used, the use of estimates obtained in this way presupposes that the structure of the model will remain sufficiently stable to enable us to assume that the past experience of relationships serves as a good guide to future performance. The extent to which this is a valid assumption will vary with the nature of the model and the period over which the structure is assumed to remain unchanged. A proper assessment must in the last analysis be pragmatic, for such models are intended as tools to aid decision making, not as sausage machines that may be cranked by unskilled labour to solve all problems. A great deal of ink has been spilled over the question of whether there is an enduring underlying economic structure that we are seeking to uncover. Many economists have felt that the model approach is too inflexible and mechanical and find it difficult to accept that a great deal of economic behaviour can be reduced to such formal framework.

The philosophical issue here need hardly detain us. The model builder seeks to add to the tool kit of the decision maker. Like the good bridge player he is concerned with the assumption he needs to make to win the game, the validity of which will ultimately meet the test of fire. It is a matter of research to establish whether calculations on the backs of envelopes, or inspired intuition can do better than elaborately constructed models. Perhaps all we need are larger envelopes. At the present stage of the game, enough has been done to encourage the researcher in this field, but not enough by far for any clear conclusion to emerge.

Models of the kind we have been discussing have two principal aims. Prima facie they should first of all assist us in the process of economic forecasting. In practice two sources of error arise in making economic forecasts. One stems from the fact that relationships in such models are not assumed to be mathematically exact, but are subject to random disturbances. It is the existence of these random disturbances that links the economic model builder with the statistician. The estimated co-efficients of the models are statistical estimates so that probabilistic criteria may be applied to attach measures of reliability both to the estimated co-efficients and to the forecasts made. We do not expect to forecast with complete accuracy or certainty but to be able to assess the probability that a random interval constructed about the point forecast of an individual variable will include the "true" value of the variable. Errors that occur in this context are model errors. The second principal source of error arises because the independent variables themselves have to be estimated. Thus for example, the level of exports may depend directly on the level of world trade that is not explained by the model. But over the forecast period the behaviour of world trade may be crucial. Some method has to be found for making this "higher order" forecast. Thus, while the model may be very good at calculating what exports would be if the future level of world trade were known, a substantial error may occur in the world trade forecast, which results in substantial errors in the model's calculated export values. In some cases, independent ininformation may be inaccurate because up-to-date figures are not known. Official statistics are continually being revised and a recurrent problem for the Government forecaster is to assess where the economy is at a point of time, let alone where it is going to be. All these factors combine to mean that even if the model used is itself a useful approximation to the economic structure, the actual forecasts made may be subject to substantial error for other reasons.

The second principal aim of model building is to provide a framework in which to analyse the effects of alternative policies. Thus the Government controls certain strategic economic variables that effect the level of economic activity. These include hire purchase regulations, the level of Bank Rate, Government spending, and tax rates and allowances of various kinds. A complete model of the economy must weave these variables into the fabric of the relationships. In that case the model may be used to compute the outcome of alternative sets of values of the policy variables. This is an ambitious task which provides the model builder with a strong incentive to combine his approach to forecasting with a knowledge of economic structure.

The past history of major work in this field is mainly confined to the United States and Holland. In both countries substantial resources have been directed to the construction of models of the type we have been discussing.

In the United States the Social Science Research Council originally sponsored a major project that resulted in a large model of around 150 equations, that is still being maintained and tested by the Brookings Institute in Washington.[1] Already they are preparing for an even larger model of between 300 and 400 equations. The Department of Commerce has recently published the model it uses to assist in understanding the behaviour of the economy.[2]

Model building work carried out in Holland has always been most closely linked with official forecasting and policy making, through the Dutch Central Planning Bureau at the Hague. Evaluations of the models have been carried out, and on the whole the performances have been encouraging.

In the remainder of this paper I want to illustrate the nature and performance of such models with specific reference to a model of the U.K. economy that is being developed at the London Business School. This model is still in its infancy. It is no more than a prototype that awaits development, but given the research resources we hope to be able to employ, we would expect it to provide a vehicle for further basic research in the field.[3] The principal aim of the model initially was to provide a framework within which to treat the explanation of the level of U.K. output, as measured by the published figure of Gross Domestic Product, in real or quantity terms.

The mathematical representation of the model, together with definitions of the relevant variables, is set out in the Appendix to this paper. I do not propose here to deal with it in detail. Instead it is worth trying to get some idea of the logic of the system in schematic terms. Many of the variables that enter into the structure in the Appendix are non-linear, i.e. they involve ratios and products of separate variables. To facilitate manipulation of the system these variables are replaced by linear approximations about the most recent values of the variables. The schematic picture is developed on the assumption that these variables are treated in this linearized form. To simplify the presentation we have aggregated

[1] *The Brookings Quarterly Econometric Model of the U.S.* Ed. by J. S. Duesenbery, G. Fromm, L. R. Klein, E. Kuh (1965.)

[2] Cf. *Survey of Current Business.*

[3] A previous large scale U.K. model was constructed in Oxford in 1956–58 Cf. L. R. Klein, R. J. Ball, A. Hazlewood and P. Vandome, *An Econometric Model of the United Kingdom 1948–56*. The building of this model was handicapped by the lack of data at that time—in particular by the absence of quarterly national income accounts.

Condensed Flow Diagram (Current Endogenous Variables)

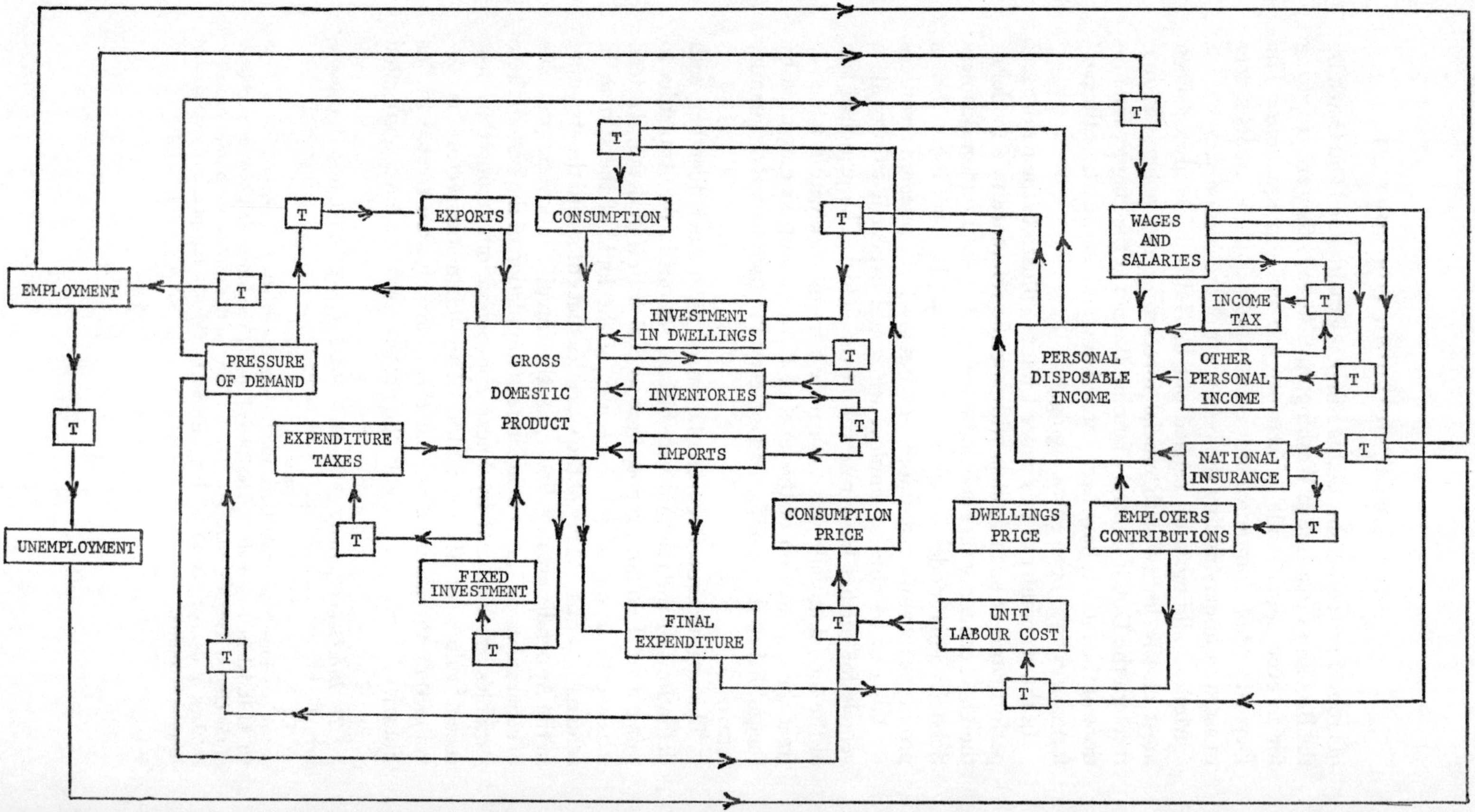

some of the equations together. The purpose of the exercise is to explain the logic not to produce exactly the model given in the Appendix.

It is convenient to start with a simplified scheme that pictures all the economic variables that the model explains. This is given in Fig. 4. In drawing this picture we ignore the exogenous variables—those not determined by the system—and the lagged values of the dependent variables that feed into the current situation. The flow diagram illustrates the interdependence between the dependent variables at a given point of time. This particular model is designed around quarterly data and so the diagram refers to a single 3-month period.

To begin with we may focus attention on the box containing Gross Domestic Product at factor cost. From Gross Domestic Product valued at Market prices we deduct expenditure taxes less subsidies so that what remains is in principle equal to the income of factors of production. The arrows feeding into G.D.P. indicate that the source must be added in or subtracted in arriving at G.D.P. Thus expenditure on exports, consumption and the different categories of investment are all components of G.D.P. All that is missing here in the equation for G.D.P. is the level of Government spending which is regarded as determined outside the system. The T-boxes represent the structural relations of the system that may be represented by structural equations that transform the information that feeds into the boxes into the outputs that follow them. Some of lines lead away from G.D.P. Thus for example G.D.P. and imports add together to give final expenditure. Following the circuit round, this helps to determine the volume of exports and wages and salaries. Wages and salaries help to determine personal disposable income which feeds into the equation for consumption expenditures, and finally by this route we return to G.D.P. Leaving by another route we see that the level of G.D.P. helps to explain the level of employment which in turn affects unemployment. In this model unemployment is used to help fix the level of national insurance contributions, which assist us in arriving at the level of personal disposable income.

To obtain estimates of the values of all the dependent variables in the model, we need to feed in all the exogenous information and the relevant lagged values of the dependent variables. In Fig. 5 we

Complete Flow Diagram

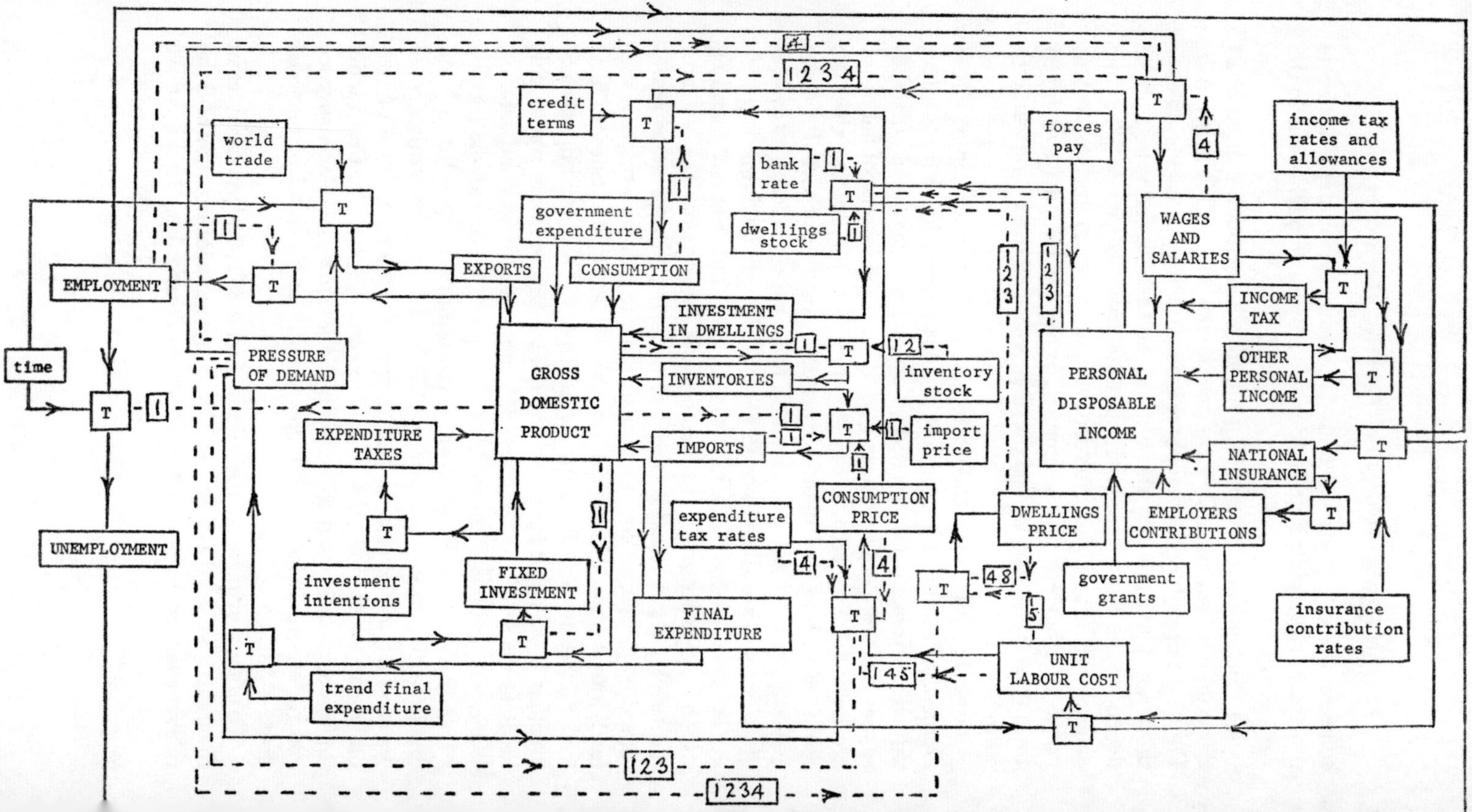

illustrate the complete system in which all this predetermined information is included. Here the dotted lines represent feed backs in time, with the numbers in circles representing the order of the lags. Thus note that employment is partly determined by employment in the previous period. The exogenous information includes the anticipated level of fixed investment, estimated from Board of Trade survey data, which helps to determine the rate of fixed investment. The level of world trade is now added to the pressure of demand and a time trend in computing exports. Expenditures on consumption are affected by hire purchase conditions as laid down by the Government, and measured here by the minimum deposit rate on durable goods, and the average monthly repayment, which is affected by Government decisions as to the maximum length of hire purchase contract.

As pointed out earlier, the network of relationships in Fig. 5 is conveniently handled in mathematical form. This makes it easy to translate the system on to an electronic computer.[1] Given the exogenous and predetermined information it is an extremely tedious process to solve for the values of the independent variables at a point of time. For a large modern computer this is almost trivial. Thus when the model has been set up and programmed for the computer, it is a comparatively easy task to examine the effects of introducing alternative assumptions about say, the level of Government spending.

The model we are illustrating is in many ways very naïve. It does not explicitly incorporate a great many factors that a complete policy model requires. Thus for example the treatment of income taxation is formally inadequate for it does not explicitly isolate several of the key "policy" levers. This is because this is only a prototype system that provides a framework for development work.[2] Nevertheless at each stage it is important to assess whether the development is along the right lines. As an aircraft progresses in development, its features may be tested by say the use of a wind tunnel to see that they are in line with calculations. In the present

[1] For this particular system, programmes have been written for the Atlas Computer of the University of London.

[2] A more adequate treatment of the tax system for this model is described in a forthcoming book by Dr. E. Balopoulos, to be published by the North Holland Publishing Company. His approach will be subsequently incorporated into the illustrative model.

case, we want to assess the overall structure of the system. This can be done in part by checking the values that are computed from the model for periods for which we have actual data of what happened. Note that this does not guarantee that even if the structure appears plausible, we have a good forecasting tool.

This is so firstly because in the subsequent illustrative runs of the model we use the actual known values of the exogenous and predetermined variables and this will not generally be the case. A dramatic illustration of this is the level of world trade which is crucial to our export performance. Even for one period predictions,

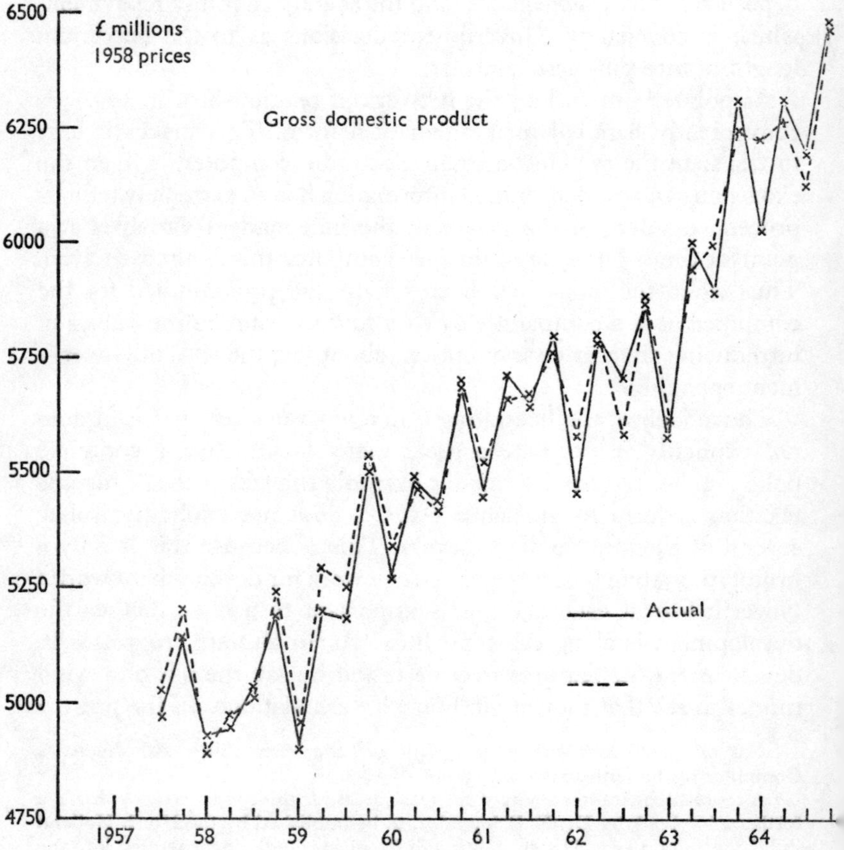

FIGURE 6

which essentially concern us here, some lagged values of endogenous variables will have to be forecast by the model, as up-to-date figures are not available. For forecasts over a longer period than one quarter, errors involved in generating predetermined variables will be of even greater significance.

Secondly, the period we examine has been used in part to estimate the structure of the individual relationships. The whole, however, is not a simple sum of its parts, and the calculations that follow are important guides to assessing weaknesses, and planning research and development strategy.

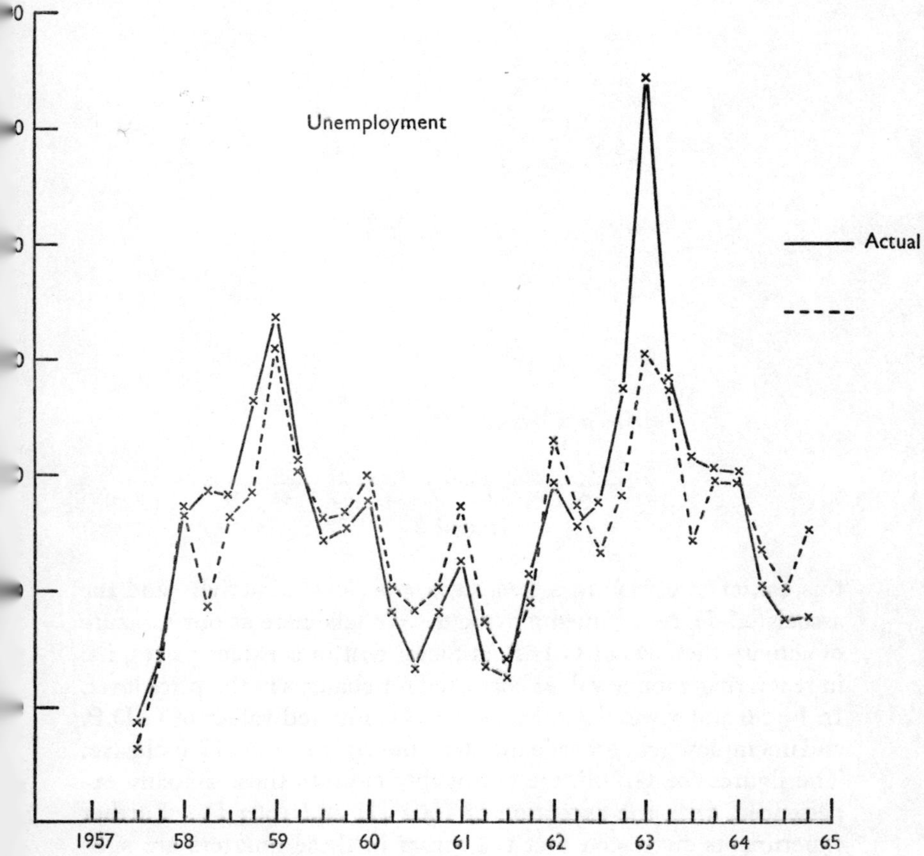

FIGURE 7

In Figs. 6–11 are plotted the actual and computed values of a number of the key dependent variables that relate to short-term policy objectives. Originally models of this type sprang from the theoretical framework of Lord Keynes that sought to throw light on the problem of how to obtain and maintain full employment. In

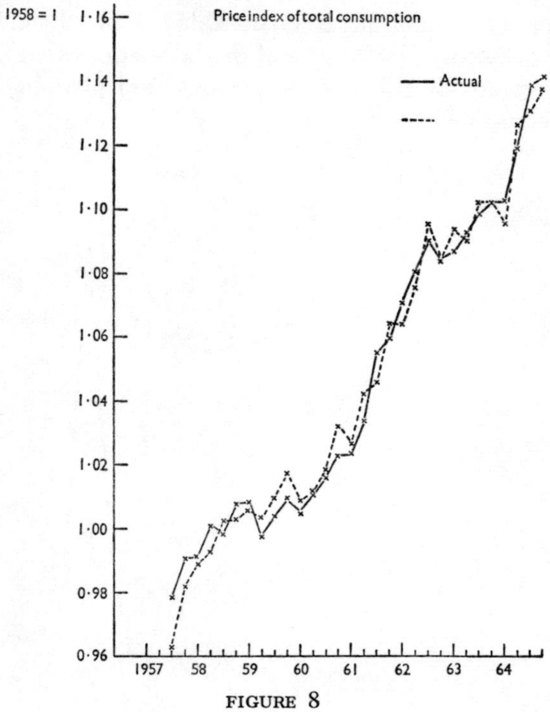

FIGURE 8

this context we wish to assess the overall level of activity and the associated degree of unemployment. We take here as our measure of activity the level of G.D.P. at factor cost in constant prices, i.e. in real terms, money values corrected for changes in the price level. In Fig. 6 and 7 we plot the actual and computed values of G.D.P. and unemployment for each quarter from 1957 I – 1964 IV inclusive. The figures for G.D.P. are reasonably close to those actually experienced, with the exception of 1962 III and 1963 IV. Further experiments suggested that the errors in these quarters are substantially affected by our failure to account adequately for the movement of inventory investment. Discoveries of this kind affect the allocation of research resources in further development. With regard to unemployment, there is a large error in 1963 I. The actual level is far above that computed by the model. This is undoubtedly due to the dramatic effect of the weather during the winter of that year, for which we do not explicitly account. The error in fact is a point in favour of the model rather than against it, for it helps to confirm the popularly held view that the high rate of unemployment in that quarter was not due to economic conditions. Indeed the difference between the actual and computed value may be treated as an estimate of the additional unemployment created by weather

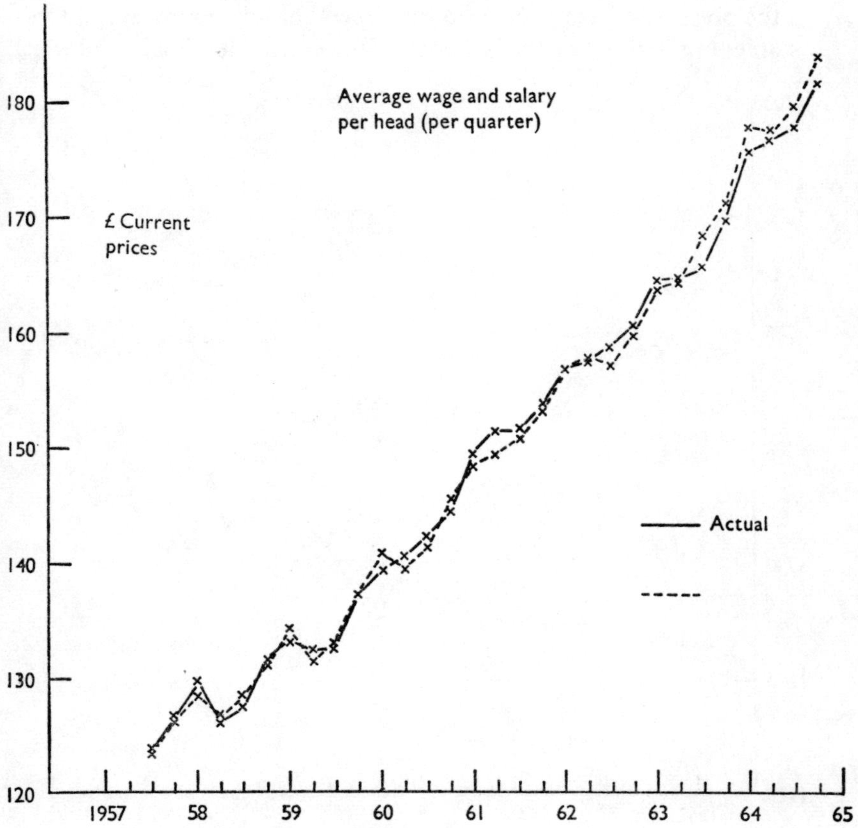

FIGURE 9

conditions, and used to adjust the published figures in providing a "normal" series, just as we correct export figures for the effect of dock strikes. In practice the result suggests that there is a case for perhaps excluding 1963 I from estimating procedures designed to yield estimates of "normal" structure.

In the short run we are also concerned with the problem of inflation and the Balance of Payments. In Fig. 8 we plot actual and calculated figures of the general level of prices, and in Fig. 9 the average wage and salary per head. Finally in Figs. 10 and 11 we plot exports and imports.

Figure 10 reflects primarily the individual structural relation immediately concerned as there is feedback to exports only through the pressure of demand. Imports depend heavily upon lagged variables but in this case the inclusion of the current level of inventories,

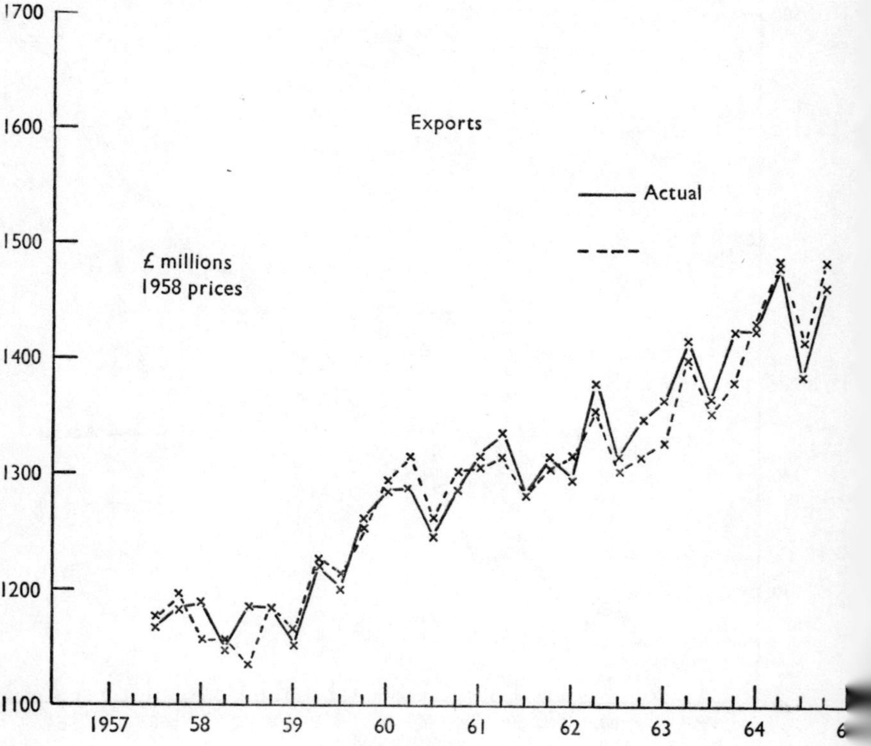

FIGURE 10

with a co-efficient of about one half, produces a substantial feedback from the system.

These figures serve to illustrate that while the model is not perfect, the structure it embodies enables us to get sufficiently close to the true values of relevant variables to enable us to use it as a basis for development. They also encourage us to begin using the system to study the effects of changes in some of the key exogenous variables. It was remarked earlier that the presence of lagged dependent variables in the system means that it is a dynamic system that feeds on its own past. In formulating say policies for full employment, it is

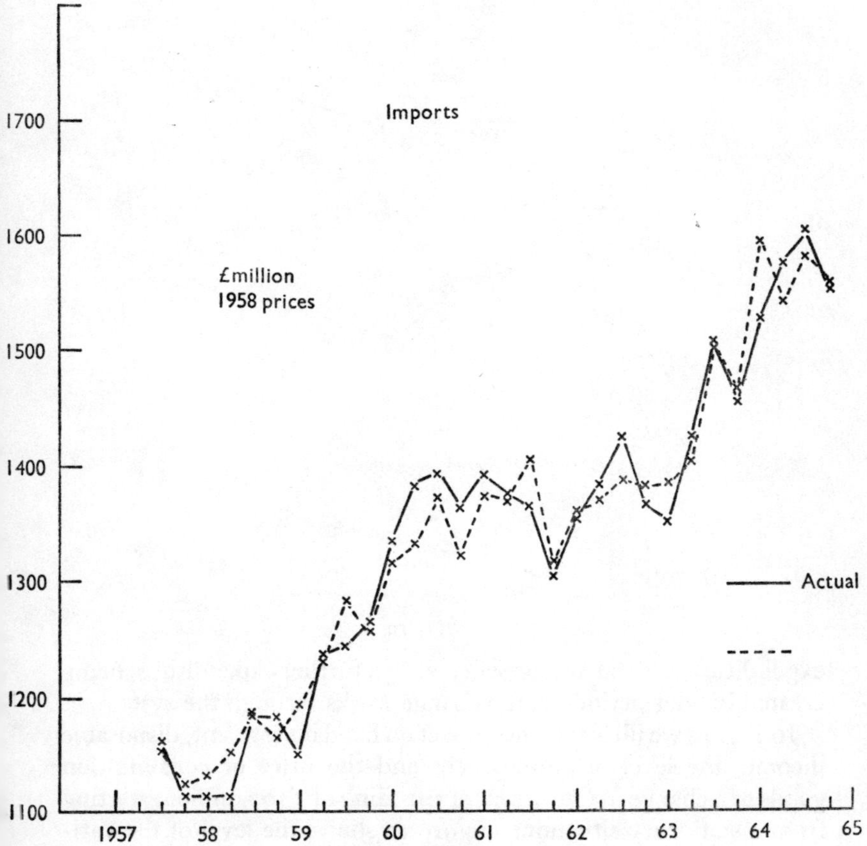

FIGURE 11

of paramount importance to get right the timing of changes in policy variables such as Government spending and hire purchase regulations and to assess their impact on the level of activity. To illustrate the point we may consider the time profile of the effects of a change in Government expenditure. The addition of an extra maintained

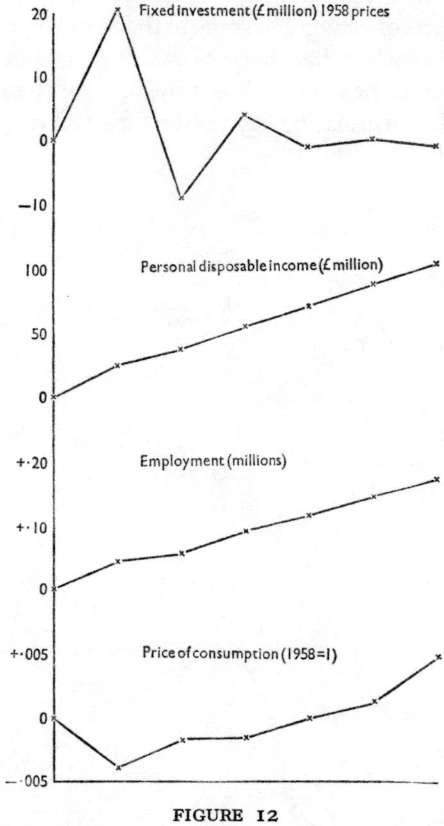

FIGURE 12

expenditure of £100 million will result in further expenditures being created in later periods as the change works through the system.

In Fig. 12 we illustrate the impact on fixed investment, disposable income, the level of employment and the price of consumption goods of a change in Government spending of £100 million, starting from a stationary situation. Figure 12 shows the level of the variables after six periods following the initial rise of Government spending by £100 million. To begin with the rise in expenditure causes an increase in the fixed investment of about £21 million. This is followed by a sharp decline and a tendency for the net increase to go to zero. This happens because in making these calculations we have made (for illustrative purposes) the unrealistic assumption that investment plans or anticipated levels of investment are unaffected by the change in Government spending. As can be seen from the Appendix, the rate of fixed investment depends on the anticipated level and on the change in Gross Domestic Product. As time goes on the impact of the change in Government spending becomes less from one period to another so the level of fixed investment tends to decline towards its initial level. The rise in Government spending also results in a rise in both the level of employment and the level of disposable income. Both these variables rise fairly steadily even after the impact on Gross Domestic Product from period to period has fallen off markedly. This is because the reaction of wages, salaries and so forth, to a change in demand for goods and services lags behind and adjusts smoothly to the new situation. Notice that in the case of the price of consumption goods there is an initial fall. This is because the initial effect of the rise in output is associated with an increase in productivity which tends to depress prices slightly, a gain which is subsequently eroded by the response of wages and salaries (costs) to the increase in demand.

In a more complete and fully articulated system, it would be possible to examine in this way the effects of changes in a variety of key policy variables, such as tax rates and allowances. As I have pointed out, the present model is primitive and illustrative, and needs considerable extension before this can be done.

It is important to emphasize that the model illustrated is a basis for developing a short run model to aid decision making, where short run may be construed as up to a year. It is not a model that can be usefully used to assess longer run trends such as would be required to develop growth policies to span a 5- or 10-year period. This model ignores, among other things, the long run effects of changes in industrial structure, industrial interdependence, and the long run impact of changes in monetary condition. It is geared to the problems of employment, current account balance, and inflation in the short run. It focuses on short-term changes in expenditure rather than long run problems of resource reallocation and growth.

This illustrates the point that in model building it is important to be clear as to the objectives of the exercise. Models are tools—part of the tool kit of the decision maker that he uses to control and interpret phenomena. At the present stage of our knowledge and abilities it is probably over ambitious to search for "the" model that can be used to deal with all problems. Nevertheless it is to be hoped that further analyses of the kind I have illustrated will add to our knowledge of short run economic behaviour and our ability to control.

Acknowledgment

In preparing this lecture I have received invaluable assistance from Terence Burns, who supervised the calculations presented and carried the burden of data preparation.

APPENDIX

A QUARTERLY MODEL OF THE UNITED KINGDOM

APPENDIX

A QUARTERLY MODEL OF THE UNITED KINGDOM

1\. (a) $$C_{nd} = \underset{(106{\cdot}99)}{521{\cdot}91} + \underset{(0{\cdot}079)}{0{\cdot}322}\,\frac{Y_d}{P_{nd}} + \underset{(0{\cdot}118)}{0{\cdot}536}\,C_{nd-1} - \underset{(36{\cdot}87)}{444{\cdot}126}\,Q_1 - \underset{(31{\cdot}95)}{91{\cdot}50}\,Q_2 - \underset{(10{\cdot}54)}{141{\cdot}32}\,Q_3$$

$$\overline{R}^2 = 0{\cdot}9948 \qquad \text{V.N.} = 2{\cdot}219$$

(b) $$\Delta C_{nd} = \underset{(10{\cdot}08)}{191{\cdot}97} + \underset{(0{\cdot}057)}{0{\cdot}308}\,\Delta\,\frac{Y_d}{P_{nd}} - \underset{(0{\cdot}122)}{0{\cdot}423}\,\Delta C_{nd-1} - \underset{(26{\cdot}25)}{455{\cdot}03}\,Q_1 - \underset{(55{\cdot}86)}{204{\cdot}7}\,Q_2 - \underset{(26{\cdot}15)}{24{\cdot}13}\,Q_3$$

$$\overline{R}^2 = 0{\cdot}9935 \qquad \text{V.N.} = 2{\cdot}208$$

2\. (a) $$C_d = -\underset{(82{\cdot}32)}{373{\cdot}46} + \underset{(0{\cdot}027)}{0{\cdot}155}\,\frac{Y_d}{P_d} + \underset{(0{\cdot}099)}{0{\cdot}761}\,\frac{NC}{P_d} - \underset{(0{\cdot}0064)}{0{\cdot}0229}\,\sum^{55} C_{d-1} + \underset{(8{\cdot}015)}{28{\cdot}25}\,Q_1 + \underset{(8{\cdot}67)}{10{\cdot}669}\,Q_2 - \underset{(7{\cdot}54)}{9{\cdot}06}\,Q_3$$

$$\overline{R}^2 = 0{\cdot}963 \qquad \text{V.N.} = 1{\cdot}426$$

(b) $$\Delta C_d = \underset{(17{\cdot}161)}{15{\cdot}767} + \underset{(0{\cdot}032)}{0{\cdot}159}\,\Delta\frac{Y_d}{P_d} + \underset{(0{\cdot}156)}{0{\cdot}851}\,\Delta\,\frac{NC}{P_d} - \underset{(0{\cdot}044)}{0{\cdot}045}\,\Delta\sum^{55} C_{d-1} + \underset{(9{\cdot}36)}{20{\cdot}47}\,Q_1 - \underset{(12{\cdot}56)}{29{\cdot}00}\,Q_2 - \underset{(10{\cdot}01)}{24{\cdot}51}\,Q_3$$

$$\overline{R}_2 = 0{\cdot}8826 \qquad \text{V.N.} = 2{\cdot}020$$

3\. (a) $$\frac{NC}{Pd} = \underset{(37{\cdot}16)}{101{\cdot}09} + \underset{(0{\cdot}063)}{0{\cdot}412}\,C_d - \underset{(0{\cdot}322)}{2{\cdot}03}\,d - \underset{(0{\cdot}02)}{0{\cdot}06}\,\frac{D_{-1}}{P_d} - \underset{(8{\cdot}92)}{1{\cdot}64}\,M^* - \underset{(6{\cdot}75)}{12{\cdot}04}\,Q_1 - \underset{(7{\cdot}34)}{2{\cdot}99}\,Q_2 + \underset{(6{\cdot}76)}{5{\cdot}96}\,Q_3$$

$$\overline{R}^2 = 0{\cdot}877 \qquad \text{V.N.} = 1{\cdot}02$$

(b) $$\Delta\,\frac{NC}{P_d} = -\underset{(3{\cdot}97)}{6{\cdot}37} + \underset{(0{\cdot}069)}{0{\cdot}353}\,\Delta C_d - \underset{(0{\cdot}455)}{2{\cdot}366}\,\Delta d - \underset{(0{\cdot}073)}{0{\cdot}009}\,\Delta\frac{D_{-1}}{P_d} - \underset{(11{\cdot}40)}{36{\cdot}34}\,\Delta M^* - \underset{(5{\cdot}69)}{6{\cdot}27}\,Q_1 + \underset{(6{\cdot}40)}{18{\cdot}52}\,Q_2 + \underset{(7{\cdot}26)-}{10{\cdot}32}\,Q_3$$

$$\overline{R}^2 = 0{\cdot}841 \qquad \text{V.N.} = 2{\cdot}468$$

4. (a) $$I_f = \underset{(34{\cdot}8)}{117{\cdot}64} + \underset{(0{\cdot}058)}{0{\cdot}725}\, I^* + \underset{(0{\cdot}062)}{0{\cdot}141}\,(Y - Y_{-1}) + \underset{(34{\cdot}12)}{53{\cdot}58}\, Q_1 - \underset{(14{\cdot}44)}{12{\cdot}93}\, Q_2 + \underset{(23{\cdot}43)}{15{\cdot}71}\, Q_3$$

$$\bar{R}^2 = 0{\cdot}842 \qquad \text{V.N.} = 1{\cdot}037$$

(b) $$\Delta I_f = \underset{(8{\cdot}78)}{32{\cdot}87} + \underset{(0{\cdot}077)}{0{\cdot}160}\, \Delta I^* + \underset{(0{\cdot}021)}{0{\cdot}046}\, \Delta(Y - Y_{-1}) + \underset{(19{\cdot}44)}{46{\cdot}08}\, Q_1 - \underset{(8{\cdot}84)}{37{\cdot}91}\, Q_2 - \underset{(14{\cdot}90)}{22{\cdot}56}\, Q_3$$

$$\bar{R}^2 = 0{\cdot}823 \qquad \text{V.N.} = 2{\cdot}251$$

5. (a) $$I_R = -\underset{(52{\cdot}06)}{194{\cdot}58} + \underset{(0{\cdot}0144)}{0{\cdot}0738}\, \tfrac{1}{4}\Sigma\frac{Y_d}{P_R} - \underset{(1{\cdot}990)}{1{\cdot}229}\, r_{-1} - \underset{0.0061}{0{\cdot}0073}\, K_{r-1} - \underset{(4{\cdot}40)}{7{\cdot}27}\, Q_1 + \underset{(4{\cdot}28)}{2{\cdot}52}\, Q_2 + \underset{(4{\cdot}29)}{1{\cdot}49}\, Q_3$$

$$\bar{R}^2 = 0{\cdot}9009 \qquad \text{V.N.} = 1{\cdot}202$$

(b) $$\Delta I_R = \underset{(7{\cdot}734)}{2{\cdot}238} + \underset{(0{\cdot}063}{0{\cdot}080}\, \Delta\tfrac{1}{4}\Sigma\frac{Y_d}{P_R} - \underset{(2{\cdot}83)}{2{\cdot}01}\, \Delta r_{-1} - \underset{(0{\cdot}062)}{0{\cdot}041}\, \Delta K_{h-1} - \underset{(4{\cdot}77)}{5{\cdot}38}\, Q_1 + \underset{(4{\cdot}706)}{9{\cdot}52}\, Q_2 + \underset{(4{\cdot}69)}{0{\cdot}151}\, Q_3$$

$$\bar{R}^2 = 0{\cdot}1757 \qquad \text{V.N.} = 2{\cdot}469$$

6. (a) $$I_h = -\underset{(314{\cdot}18)}{1040{\cdot}97} + \underset{(0{\cdot}0845)}{0{\cdot}4635}\, Y - \underset{(0{\cdot}1155)}{0{\cdot}2705}\, Y_{-1} + \underset{(0{\cdot}1666)}{0{\cdot}3931}\, K_{h-1} - \underset{(0{\cdot}1405)}{0{\cdot}5107}\, K_{h-2} + \underset{(56{\cdot}926)}{348{\cdot}237}\, Q_1 + \underset{(20{\cdot}373)}{113{\cdot}533}\, Q_2 + \underset{(29{\cdot}602)}{178{\cdot}385}\, Q_3$$

$$\bar{R}^2 = 0{\cdot}7665 \qquad \text{V.N.} = 2{\cdot}327$$

(b) $$\Delta I_h = -\underset{(28{\cdot}59)}{172{\cdot}56} + \underset{(0{\cdot}094)}{0{\cdot}460}\, \Delta Y + \underset{(0{\cdot}124)}{0{\cdot}162}\, \Delta Y_{-1} - \underset{(0{\cdot}188)}{0{\cdot}484}\, \Delta K_{h-1} + \underset{(0{\cdot}181)}{0{\cdot}266}\, \Delta K_{h-2} + \underset{(69{\cdot}08)}{356{\cdot}09}\, Q_1 + \underset{(53{\cdot}94)}{161{\cdot}16}\, Q_2 + \underset{(45{\cdot}67)}{143{\cdot}53}\, Q_3$$

$$\bar{R}^2 = 0{\cdot}836 \qquad \text{V.N.} = 2{\cdot}105$$

7. (a) $$\frac{E}{T_w} = \underset{(6.316)}{69.425} - \underset{(0.014)}{0.427}\,t - \underset{(6.36)}{16.13}\,\frac{(Y+M)}{(Y+M)_T} + \underset{(0.421)}{2.596}\,Q_1 + \underset{(0.4202)}{2.102}\,Q_2 + \underset{(0.409)}{2.145}\,Q_3$$

$$\bar{R}^2 = 0.966 \qquad \text{V.N.} = 1.906$$

(b) $$\Delta\frac{E}{T_w} = -\underset{(0.361)}{2.549} + \underset{(10.81)}{36.75}\,\Delta\frac{(Y+M)}{(Y+M)_T} + \underset{(0.525)}{4.711}\,Q_1 + \underset{(0.528)}{1.397}\,Q_2 + \underset{(0.511)}{2.437}\,Q_3$$

$$R^2 = 0.710 \qquad \text{V.N.} = 2.636$$

8. (a) $$M = \underset{(264.63)}{496.48} + \underset{(0.129)}{0.512}\,I_h + \underset{(0.058)}{0.201}\,Y_{-1} - \underset{(177)}{538}\left(\frac{P_m}{P_{c-1}}\right) + \underset{(0.196)}{0.185}\,M_{-1} - \underset{(34.0)}{71.9}\,Q_1 - \underset{(21.26)}{0.054}\,Q_2 - \underset{(21.83)}{4.82}\,Q_3$$

$$R^2 = 0.9599 \qquad \text{V.N.} = 2.025$$

(b) $$\Delta M = \underset{(15.323)}{11.768} + \underset{(0.087)}{0.296}\,\Delta I_h + \underset{(0.075)}{0.159}\,\Delta Y_{-1} + \underset{(351.39)}{312.55}\,\Delta\left(\frac{P_m}{P_{c-1}}\right) - \underset{(0.161)}{0.349}\,\Delta M_{-1} - \underset{(40.60)}{64.37}\,Q_1 + \underset{(21.51)}{64.94}\,Q_2 + \underset{(28.62)}{3.064}\,Q_3$$

$$\bar{R}^2 = 0.5314 \qquad \text{V.N.} = 2.2297$$

9. (a) $$(Tx - S) = -\underset{(52.28)}{257.32} + \underset{(0.009)}{0.184}\,Y - \underset{(11.95)}{0.4425}\,Q_1 - \underset{(11.52)}{28.75}\,Q_2 - \underset{(11.37)}{25.16}\,Q_3$$

$$\bar{R}^2 = 0.923 \qquad \text{V.N.} = 0.710$$

(b) $$\Delta(Tx - S) = \underset{(10.213)}{41.797} + \underset{(0.035)}{0.112}\,\Delta Y - \underset{(19.66)}{59.89}\,Q_1 - \underset{(9.06)}{52.03}\,Q_2 - \underset{(12.89)}{42.53}\,Q_3$$

$$\bar{R}^2 = 0.826 \qquad \text{V.N.} = 2.510$$

10. (a) $$N = \underset{(1{\cdot}67659)}{5{\cdot}26835} + \underset{(0{\cdot}0000906)}{0{\cdot}0003324}\,Y + \underset{(0{\cdot}0884)}{0{\cdot}7065}\,N_{-1} - \underset{(0{\cdot}04913)}{0{\cdot}10892}\,Q_1 + \underset{(0{\cdot}04295)}{0{\cdot}07547}\,Q_2 + \underset{(0{\cdot}04083)}{0{\cdot}16525}\,Q_3$$

$$\overline{R}^2 = 0{\cdot}9660 \qquad V.N. = 1{\cdot}646$$

(b) $$\varDelta N = -\underset{(0{\cdot}06305)}{0{\cdot}07854} + \underset{(0{\cdot}0001807)}{0{\cdot}0003538}\,\varDelta Y + \underset{(0{\cdot}181)}{0{\cdot}176}\,\varDelta N_{-1} - \underset{(0{\cdot}10742)}{0{\cdot}004756}\,Q_1 + \underset{(0{\cdot}07767)}{0{\cdot}16465}\,Q_2 + \underset{(66{\cdot}37)}{0{\cdot}23967}\,Q_3$$

$$\overline{R}^2 = 0{\cdot}649 \qquad V.N. = 2{\cdot}084$$

11. (a) $$U = \underset{(1{\cdot}2572)}{7{\cdot}7478} - \underset{(0{\cdot}0654)}{0{\cdot}2567}\,N + \underset{(0{\cdot}0029)}{0{\cdot}02719}\,t - \underset{(0{\cdot}0001034)}{0{\cdot}0003121}\,Y_{-1} + \underset{(0{\cdot}03972)}{0{\cdot}08852}\,Q_1 - \underset{(0{\cdot}02619)}{0{\cdot}06982}\,Q_2 - \underset{(0{\cdot}2585)}{0{\cdot}01043}\,Q_3$$

$$\overline{R}^2 = 0{\cdot}799 \qquad V.N. = 0{\cdot}8745$$

(b) $$\varDelta U = \underset{(0{\cdot}0149)}{0{\cdot}0579} - \underset{(0{\cdot}070)}{0{\cdot}461}\,\varDelta N - \underset{(0{\cdot}000085)}{0{\cdot}000027}\,\varDelta Y_{-1} - \underset{(0{\cdot}0379)}{0{\cdot}0478}\,Q_1 - \underset{(0{\cdot}0277)}{0{\cdot}0882}\,Q_2 - \underset{(0{\cdot}0326)}{0{\cdot}00218}\,Q_3$$

$$\overline{R}^2 = 0{\cdot}80 \qquad V.N. = 1{\cdot}67$$

12. (a) $$OPY = -\underset{(36{\cdot}30)}{114{\cdot}92} + \underset{(0{\cdot}0099)}{0{\cdot}327}\,WS + \underset{(15{\cdot}67)}{42{\cdot}85}\,Q_1 + \underset{(15{\cdot}66)}{90{\cdot}78}\,Q_2 + \underset{(15{\cdot}26)}{115{\cdot}53}\,Q_3$$

$$\overline{R}^2 = 0{\cdot}968 \qquad V.N. = 1{\cdot}517$$

(b) $$\varDelta OPY = -\underset{(20{\cdot}79)}{83{\cdot}44} - \underset{(0{\cdot}199)}{0{\cdot}054}\,\varDelta WS + \underset{(18{\cdot}76)}{139{\cdot}8}\,Q_1 + \underset{(22{\cdot}01)}{138{\cdot}97}\,Q_2 + \underset{(18{\cdot}70)}{123{\cdot}57}\,Q_3$$

$$\overline{R}^2 = 0{\cdot}7007 \qquad V.N. = 3{\cdot}16$$

13. (a) $$\text{NIHC} = \underset{(5\cdot717)}{-3\cdot602} + \underset{(0\cdot00132)}{0\cdot04773}\,[\text{Nn}^* + \text{Uu}^*] + \underset{(0\cdot0006)}{0\cdot0133}\,\text{WS}^{\text{D}} - \underset{(5\cdot014)}{28\cdot665}\,\text{D} - \underset{(2\cdot128)}{0\cdot636}\,\text{Q}_1 - \underset{(2\cdot194)}{0\cdot120}\,\text{Q}_2 + \underset{(2\cdot068)}{0\cdot922}\,\text{Q}_3$$

$$\overline{\text{R}}_2 = 0\cdot995 \qquad \text{V.N.} = 0\cdot7897$$

(b) $$\Delta\text{NIHC} = \underset{(1\cdot1995)}{-0\cdot8341} + \underset{(0\cdot0040)}{0\cdot04538}\,\Delta[\text{Nn}^* + \text{Uu}^*] + \underset{(0\cdot0015)}{0\cdot0118}\,\Delta\text{WS}^{\text{D}} - \underset{(3\cdot98)}{20\cdot56}\,\Delta\text{D} + \underset{(1\cdot743)}{1\cdot494}\,\text{Q}_1 + \underset{(1\cdot816)}{1\cdot335}\,\text{Q}_2 + \underset{(1\cdot860)}{2\cdot558}\,\text{Q}_3$$

$$\overline{\text{R}}^2 = 0\cdot877 \qquad \text{V.N.} = 2\cdot884$$

14. (a) $$\text{EC} = \underset{(4\cdot550)}{51\cdot043} + \underset{(0\cdot016)}{0\cdot875}\,\text{NIHC} + \underset{(3\cdot113)}{0\cdot942}\,\text{Q}_1 + \underset{(3\cdot108)}{1\cdot621}\,\text{Q}_2 - \underset{(3\cdot025)}{2\cdot437}\,\text{Q}_3$$

$$\overline{\text{R}}^2 = 0\cdot9875 \qquad \text{V.N.} = 0\cdot408$$

(b) $$\Delta\text{EC} = \underset{(0\cdot398)}{2\cdot555} + \underset{(0\cdot021)}{0\cdot483}\,\Delta\text{NIHC} - \underset{(0\cdot582)}{0\cdot782}\,\text{Q}_1 + \underset{(0\cdot603)}{1\cdot304}\,\text{Q}_2 - \underset{(0\cdot619)}{0\cdot497}\,\text{Q}_3$$

$$\overline{\text{R}}^2 = 0\cdot9463 \qquad \text{V.N.} = 2\cdot454$$

15. $$\frac{\text{W} - \text{W}_{-4}}{\text{W}_{-4}} = \underset{(0\cdot0785)}{-0\cdot5451} + \underset{(0\cdot082)}{0\cdot612}\,\frac{1}{4}\sum_{0}^{-3}\frac{(\text{Y}+\text{M})}{(\text{Y}+\text{M})_{\text{T}}} + \underset{(0\cdot061)}{0\cdot023}\left[\frac{(\text{Y}+\text{M})}{(\text{Y}+\text{M})_{\text{T}}} - \frac{(\text{Y}+\text{M})}{(\text{Y}+\text{M})_{\text{T}-4}}\right] - \underset{(0\cdot122)}{0\cdot176}\left(\frac{\text{W}_{-4} - \text{W}_{-8}}{\text{W}_{-8}}\right) -$$

$$\overline{\text{R}}^2 = 0\cdot72 \qquad \text{V.N.} = 1\cdot8$$

16. $$\text{P}_{\text{c}} - \text{P}_{\text{c}-4} = \underset{(0\cdot00196)}{0\cdot01122} + \underset{(0\cdot1204)}{0\cdot3941}\,(\text{ULC} - \text{ULC}_{-4}) + \underset{(0\cdot1069)}{0.2276}\,(\text{ULC}_{-1} - \text{ULC}_{-5}) + \underset{(0\cdot00030)}{0\cdot00131}\,(\text{tx} + \text{tx}_{-4})$$

$$\overline{\text{R}}^2 = 0\cdot7636 \qquad \text{V.N.} = 1\cdot642$$

17. $$P_{nd} - P_{nd-4} = \underset{(0{\cdot}00220)}{0{\cdot}01599} + \underset{(0{\cdot}1349)}{0{\cdot}2622}(ULC + ULC_{-4}) + \underset{(0{\cdot}1198)}{0{\cdot}2479}(ULC_{-1} - ULC_{-5}) + \underset{(0{\cdot}000339)}{0{\cdot}001415}(tx - tx_{-4})$$

$$\bar{R}^2 = 0{\cdot}683 \qquad V.N. = 1{\cdot}436$$

18. $$P_d - P_{d-4} = -\underset{(0{\cdot}1183)}{0{\cdot}3946} + \underset{(0{\cdot}168)}{0{\cdot}614}(ULC - ULC_{-4}) + \underset{(0{\cdot}120)}{0{\cdot}385}\,\tfrac{1}{4}\sum_{0}^{-3}\frac{(Y+M)}{(Y+M)^T} - \underset{(0{\cdot}0064)}{0{\cdot}0487}\,D_1$$

$$R^2 = 0{\cdot}801 \qquad V.N. = 1{\cdot}351$$

19. $$P_R - P_{R-4} = -\underset{(0{\cdot}1325)}{0{\cdot}5964} + \underset{(0{\cdot}166)}{0{\cdot}407}(ULC_{-1} - ULC_{-5}) + \underset{(0{\cdot}0003)}{0{\cdot}0002}\,t + \underset{(0{\cdot}1367)}{0{\cdot}6034}\left[\frac{1}{4}\sum_{0}^{-3}\frac{(Y+M)}{(Y+M)^T}\right]_{-1} - \underset{(0{\cdot}0948)}{0{\cdot}2108}(P_{R-4} - P_{R-8}) + \underset{(0{\cdot}00629)}{0{\cdot}03426}\,D_2$$

$$\bar{R}^2 = 0{\cdot}7798 \qquad V.N. = 1{\cdot}108$$

20. $$W = \frac{WS}{N}$$

21. $$ULC = \frac{WS + EC}{Y + M}$$

22. $$(Y + M)_T = \underset{(74{\cdot}033)}{5776{\cdot}908} + \underset{(2{\cdot}327)}{50{\cdot}84}\,t - \underset{(75{\cdot}946)}{279{\cdot}378}\,Q_1 - \underset{(75{\cdot}77)}{91{\cdot}22}\,Q_2 - \underset{(75{\cdot}66)}{144{\cdot}06}\,Q_3$$

$$\bar{R}^2 = 0{\cdot}928447 \qquad V.N. = 0{\cdot}5897$$

23. $$Y^d = WS + EP + EC + CGG + OPY - PYT - NIH$$

24. $$Y = C_{nd} + C_d + I_f + I_R + I_h + I_f^G + I_R^G + G + E - M - Tx + S$$

1. C_{nd} = Consumers' expenditure on non-durable goods and services at market prices (£ million 1958).
2. Y_d = Total personal disposable income (£ million current).
3. P_{nd} = Price index of non-durable goods.
4. C_d = Consumers' expenditure on durable goods and services at market prices (£ million 1958).
5. P_d = Price index of durable goods.
6. NC = New credits extended to the consumer sector (£ million current).
7. D = Hire purchase debt for consumers (£ million current).
8. d = Minimum average deposit rate (per cent.) for consumer sector.
9. M^* = Minimum average monthly payment as per cent. of price (involving a maximum contract length of three years where no legal maximum exists).
10. If = Private non-dwellings gross domestic fixed capital formation at market prices (£ million 1958).
11. Y = Gross domestic product at factor cost (£ million 1958).
12. I^* = Private investment forecasts (January) for manufacturing, distributive and service industries (£ million 1958).
13. I_R = Private dwellings gross domestic fixed capital formation at market prices (£ million 1958).
14. P_R = Price index of total dwellings gross domestic fixed capital formation.
15. K_R = Cumulated sum of I_R from 1955
16. r = Bank Rate.
17. I_h = Value of physical increase in stocks and work in progress at market prices (£ million 1958).
18. K_h = Cumulated sum of I_h from 1955.
19. E = Exports of goods and services at market prices (£ million 1958).
20. T_w = World trade exports ($ 1958).
21. t = Time trend.
22. $(Y + M)_T$ = Predicted values from a linear regression of (Y + M) upon time and seasonal dummies.
23. M = Imports of goods and services (£ million 1958).
24. P_m = Price index of imports.
25. P_c = Price index of total consumption.
26. (Tx − S) = Taxes on expenditure less subsidies (i.e. adjustment to factor cost) valued at average 1958 rates (£ million).

27. N = U.K. civil employment less temporarily unemployed (million).
28. U = U.K. unemployed (including temporarily unemployed) (million).
29. OPY = Other personal income (£ million current).
30. WS = Wages and salaries (£ million current).
31. NIHC = National insurance and health contributions (£ million current).
32. n* = Average weekly flat rate contribution (employer and employee) in pennies for employed and self-employed.
33. u* = Average weekly flat rate contribution in pennies for unemployed.
34. WS^D = Dummy variable taking value zero for 1955 to 1961 (I) and value of WS from 1961 (II).
35. D = Dummy variable taking value 1 for 1961 (II) and zero elsewhere.
36. EC = Employers' contributions to national insurance and health and pension funds, etc. (£ million current).
37. D_1 = Dummy variable taking value 1 for 1963 and zero elsewhere.
38. D_2 = Dummy variable taking value 1 for 1963 and 1964 and zero elsewhere.
39. FP = Forces pay (£ million current).
40. CGG = Current grants from public authorities (national insurance benefits, family allowances, assistance grants, war pensions and service grants, etc.) (£ million current).
41. PYT = U.K. taxes on income (payments) plus transfers abroad (£ million current).
42. I_f^G = Public non-dwellings gross domestic capital formation at market prices (£ million 1958).
43. I_R^G = Public dwellings gross domestic capital formation at market prices (£ million 1958).
44. G = Public authorities current expenditure on goods and services at market prices (£ million 1958).
45. tx = Ratio of Taxes on expenditure minus subsidies at current and 1958 prices with a base of 100.

N.B. (a) The basic data used is that published in *Economic Trends*, October, 1965, which begins with 1955 (I).
(b) The sample periods vary from 1955 (II)–1964 (IV) to 1957 (III)—1964 (IV) depending upon
(i) the lag structure;
(ii) the existence of data for the investment intentions and credit variables.
(c) The price indices are the ratios of the variables expressed in current and 1958 prices, with a base of unity not 100.

13

SENSE AND NONSENSE IN BUDGETARY POLICY

A. R. PREST

Leeds, August, 1967

WHEN I think of the long line of eminent men who have delivered a Presidential Address to Section F—I observe that, for instance, Alfred Marshall spoke at the Leeds meeting in 1890 on "Some Aspects of Competition" and D. H. Macgregor at the 1927 meeting in Leeds on "Rationalization in Industry"—I can only reflect with sadness on the decline in standards evidenced by my filling this position today. The contrast is further heightened by the increase in the prestige of the social sciences generally, and that of economics in particular, over the years. To illustrate this, there is the delightful story about the 1870s in Lady Longford's biography of Queen Victoria.[1] A party of social scientists asked to be allowed to visit Balmoral in 1877. The Queen gave instructions that they could be allowed in the grounds, but not on any account in the house itself. She subsequently asked Sir Henry Ponsonby what they were like, and had the reply that he had seldom seen a slummier lot. One likes to think that the standing of social scientists, deservedly or undeservedly, is a little higher today.

My concern is to look at some of the major themes of Budgetary Policy in this country over the last twenty years or so and try to highlight lessons which should have been learned from these experiences. I should like to amplify this statement in several ways. First, I am using the word "budgetary" as a short-hand for "revenue and expenditure." My coverage will therefore be wider than what is often implied by the term "fiscal" policy;

[1] Elizabeth Longford, *Victoria R.I.* (London: Weidenfeld & Nicolson, 1964), p. 420

on the other hand, I shall not trench on the many other issues, e.g. monetary policy, controls on overseas capital movements and so on, which Chancellors of the Exchequer frequently discuss in their Budget Speeches. Second, I am taking a highly subjective view: I am not bold enough to say what lessons have been learned, but am only putting forward my view, with which many may disagree, about what ought to have been learned. Third, with a subject as vast as this, I must be highly selective if I am to satisfy the time constraint. I shall in fact concentrate on the following three themes:

The adjustment of aggregate demand and supply.
Investment stimuli.
Particular tax concessions and subsidies.

It will at once be obvious that there are many important topics (e.g. social security) which I shall not cover at all and that, even so, some of my remarks will perforce be of a very general, not to say superficial, character.

I

If one had to select a single point of time from which it could be said that henceforth a guiding principle of budgetary policy in this country should be the adjustment of aggregate demand to aggregate supply, the choice would almost certainly be Sir Kingsley Wood's Budget of 1941, with its explicit references to the need to judge proposals for tax increases in the light of the prospective inflationary gap.[1] It is no secret that Keynes played a major part in formulating these ideas; and it is also no secret that the ideas were somewhat beyond the Chancellor.[2] However, by the end of the war the general principles were widely accepted and already enshrined in such classic documents as Beveridge's *Full Employment in a Free Society*[3] and the 1944 White Paper.[4] Indeed, at that time it was sometimes asserted that the regulation of overall demand

[1] Hansard (Commons), 1940–41, Vol. 370, Cols. 1297–335.

[2] One hard-bitten Parliamentary observer of the time is alleged to have said that he had on many occasions listened to speeches by Ministers which they had not written; but this was the first time he had heard a speech which the Minister had neither written nor understood.

[3] Sir William Beveridge, *Full Employment in a Free Society* (London: Allen & Unwin, 1944).

[4] *Employment Policy*, Cmd. 6527 (London: H.M.S.O., 1944).

relatively to supply was the only Budget principle that really mattered and that, furthermore, it was a relatively easy principle to put into effect. In re-reading some of the early post-war Economic Surveys and Budget Speeches one is struck by the confidence of the authors that they could estimate prospective demands in the year ahead, the likely supply potential and the likely inflationary gap—at a time when national accounts were far less detailed than they are today, when there was no adequate official index of industrial production, no up-to-date Census of Production, no surveys of intended private capital expenditure and so on.[1] It was in reality a classic case of the belief that faith could move mountains. Some sceptics raised their voices in disbelief at some of the more extravagant claims,[2] but, by and large, it seems fair to characterize the predominant view of the time as one of being roughly 101 per cent. certain of the rightness of the principles of Keynesian fiscal policy and 99 per cent. certain of their practicality.

What in reality has been our experience in this country? Clearly one cannot summarize in a few words the economic history of a major country over a twenty-year period, and so the following remarks do no more than touch the top of a very large iceberg. The first observation is surely that we have been extraordinarily successful in maintaining full employment, whether judged by the standards of the past or by those of other countries. To keep at least 97 per cent. (and sometimes as much as 99 per cent.) of the working population in employment over a twenty-year period is an achievement in which we really can take pride. Unfortunately the employment percentage is not the only test of policy success. As Sir Roy Harrod has recently pointed out, the relatively stable percentage employment figures conceal much larger fluctuations in industrial production.[3] The balance-of-payments crises and the gyrations of the economy in the successive phases of "stop" and "go," the low growth rate of output and the high growth rate of

[1] In fairness, one should add that some private activities were very much dependent on public controls, and so forecasts could be made on that basis.

[2] See, for instance, Sir Hubert Henderson, *The Uses and Abuses of Economic Planning* (Cambridge: Cambridge University Press, 1947).

[3] E.g. whereas from 1955 last quarter to 1958 last quarter industrial production fell at the rate of 0·5 per cent. per annum, it rose at a rate of 9·0 per cent. per annum between 1958 last quarter and 1960 second quarter. Cf. Sir Roy Harrod, *Towards a New Economic Policy* (Manchester: Manchester University Press, 1967), pp. 13 and 19.

prices are too well known to require documentation in detail. Nor is there any convincing evidence that forecasting of prospective crises—or at any rate appropriate action emanating from accurate forecasts—has improved over the period. At the beginning of the period we had the severe crisis of summer 1947 followed by the devaluation of September 1949; and at the end we had the autumn crisis of 1964 followed, *inter alia*, by the summer crisis of 1966. It is worth noting in relation to the most recent of our trials that the Chancellor remarked in his Budget preview in Parliament on 2nd March, 1966, that he did not foresee the need for severe increases in taxation, that in his Budget of 3rd May, 1966, he expected a lull in consumer spending in the months immediately ahead, but by July some of the most drastic economic measures ever undertaken in this country in peacetime had to be introduced by the Prime Minister in person.

Mr. Dow has studied the United Kingdom economy from 1945 to 1960 with greater thoroughness than anyone else.[1] Two of his many important conclusions are relevant at this stage. On p. 65 he declares:

> "It is mostly by accident that for most of the time most Chancellors have been successful."

And on p. 384 he concludes:

> "As far as internal conditions are concerned then, budgetary and monetary policy failed to be stabilizing and must on the contrary be regarded as having been positively destabilizing. . . . Had tax changes been more gradual and credit regulations less variable, demand and output would probably have grown much more steadily."

It is true that some reviewers have not been able to accept the latter conclusion, but nevertheless one of the more critical still agreed that interventions were excessive.[2]

[1] J. C. R. Dow, *The Management of the British Economy 1945–60* (Cambridge: Cambridge University Press, 1964).

[2] I. M. D. Little, *Economic Journal*, December, 1964, p. 983.

It might be added that the conclusion that government policy in the United Kingdom had probably been destabilizing was reached independently by D. J. Smyth, "Public Finance Policy and Techniques for Economic Stability and Balanced Economic Growth" (International Institute of Public Finance, *Public Finance Policy and Techniques for Economic Stability and Balanced Economic Growth*, Saarbrücken, 1966).

Why has there been this size of gap between performance and promise? One view on this is to parody the famous lines of Canning and say:

> "In matters of finance the fault of the British
> Is consuming too much and acting too skittish."

But a general statement of this sort does not get us very far. I should be inclined to classify the reasons under two main headings: first, over-simplification of all the issues involved, and second, increasingly ambitious aims over the years.

Over-simplification has many dimensions. At the more theoretical level, one could say that earlier ideas about the stability of the consumption function, and hence the investment–income relationship, were far too naïve; so also was the notion that there was a single point of equilibrium below which there was less than full employment and beyond which prices started to rise. Nor was anything like adequate allowance made for the pervasive effects of world influences on a highly open economy. Another point is the self-generating character of some economic phenomena. E.g. a low level of unemployment has become a built-in feature of the post-war economy; and when the situation is such that today no one under 40 can remember a period when prices were not rising, is it surprising that economic actions become more and more based on the assumption that this is a permanent state of affairs? Finally, one might point to the theoretical complications of stabilization policy—the danger that government attempts at correction might easily have perverse effects, as shown by the work of Friedman and Phillips.[1]

Many of the more practical difficulties of applying "the nicely calculated less or more" in the context of macro-economic policy were also underestimated. There have been a number of instances in the post-war years when budgetary policy went badly astray. Dow[2] takes as clear examples the periods 1952–55 and 1958–60.

[1] M. Friedman, "The Effects of a Full-Employment Policy on Economic Stability", in *Essays in Positive Economics* (Chicago: University of Chicago Press, 1953). A. W. Phillips, "Stabilisation Policy in a Closed Economy", *Economic Journal*, June, 1954, and "Stabilisation Policy and the Time-Form of Lagged Responses", *Economic Journal*, June, 1957.

[2] Op. cit., p. 384. There have, of course, been failures elsewhere as well, e.g. there were errors in 1953, 1954, 1959 and 1962 in the United States. (*Annual Report, Council of Economic Advisers*, Washington, D.C., January, 1966, p. 174.)

Nearer to the present day, the failure to take action in the summer of 1964 to combat the mounting foreign-exchange crisis is another example. The reasons for these failures are manifold. There have been some cases where events or prospects changed so rapidly that it would have been extremely difficult for any government, however well-equipped and well-intentioned, to have done any better, e.g. the consequences of the Korean War for import prices or the quick deterioration in the balance-of-payments prospects during the early spring of 1964.[1] There are other cases where one suspects that the forecasting machinery was not as smooth-running as it might have been, but with the many improvements in statistical material and techniques one hopes that this will be a diminishing factor in the years to come.[2] Finally, there are some cases where what might be called electoral cost–benefit analysis would appear to have played an important role, e.g. the relaxation of April, 1955, in advance of the election of the following month.

Then we have the inability of the government machine to act in a co-ordinated fashion, in such wise that revenue and expenditure policies are reinforcing rather than pulling against one another. If one takes quarterly deseasonalized data of all public expenditure on goods and services from 1955 to 1966 (inclusive) and plots the unused resources[3] one gets the picture shown in Fig. 1. The correlation coefficient between the two series is—0·603.[4]

Obviously, no simple deduction about the perverse influence of government spending policy on the pattern of cycles in the last few

[1] The 1964 balance of payments on current and long-term capital account was forecast as −£165 million in the February issue of the National Institute *Economic Review*; and as −£300 million in the May issue.

[2] After explaining that it was very difficult to compare the forecast and actual changes in output between 1958 and 1959 because the actual outcome was still uncertain several years later, Treasury witnesses did declare that they now considered that statistical deficiencies were unlikely to lead to errors in forecasting the domestic economy in future (Fourth Report, Estimates Committee, 1966/67, *Government Statistical Services* (London: H.M.S.O., 1966), paragraphs 1381–3).

[3] From F. W. Paish and J. Hennessy, *Policy for Incomes* (Hobart Paper 29, Institute of Economic Affairs, London, 3rd Edition, 1967). I am indebted to Professor Paish for making additional figures available to me.

[4] The time trend fitted to public expenditure was $Y = 1{,}204{\cdot}7 + 10{\cdot}68X$ (where Y = public expenditure and X = time). If one fits a time trend to the series for the margin of unused resources one gets substantially the same results. And the same is true if one measures unused resources by the deseasonalized excess demand for labour data in the National Institute *Review*.

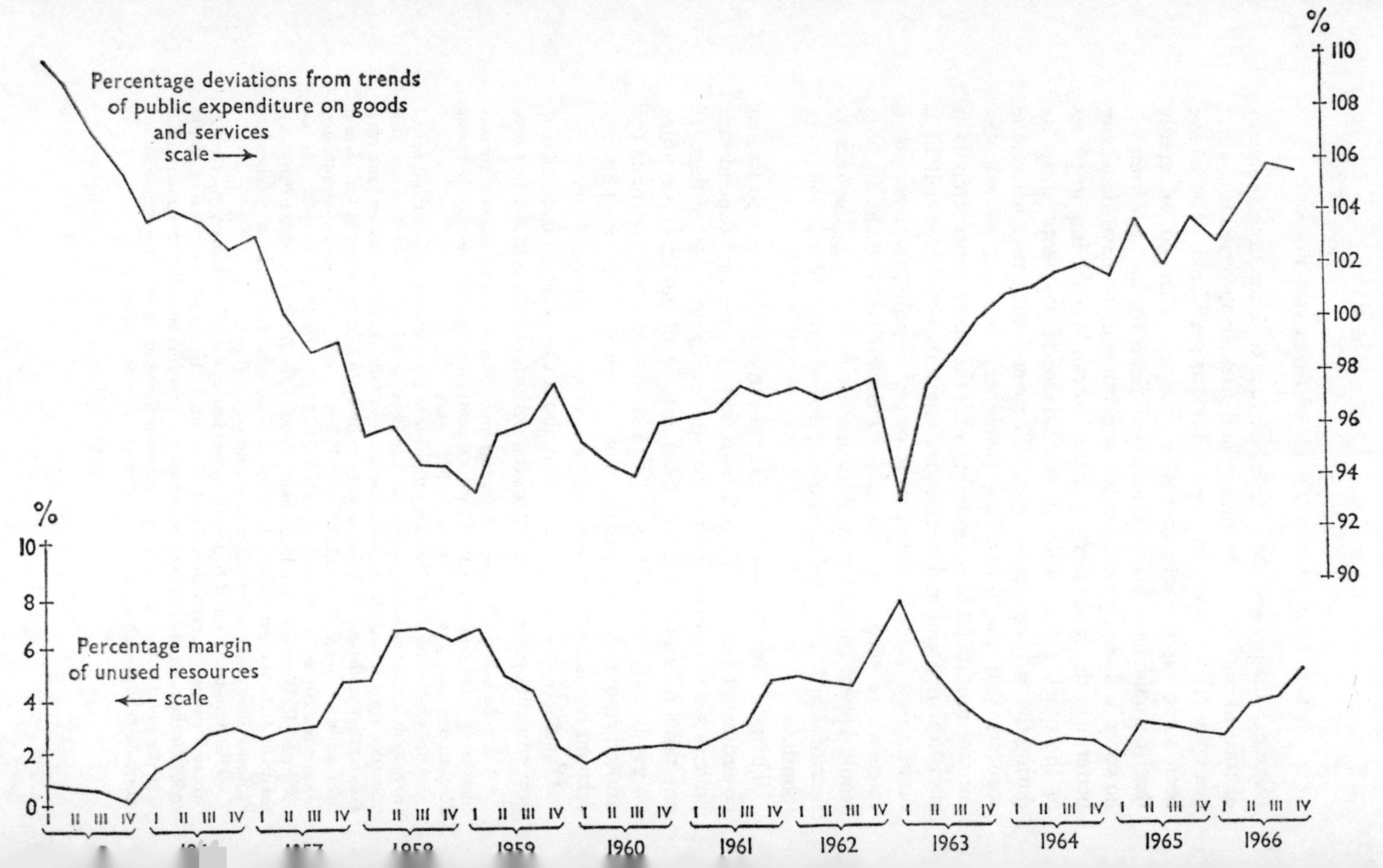
Percentage deviations from trends of public expenditure on goods and services
scale →
%
110
108
106
104
102
100
98
96
94
92
90
Percentage margin of unused resources
← scale
%
10
8
6
4
2
0
1960
1961
1962
1963
1964
1965
1966

years can be drawn from this picture; but at least one can hardly say, when the correlation coefficient is negative and not positive, that public expenditure has followed the pattern one might have expected on simple macro-economic grounds. It would take too long to explore the reasons for all this, but one can say in general that it is extremely difficult to co-ordinate the current or capital expenditure patterns of a highly diversified and multifarious group of authorities;[1] and, more particularly, that very recently we seem to have had a case where local-authority spending has been the rogue elephant.[2]

There have also been cases where budgetary policy has not been well co-ordinated with monetary policy. One would like to think that the position had improved over the years since the débâcle of the Dalton era. But when it is observed that over the calendar year 1965, a year of alleged retrenchment, the stock of money rose by £915 million or some 7·5 per cent.[3] one has some doubts.

Our analysis of the gap between expected and realized results of short-term stabilization measures has so far been cast in terms of over-simplification. We now come to the second major heading: the more ambitious aims of policy-makers over the years. The basic point here is that some of our difficulties have been due to the standards we have set ourselves. The Beveridge Full Employment case was based on the assumption that the *average* employment rate would be 97 per cent.; the average rate and the deviations about it have been such that 97 per cent. has been just about the *minimum* at any time since the war. Although employment data are not entirely satisfactory as a measure of excess demand, there can be little doubt that if we had chosen to run the economy with 97 per cent., or even 97 per cent. average employment, instead of

[1] It was stated in *Public Investment in Great Britain*, Cmnd. 1203 (London: H.M.S.O., 1960), that responsibility for investment expenditure was widely diffused with, for instance, 27 gas and electricity boards, 180 local education authorities, 950 government water undertakings, 1,600 sewerage authorities and 1,700 local housing authorities. The result was that it would take six months for a decision to change capital expenditure to have significant effects; and twelve for full effects.

Although the numbers in some of these categories are less today, the general problem remains.

[2] Cf. Sir John Hicks, *After the Boom* (London: Institute of Economic Affairs, 1966).

[3] *Financial Statistics* (London: H.M.S.O., March, 1967).

I

something much nearer to 98·5 per cent., we should have had less trouble in the way of cost inflation, imbalance of payments and so on. Although United States unemployment data are not directly comparable with United Kingdom, it is reasonably clear that the United States authorities have operated with a lower pressure of demand than in the United Kingdom and that difficulties became apparent in 1966 when their position became more like that usually found in the United Kingdom.

Another most important sense in which ambitions have grown has been the attempt to fit stabilization policy into a long-term framework. Although there have been many scattered attempts at framing Budgetary policy in the context of long-term developments,[1] it is only in recent years that emphasis has been placed on the idea of matching the growth rate of demand with that of supply potential, as given by the forces of population increase, technical progress and so on. This is clearly a much more complex set of aims. First, one has to estimate the growth rate of both demand and supply potential with some finesse. Second, circumstances are likely to arise in which short-run considerations dictate a slower or faster rate of growth of demand than long-term ones, with the obvious possibility of output movements diverging from the trend line. Then there is scope for a good deal of argument about the relationships between the pressure of demand and the actual growth rate, e.g. is an employment rate of 98·5 per cent. more conducive to a high growth rate than one of 97·5 per cent., and what is the effect of fluctuations in the pressure of demand on the rate of growth? One also now has to be careful about specifying the appropriate saving ratio: for instance, Harrod-neutral technical improvements would require a constant savings ratio, and a rising capital–output ratio would require a rising savings ratio. There are many more complications which we cannot go into here.

To summarize, the conclusion is simply that if one stipulates that policy should be aimed at a very high employment ratio and at the achievement of a growth rate permanently in line with that of a productive potential one is pitching one's sights much higher than

[1] In what was possibly the most outstanding Budget performance of all time, Gladstone in his 1853 Budget set out a seven-year plan for reducing the income tax to zero; it failed.

was common even a few years ago. So it is not surprising that we have experienced a number of setbacks in these endeavours.

What sorts of lessons can be drawn, however tentatively, from these experiences? There are certain points on which there is a widespread agreement: for instance, the need for more detailed, more reliable and more up-to-date statistics. On another issue, whether to run the economy at, say, 97·5 per cent. or 98·5 per cent. employment, there is a great deal of disagreement. My own belief is that the former is much more likely to make sense than the latter, but I would not maintain that as yet it has been settled beyond all question. If, for very differing reasons, we leave both these matters on one side there is still another wide-open question about the proper use of Budgetary policy. One school of thought is that government should concentrate on a steady rate of growth of demand in line with the long-run growth rate of productive potential. Another is that government should always be ready to take short-term corrective measures, if necessary on a week-by-week, or even a day-by-day, basis. There is obviously some conflict between these two views—though this has not stopped some intellectual acrobats from clinging to both simultaneously!

The former view has, in differing forms and for different reasons, some very distinguished supporters—one of the most recent (albeit in the form of monetary rather than fiscal expansion) being the 1967 United States Congressional Joint Economic Committee Report on the President's *Economic Report*. The arguments for this kind of policy are manifold: the importance of generating growth at the full natural rate, the advantages of long-term planning of government expenditure on goods and services on both current and capital account, the political and economic disadvantages of frequent variations in the injection of purchasing power into the economy and so on. On the other hand, we still live in a world where there are substantial short-term changes; and these are of especial significance for a highly open economy, such as ours. There is also the danger that over time British costs and incomes may gradually move out of alignment with those overseas. There is a variety of ways in which one can try to cope with such disharmonies within the framework of stable long-term government budgetary policies. One is variations in exchange rates; another is a combination of import controls and other internal measures, especially incomes policy; another is to plead for world monetary reform. None of these is free from snags, e.g. the need to maintain higher interest rates at home than abroad if the usual expectation is that sterling will move down, the well-known dangers of import controls, the unlikelihood of sufficient success in the immediate future in securing effective incomes policies or world monetary reform. There is also a further problem. If one goes so far as to argue that government expenditure on goods and services should continue to grow steadily whatever the degree of short-term upset, one is really saying that the burden of any adjustment should fall on the private sector.[1] This is a particularly important result when, as in the United Kingdom, the public sector absorbs a large proportion of G.N.P.

The second view—the need for "fine tuning" or continuous government budgetary intervention to adjust aggregate demand—also has many supporters. Some perfectly good reasons exist for this. Short-period imbalances can arise rapidly, as we all know only too well; there is no reason why we should be slaves of tradition in Budgetary procedure, insisting on one (or perhaps two) major series of changes per annum and at pre-ordained times of the year. Policy on such lines is also feasible. Even though one cannot always engineer quick changes in government spending,[2] there are ways in which tax rates can be varied quickly in this country—in marked contrast to the United States.

Equally clearly, there are objections to this type of policy. First, there is a major constitutional problem: it may not always be easy to fit quick changes into the Parliamentary legislative programme and, if it is not, how much discretion is it right and proper to give to the executive in such matters? Second, greater frequency of intervention may do more to destabilize than to stabilize, in so far as incorrect predictions are made, lags insufficiently allowed for and so on. During the period October 1964–July 1966 the number of "mini-Budgets" was so great that more or less the only way of keeping up with them was constant perusal of all economic intelligence—in much the same way as Horace Walpole is alleged to

[1] This was the (unstated) implication of the argument in favour of stability of government programmes in the Plowden Committee Report, cf. *Report of Committee in Control of Public Expenditure*, Cmnd. 1432 (London: H.M.S.O., 1961).

[2] For technical and organizational reasons in the case of goods and services; for institutional reasons in the case of transfer payments.

have said in the *annus mirabilis* of 1759 that he had to inquire every day whether there had been another victory, in case he missed one. Nevertheless, it was still necessary to supplement all these measures with the severe deflationary package of 20th July, 1966: the very kind of intervention that constant small adjustments are supposed to obviate.

Finally, it is not clear how businessmen react to frequent small-scale changes rather than infrequent larger ones. Are they more likely to go ahead with plans for expansion or installation of new equipment if they never know where they are than if they only have to face occasional changes, even though the latter may be on a larger scale?

My own preference is for a policy intermediate between these views: i.e. one which tries to ensure a reasonably adequate long-term growth of demand without completely sacrificing short-term adaptability. It should not be thought that this is easy. To illustrate, take the question of the built-in flexibility of taxation. Short-term domestic fluctuations are likely[1] to be eased the more the revenue structure has this characteristic; but externally led fluctuations raise further issues. Then over the long run revenue bouyancy may be embarrassing and the economy become subject to "fiscal drag," if conditions are of the United States type; but if public expenditure threatens to forge ahead, as appears to be the prospect in the United Kingdom in the next few years, revenue buoyancy is needed to hold down the rate of growth of private demand. Despite these and other complications, one would hope that a reasonable degree of built-in flexibility would cut down the need for frequent short-run tax-rate changes. If there were also an extension of Regulator powers, whereby the executive is permitted to make strictly circumscribed adjustments to tax rates without prior reference to Parliament,[2] one should then be able to secure a reasonable degree of short-term adjustment without losing sight of longer-term changes.

Prescriptions of this sort are inevitably subject to the charge that they are no more than common sense. But in a field where, more

[1] *Not* certain. Cf. D. J. Smyth, "Can Automatic Stabilisers be De-Stabilising?" *Public Finance*, Vol. IV, 1963.

[2] I should, incidentally, say that my own preference is for the Regulator in its original (1961) form when all the relevant rates had to be changed in the same proportion rather than the new (1964) form, which allows for greater discretion.

often than not, the modern version of Gresham's law prevails ("wishful political thinking drives out economic common sense") this may be no bad thing.

II

Our next concern is budgetary investment stimuli. The history of these in the post-war period is complicated, with the mixture of initial allowances, investment allowances, free depreciation and investment grants, but sufficiently well known in outline not to need repetition. Instead we shall concentrate on three questions:

1. The effectiveness of such devices in stimulating investment.
2. The effects of stimulating investment on the level and growth rate of G.N.P.
3. A possible alternative policy.

1. Evidence is mixed on this. On the one hand, one can point to the fact that by and large investment stimuli have become more generous over the post-war period and that the gross investment/G.N.P. ratio has also risen. And, in particular, one can single out the investment boom of 1955 and argue, with some show of reasonableness, that this was not unconnected with the introduction of investment allowances in 1954. On the other hand, a variety of inquiries conducted in recent years[1] among businessmen seemed to suggest that initial and investment allowances had very little influence on decisions to invest. It is too early to say whether the response to the new investment grants is likely to be different, but unless and until there is some positive evidence that it is—and such evidence may be extremely hard to establish for the current period in view of the simultaneous changes in other likely determinants of investment—one must remain sceptical about the magnitude of any change in attitudes.

It is easy to pick holes in both views. On the first, one can say that it is hard to distinguish cause and effect—and to isolate the influence of these measures on the higher level of investment. On

[1] See, e.g. *Report of Committee on Turnover Taxation*, Cmnd. 2300 (H.M.S.O., 1964); R. R. Neild, "Replacement Policy", *National Institute Review*, November, 1964; D. C. Corner and Alan Williams, "The Sensitivity of Businesses to Initial and Investment Allowances", *Economica*, February, 1965; N.E.D.C., *Investment in Machine Tools* (H.M.S.O., 1965).

the second, there are all the old problems of business men rationalizing answers to such questions. The most likely answer in our present state of knowledge is that such stimuli have a minor but not a major effect on the level of investment and the ratio of investment to G.N.P.

2. The effects of investment on the level of G.N.P. and its rate of growth is the subject of an enormous volume of literature, both at theoretical and applied levels. Confining ourselves entirely to the latter, one can again find conflicting evidence. For instance, Sir Robert Shone[2] has argued as if there is a causal connection between the fact that the investment ratio rose from 14 per cent. in 1947–52 to 19 per cent. in 1964, and that productivity rose substantially over the same period. On the other hand, more extensive investigations of these matters have not found a very substantial connection. For instance, Professor Matthews[3] found that from 1948 to 1962 the average annual percentage increase in G.D.P. per man-year was 1·9 per cent., but only 0·6 per cent. could be explained by changes in capital per man, leaving a residual factor of 1·3 per cent.[4] Other studies, both of this country and of others, have come out with similar sorts of conclusions.[5]

There is obviously a great deal more to be done in this field (e.g. the further development of the vintage approach pioneered by Salter and Solow),[6] and it would be the height of foolishness to proclaim that we are anywhere in sight of certainty in such studies.

At the same time it does look as if some of the earlier notions that all that one needed to do to push an economy along faster was to raise the investment rate were far too *simpliste*. It may be that we shall in the end find that there are one or two simple things—whether in some form of capital investment or another easily

[2] Sir R. Shone, *Investment and Economic Growth* (University of London, Athlone Press, 1966), p. 7.

[3] R. C. O. Matthews, "Some Aspects of Post-War Growth in the British Economy in Relation to Historical Experience", *Transactions of Manchester Statistical Society*, 1964–65, p. 3.

[4] It should be added that this residual factor was absolutely higher in the post-war period than in the pre-war one, but lower relatively to the capital factor.

[5] Cf. W. Beckerman *et al.*, *The British Economy in 1975* (Cambridge: Cambridge University Press, 1965), p. 41.

[6] See, e.g. W. E. G. Salter, *Productivity and Technical Change* (Cambridge: Cambridge University Press, 1960); and R. M. Solow, *Capital Theory and the Rate of Return* (Amsterdam: North Holland, 1963).

distinguished element of input—which reveal all the secrets. But may it not also be that such quests are as fruitless as those for the philosopher's stone or the secrets of longevity? Time may, or may not, tell.

3. If, in the meantime, we must accept as a working hypothesis that the connections between investment stimuli and investment and those between investment and the growth rate are unclear it may be that there is a case for reconsidering the ways in which budgetary measures can be used to help in the growth process. Of course, there is no shortage of suggestions of suitable measures—maintaining a steady growth of demand in line with the growth of productive potential, measures to push exports, technology, education, training and so on *ad infinitum*. What I fear, however, is that if the growth process is so subtle and complex we may well find ourselves in a continuing situation whereby we prostrate ourselves to one of these new gods for a time, then discover—no doubt after suitably large expenditure of public funds—that it does not hold the keys to the promised land, and reject it for another one—and so on.

It may be preferable to seek a more direct line of approach. Like most ideas in economics, this is not a new one. Indeed, claims to originality in such matters are much more frequently a sign of inadequate reading of the literature than of anything else. In 1961 Professor K. Knorr and W. J. Baumol edited a book[1] in which the idea was mooted that an appropriate fiscal stimulant would be to grant a rebate to firms on the basis of their additions to value added between one year and the next. Although Professor Baumol would apparently now like to modify his original proposals,[2] my own view is that they do still contain a great deal of merit.

The fundamental point is that one is then tackling the problem directly by giving larger fiscal rewards to those firms which register larger increases in output—a kind of payment by results scheme on a large scale. If a major policy aim is to encourage output growth, and if we are uncertain about the relative strengths of the many reasons for output growth, surely it may make better

[1] *What Price Economic Growth?* (Englewood Cliffs, New Jersey: Prentice Hall, 1961).

[2] Cf. "A Possible Tax Stimulus for Productivity", *Financial Times*, 4th August, 1966.

sense to approach it in this direct fashion, rather than making one grant here for investment in physical capital, another there for expenditure on research and another there for retraining labour and so on.

Needless to say, there are many detailed problems. It would obviously be much easier to operate a scheme of this sort if one already had a value-added tax in existence. But there are clearly a number of reasons for thinking that this is a possible development in any case. Then there would be difficulties about the basis of calculating value added. Whereas, for tax purposes, it is usually accepted that the most appropriate computation is one which excludes capital-investment expenditure, the more relevant basis for rebate or subsidy would be the annual differences in gross value added, before deducting capital expenditure. Otherwise increments in value added, and hence rebates, would *pro tanto* be smaller, the greater the investment spending in a period. Whilst one may have doubts about the strength and nature of the influence of investment on output growth, there is certainly no need to go to the other extreme and penalize investment.

One point which troubled the authors in the original exposition[1] was the need to correct additions to value added for price changes. In so far as these are due to general changes in the price level, my worries would not be so great: the fact that a government knows that the rebates to be granted will be greater, the more it allows inflation to develop might even make for less official complacency about prices. In so far as the price changes are due to exercising a monopoly position, the position is more difficult, but even here it might be a once-for-all process (if exploiting previously neglected opportunities) or a sign of weakness of other policies (if successive increases in monopoly power over the years go unchecked).

Many other problems arise. One might be called on to square a policy of this sort with one of succouring declining industries or regions; if so, differential excise or payroll taxes could do a good deal, though this raises further complications, as we shall see later. If one works on the principle that rebates are given for increases in value added but that the process is asymmetrical (i.e. no additional liabilities are incurred if there is a fall in value added) one may then have considerable differences in treatment between

[1] Op. cit., p. 36.

firms with highly fluctuating records and those with records of steady growth. For instance, if two firms had the same increment in value added over a five-year period but one achieved it by a succession of small increments the former would get a larger rebate over the whole period. However, if the fluctuations in output are a reflection of great risks undertaken this may not be a bad result. There are also further problems of newborn and dying firms to be thought about, but we should overrun our time if we tried to go into them here.

No doubt many other points arise in such a complicated change. But I would strongly argue that a direct approach of this sort should certainly not be ruled out, except after most searching and far-reaching inquiries.

III

We have said something about lessons to be learned from the attempts to keep aggregate demand and supply balanced and the attempts to stimulate growth through investment. We now pass to a field which is both wider and narrower—wider in the sense that there have been a large number of measures or non-measures relatively unconnected with one another and yet narrower in the sense that rather more limited objectives have usually been in mind.

There are clearly problems of definition (e.g. what do we mean by neutrality, non-discrimination, etc?) when discussing the range and size of specific government subsidies, tax remissions, etc., for particular purposes. Rather than take up time in attempting to make precise definitions—and probably not succeeding—we shall try to indicate by a number of examples the sorts of considerations in mind.

One might start by quoting the answers given in Parliament to questions about recent changes in subsidies, grants, etc.[1] However, broad answers of this sort do not get us very far, and we can probably do better by singling out some of the more obvious cases, even if this does involve the risk of bias in selection. One particular field is road transport. Many people have argued the case for a

[1] See, e.g. Hansard (Commons), 10th March, 1966, Cols. 658–660, and 23rd March, 1967, Cols. 354–8.

congestion tax[1] in city centres, and we need not repeat the arguments here. So far, although there have been promises of further study at official levels, that seems to be about all. But among the consequences of the present implicit subsidy to city vehicle users are the increasingly obvious difficulties of public urban transport—buses are held up because of road congestion, fares are raised to try to cover costs, more people turn to private transport, further financial difficulties arise—leading eventually to substantial subsidies to public transport. This is a clear case of one form of "subsidy" breeding another one, with the consequences of overall cheapening of passenger transport, encouragement of commuting and so on.

In the case of the coal industry there has been a variety of means of protection—bans on imports, the tax on heavy fuel oil and "persuasion" of the electricity industry to build coal-fired power stations. The validity of the arguments for coal protection might in turn provoke less scepticism if we did not hear the exact opposite of the declining industry argument in other cases, e.g. computers. If, as a matter of general principle, government help is needed both for declining and for growing industries, how much is left which does not need help?

In the last year or so policy differentiation has taken another form. The restriction of investment grants to manufacturing and extractive industry, the introduction of Selective Employment Tax with its differential refunds and more recently the proposal to introduce still further differentiation in the repayments to manufacturing industry in Development Areas[2] are all of a pattern. It is perhaps not entirely fortuitous that an intellectual argument for such provisions is to be found in Professor Kaldor's inaugural lecture at Cambridge.[3] Whatever the merits of the arguments

[1] Cf. *Road Pricing: The Economic and Technical Possibilities* (Ministry of Transport, London, 1964); A. A. Walters, "The Theory and Measurement of Private and Social Costs of Congestion", *Econometrica*, October, 1961; G. J. Roth, *A Self-financing Road System* (London: Institute of Economic Affairs, 1966); and *Better Use of Town Roads* (H.M.S.O., London: June, 1967).

[2] *The Development Areas: a Proposal for a Regional Employment Premium* (H.M.S.O., April, 1967) and *The Development Areas: Regional Employment Premiums* (H.M.S.O., June, 1967). A welcome should be given to the open invitation to advance discussion of this proposal.

[3] *Causes of the Slow Rate of Economic Growth of the U.K.* (Cambridge: Cambridge University Press, 1966).

about increasing returns and learning by doing in the manufacturing sector, it can hardly be contended that all the consequences of the new system were fully foreseen. The need to consider new help to Development Areas; the report in March 1967 of the N.E.D.C. "little Neddy" on Distribution; and the 1967 changes in respect of part-time workers are sufficient evidence. And some of the more bizarre results, such as the tribulations of local authorities[1] or the argument[2] that the Area Electricity Boards (not subject to tax) should raise the prices they quote for contract work when in competition with private contractors (subject to tax) at a time when there was an official price-freeze policy have to be spelled out to be believed.

A great deal could be said about regional policy. First, there are a number of Ministries involved in important ways, e.g. the Department of Economic Affairs, the Board of Trade and (through both control over physical planning and the system of grants to local authorities) the Ministry of Housing and Local Government. Their policies have changed frequently in recent years, and it is by no means clear that they have always been closely co-ordinated, to put it mildly. We have a variety of different subsidies, some of which are certainly pulling against one another. How far, for instance, would the pull of London be reduced, and the regional need for grants, etc., be alleviated if Londoners did not receive transport subsidies? And although one can see some arguments in favour of the recent proposals for additional S.E.T. refunds in the Development Areas, the fact remains that with one measure (investment grants) one is encouraging capital-intensive industries or methods and with the other (S.E.T. refunds) one is encouraging labour-intensive industries or methods. It is difficult to believe that such a combination is appropriate for the whole of manufacturing industry (but no other industries) in the whole of the Development Areas (but no other areas).

Turning to general policy on income distribution, one can find a very similar state of affairs. Merrett and Monk[3] have recently argued that a large part of the redistributive side of taxation (as

[1] See H. R. Page, "Sense and Nonsense", *Local Government Finance*, December, 1966.

[2] See *The Guardian*, 11th October, 1966.

[3] A. J. Merrett and D. A. G. Monk, "The Structure of U.K. Taxation 1962/3", *Oxford Bulletin of Statistics*, August, 1966.

distinct from transfer payments) in this country is more apparent than real and that the 1962/63 tax system (other than company taxes, death duties and surtax) could have been replaced by a uniform sales tax of about 28 per cent. without any important distributional consequences between income groups. Although I have reservations about these particular calculations and about the suggested alternative,[1] the proposition that a lot of the alleged redistributional effects of taxation are mythical takes a lot of controverting.

More specific measures in the income redistribution field are legion, but let us take housing as an example. The final elimination of Schedule A tax for owner-occupiers in 1963 was greeted with loud applause. Now it has been realized that this opened a Pandora's Box, in that by leaving the whole of any mortgage interest payments by an owner-occupier to be claimed as a deduction against ordinary income the effective cost of such housing is now less the higher the individual's tax rate. Therefore legislation has now been introduced to give hand-outs in the form of option mortgages to those paying tax at low or zero rates. As another example from the housing field, we have the report that in one Scottish city tenants occupying low-rented municipally provided houses object to paying realistic rents for garages on the grounds that garage rents might then be higher than house rents; but if one cannot charge realistic rents for garages, how can one charge realistic prices for parking in city streets—and so on?

As another example, take the argument about large families. Simultaneously, there seem to be signs of official moves in 1967 to reform the Family Allowances system so as to give more help to larger families and at the same time to subsidize birth-control

[1] There is surely a great deal to be said for ensuring that a substantial part of the total tax burden is placed on individuals in the form of direct taxation. The more one moves away to a system where nobody knows what he is paying or even that he is paying, the less interest the average citizen is likely to take in the role and scope of government spending. Hence the more likely it is that this will expand without let or hindrance. A rise in personal income tax comes home to the individual much more than a rise in Value Added tax or Corporation Tax. It is the progression rather than the principle of direct taxation which is at fault.

For analogous reasons, I am not at all persuaded of the desirability of the recent legislation to shift part of the burden of local rates away from the domestic ratepayer.

measures. If extra support for larger families were limited to those already in being there would be no conflict; but as it is, the Government is open to the charge that it is simultaneously encouraging larger and smaller families.

As a last example, I cannot refrain from reproducing a passage from *The Guardian* of 25th April, 1967. Although it is not a matter of revenue and expenditure policy, and so really falls outside the scope of this paper, it is such a perfect example of the dangers of trying to govern in excessive detail that it simply must be recorded. I reproduce the passage more or less in full; comment is totally superfluous.

> "Joanna Wilkinson, aged 9, of Nottingham complained to her M.P. when the cost of a packet of marbles at the local shop went up by a penny to sevenpence. Mr. Michael English (Labour, Nottingham West) took up the matter with the Board of Trade and after a full investigation Joanna has had her penny refunded and the cost of marbles has been adjusted.
>
> "Joanna . . . told her M.P. that she thought sixpence was enough to pay for a packet of marbles. Mr. English found that the shopkeeper was only passing on to her a price increase he had to pay when buying the marbles."

Surely some lessons can be learned from this small sample of examples, culled from a large population. The main conclusion is analogous to one made above: in just the same way that it is far from clear that increased frequency of government intervention assures stability of the economy, so it is very possible that an increasingly complex pattern of subsidies, tax reliefs and so on is self-defeating, whether in defending one industry, one region or one person against another. There are clearly some cases where a second measure has to be taken to make sure that the first is effective, but at least as often the second step may, by design or accident, offset the first one. If the first step was misguided the self-cancellation process may be desirable, anyway; but it would be even more desirable to have neither measure.

Another point is surely that one must be very inquisitive about the precise reasons for steps of this kind. Vague phrases such as "the public interest" and "social priorities" are meaningless as they stand; and given a tiny bit of ingenuity, well within the bounds of any industrial or regional spokesmen, external economies or growth arguments can always be made to sound convincing, whatever the context.

One must also beware of the dangers that arise through unnecessary splitting of functions between departments. We noticed the danger in connection with regional policy. The same phenomenon has also arisen in recent years with investment stimuli (investment grants through the Board of Trade; and initial allowances through the Inland Revenue) and with S.E.T. refunds (responsibility being shared between the Ministry of Labour, the Ministry of Social Security and the Ministry of Agriculture). Such fragmentation is bound to lead to lack of co-ordination as well as to additional administration costs.[1]

More generally, the older role of Parliament was to protect the tax-payer against the Crown or executive. A little more attention to this role today would surely not come amiss. For there is little sign that the executive itself is distinguished by its capacity for learning by misdoing.

IV

How can I possibly summarize this long and wide-ranging address without being even more superficial? Clearly I must try, whatever the risks.

By and large, one must conclude that our record with revenue and expenditure policy has not been a particularly glorious one in the last twenty years. Whether one looks at the succession of stop–go crises, the growth history or the series of *ad hoc* devices to shore up particular interests, we have a mixed record. It is worth noting, *en passant*, that the old argument that our budgetary problems are so much worse than our predecessors' because of the pace of scientific advance, technological change, etc, is far from convincing. To take one example, Mr. Robert Blake points out, in his biography of Disraeli,[2] that when Disraeli was Chancellor for the second time in 1858 he was faced with all the financial

[1] One great attraction of the proposals for a negative income tax, currently under intensive discussion in the United States, is that they are a means of integrating social-security payments with the income-tax machinery, thereby eliminating, rather than increasing, duplication between government departments.

[2] R. Blake, *Disraeli* (London: Eyre and Spottiswoode, 1966), p. 398.

implications of a complete revolution in naval requirements in that simultaneously wooden ships had to be replaced by iron, armour plating was added, and the screw and steam came into use. Nevertheless, he and his successors managed.

More rewarding than an analysis of all the reasons for our mixed record is one of where economists in particular have been at fault. Surely there can be no question that many have been too ambitious. On far too many occasions policies have been advocated on the basis of untested, or insufficiently tested, hypotheses and a far too casual acquaintance with the facts. Statistical limitations and deficiencies have too often been minimized or ignored in the anxiety to advocate some new gimmick. And consultations with industrialists and others with their feet on the ground have been less frequent than they ought to have been. One hopes that some of these lessons may have been learned from recent events. But if the professional reputation of economists is not to be further tarnished there is another point of major importance: one role of the economist is surely to resist at all times the idea that one can disguise weak policies by jargon, claptrap or pretentious names or that one should accept a programme containing weak policies as a means of securing acceptance of some strong ones. Abnegation of professional standards for political purposes is the surest way to self-destruction.

I began this Presidential address by referring to that by Alfred Marshall in 1890. Perhaps I may end by a quotation from that extraordinarily sagacious man:

> "Every statement in regard to economic affairs which is short is a misleading fragment, a fallacy or a truism. I think this dictum of mine is an exception to the general rule: but I am not bold enough to say that it *certainly* is."[1]

I leave it to others to decide whether my discussion has or has not escaped these traps.

[1] A. C. Pigou (ed.), *Memorials of Alfred Marshall* (Macmillan, 1925), p. 484.

PART THREE

ECONOMICS OF GROWTH

14

PROBLEMS OF ECONOMIC GROWTH

C. F. CARTER

Evening Discourse, Aberdeen, August, 1963

I BEGIN by asking you a question: what discovery of the last thirty years has been of the greatest material benefit to mankind? Is it to be found in the exploitation of atomic energy, or the development of new materials, or the killing of pests, or the control of human diseases, or the breeding of better plants or animals? These have all been important; but they are outclassed by the discovery of a new economic policy, which has passed into orthodoxy largely because of the strong logic and persuasive advocacy of Lord Keynes. It is a matter of conjecture what this country would have lost in material production if the policies of the 1920's had been applied in the 1950's, but I cannot suppose that it would have been less than £10,000 million. The value of Keynes to the world must be related, not only to the avoidance of mass unemployment and disturbing economic fluctuations in the developed countries, but also to the avoidance of still worse poverty in the underdeveloped world. If we assessed it, so far, at £100,000 million we would certainly not be exaggerating; and this is a figure perhaps a hundred times greater than all that the world has ever spent on the support of the science of economics.

It is no disrespect to Lord Keynes to say that the benefit of his ideas stems from a quite simple observation, that the economic policy appropriate to a whole society or nation is not the same as the policy appropriate to its parts. The social sciences may still have truths as simple and as beneficial as this to discover. Generally, however, it is very difficult to find simplicity in the maze of interrelated units and half-understood human motives and actions which make up a social or economic system; and this is perhaps why progress is disappointingly slow, and why the efforts of social scientists leave an impression more of quackery or alchemy than of the austere perfection of a developed science. (It is significant that though this Association has long contained sections concerned with the social sciences, and though our distinguished natural scientist Presidents have often chosen to speak on social and economic matters, it is virtually unknown for a social scientist to be chosen as President.)

The problem of economic growth is an example of a complex and unsatisfactory subject, on which a vast outpouring of professional literature has failed to find a simple unifying thought. At most times most of mankind has lived in conditions of fluctuating but severe poverty, often without any appreciable improvement in standards of living for periods of many centuries. At times, however, certain communities have had some sort of release of energy, which has enabled them in a short time to achieve great economic advance. This advance is not simply a by-product of scientific or technological discovery, for other communities remain in static poverty although the stock of the world's scientific knowledge is in principle available to them. The nations which have jumped to a higher standard of living ought in theory to be able to sustain a continued growth, in accordance with that great economic law "To him that hath shall be given"; but it is observed that they show great differences in their performance, and these are difficult to explain.

Thus described, there are two problems of growth; one is how to begin and sustain the process in those countries which remain very poor; and the other is how to influence the rate of growth of developed countries. In discussing these, it is important to keep a firm control of our time perspective. A compound rate of growth of production per head at 5 per cent per annum is sufficient to give an increase of $11\frac{1}{2}$ times in 50 years (which is enough to get the Indian standard of living within striking distance of that at present enjoyed by the United States), or of 132 times in a century. Small differentials in growth rates, operating over quite a short time in the history of the human race, are sufficient to produce large differences between rich and poor nations. High *per capita* growth rates (of the kind, for instance, which we hope to achieve through the National Economic Development Council) must necessarily be a short-lived phenomenon, when considered against the whole scale of history. It is plausible that, with the substitution of new materials and sources of energy, the world can produce five times what it now produces; it is not plausible that it can produce a hundred times as much, either in total or per head, nor does it seem very likely that the human race would desire to create material wealth on this scale. During the next century the increasing difficulty and real cost of winning extra supplies, and the cost of finding or making substitutes for easily-won natural materials, may slow down the achievable rate of growth below the rate of rise of population, so that the world average income per head would necessarily fall.

It follows that, so far from the future holding a promise of Cadillacs for Indian farmers and ever-larger television screens in the villages of Africa, our grandchildren or great-grandchildren might belong to (on average) the richest generation ever to dwell on this planet, at least until the human race learns to control its numbers; and the peak would be reached at a time when serious poverty was still the fate of a large part of the human race. Beyond that time there would be a direct conflict between the relief of poverty and the desire of the rich to become still richer. But it may well be asked whether this conflict does not already exist. It is fashionable, for instance, to consider it a "problem" that the United States and Britain are showing lower growth rates than Western Europe, the Soviet Union or Japan. A low position in the league table of growth is a cause for even the rich to hang their heads in shame. It is considered self-evident that something must be done about it:

I do not believe that any thoughtful American could look at the statistics and impartial facts about this Nation's economy and not conclude that we need to step up our growth. (President Kennedy, 25th February, 1963.)

There are certainly many needs, both in the United States and Britain, still unmet; and some of them (such as tearing down a large part of Glasgow and rebuilding it) would absorb a lot of economic effort. But we cannot accept it as self-evident that low growth rates in developed countries are a bad thing, without first satisfying ourselves on two points. First, is additional wealth in the form of motorways, bowling alleys, outsize steaks, and other products of the affluent society (good or bad) won without harm to those countries currently in poverty? Second, is it won at the cost of future generations? To the first of these one can give Croesus a reasonably comforting answer. The purchasing power of the rich stimulates the growth of the poor. Whatever may happen in a century's time, at this stage of history the goods produced by the under-developed world tend to be cheap and in excess supply, and it is to their interest that the rich nations should get richer as fast as possible. This is why news of recession in the United States is a shock to confidence throughout the poorer parts of the non-Communist world.

To the second question, however, the answer must be more gloomy. Every increase in the rate of exploitation of the world's resources brings closer the time when the ingenuity of science and technology will be inadequate to offset the increasing difficulty and cost of meeting human needs. We are paying more for energy today because our forefathers used the easily-won seams of coal first, just as we are paying more for wood and paper because they cut down the forests. There is of course every reason to think that we shall go on finding new ways of meeting human needs—the development of atomic power being a most striking example. But there is no certainty that the new methods will be as easy and cheap as the exploitation of simple natural products, nor that they will enable us to keep pace with the explosive growth of world population. Malthus may have cried "wolf" too soon, but his wolf is not an imaginary beast.

There are few who worry about conservation; our time-horizon is too close, perhaps closer than in past generations. We live in the present; to double our standard of living in twenty-five years is attractive, because most people hope still to be here in twenty-five years, and we do not greatly care if the comfort of the present is won at the expense of our successors. The human race is still acting as though it were a temporary visitor to this planet. Perhaps it is.

In what follows, I shall accept the conventional wisdom, and assume that growth, whether in rich or in poor communities, is a good thing. What can we say about its causes? The flow of wealth is created by the application of human effort, skill and ingenuity to the resources provided by nature and to the stock of capital goods created in past times, within the framework of a particular method of organizing production and exchange. It follows that economic growth requires one or more of the following:

More human effort
More skill and ingenuity (including here the use of a more advanced technology)
The discovery of more natural resources
More capital goods (of an appropriate kind)
More appropriate organization.

This list involves ideas both of stock and of flow. Human effort and skill is expressed in a flow of actions over time; certain natural resources are also of the nature of a flow, for instance annual rainfall, or a year's growth of a forest. But human knowledge is a stock, to which additions are constantly being made; losses are on the whole small (for the stock of knowledge can be used without being diminished), though there is increasing difficulty in retrieving a particular item on demand. Certain natural resources, such as reserves of oil or iron-ore, are stocks subject to depletion by use; so are the machines, buildings, roads, drainage systems and other man-made improvements which constitute the stock of capital, with the important distinction that in this case the depletion can be made good by replacement or repair.

Economists have sometimes given the impression that *the* key factor in economic growth is the size of the stock of capital. In consequence a country wishing to achieve rapid growth was to tighten its belt, to use less for its immediate needs, and to divert its effort to the creation of a capital stock to produce wealth in the future. This, we were told, was the great secret of the growth of the Soviet economy. It was an unhappy implication that those countries most in need of growth would find it hardest to achieve, because they would be too poor to divert resources from current consumption.

Now, since economic growth usually involves the production of new kinds of goods, it is no doubt generally true that it involves the creation of new capital to make those goods. But where several influences work together to create a result, it is dangerous to label one as a "key factor". It seems *a priori* more likely that the most important influences on growth will differ from one country to another and from one period to another. Furthermore, the influence of a stock (whether of capital, natural resources, or knowledge) depends not only on its absolute size but also upon the effectiveness of its exploitation. Machines which work one shift can be made to work three; railway lines which carry trains once an hour can carry them every ten minutes. It does not follow that because the British rate of growth is low, therefore we immediately need a lot more capital. Perhaps (for a considerable period) we need only make better use of what we have got already.

Let me illustrate the importance of alternative influences on growth (and give myself an opportunity of exploring further complexities) by setting down a series of propositions.

(1) "In the short period, Britain could have a 5 per cent. growth rate if people worked harder and longer." Such a proposition might not be true if applied to an Indian village, where people already work as hard as a diseased and undernourished state allows. But few of us in this country have reached the limit of our capacity to work; and we often, in common gossip, ascribe our lack of economic progress to our failure to work as hard as (say) the Germans or the Japanese. Why, then, do we not work harder? Or (to put it another way) why are there periods in which the energies of a community are easily stimulated and released, and other periods when men demand action of others which they will not give themselves?

The question is an obvious one, but it is not answered by sermons, political speeches, or leaders in *The Times*, calling for a "new sense of national purpose". This only states the problem: why does the sense of national purpose vary? The social influences on ntensity of effort remain, in fact, somewhat mysterious, despite the many millions of words which have been written about them—probably, again, because they are various, and operate in different combinations and to different degrees at different times and places. I select a few pointers:

(*a*) People will not work hard to create material wealth unless it is considered desirable and respectable to enjoy the fruits of their labour; in this sense economic growth requires a "materialistic" society.

(*b*) They will not work hard unless they can imagine themselves attaining the desirable consequences. Energy is released by the spread of the use of money in an economy formerly producing for subsistence within closed village or family communities, for money carries the power to break out into a new kind of life, to buy the products of the towns or to emigrate. In a developed community, energy is stimulated by strong social pressure to keep up with the neighbours; the best achieved within our social group is the object of our own imaginings.

(*c*) It follows that a society with marked class or caste or racial barriers will offer an inferior stimulus; if a man knows or believes that he cannot rise far, why should he bother? Why work to get a Rolls-Royce if one is confined for life to a social group satisfied with a Mini-Minor?

(*d*) The extent of people's effort depends on the weight which they put on the co-operative, as against the competitive, aspects of society. All economic life, in any society, involves elements both of co-operation and of conflict. But in some societies a man who works harder sees his efforts as benefiting "Them"—the bosses, the shareholders, the Government—while in others he sees first the benefit to himself and to "Us", the common interest in economic growth. These points of view bear no apparent relation to the actual division of the benefits, though they are perhaps related to the extent to which social divisions run along lines which separate economic functions.

(*e*) People will not work hard if they see the results of their efforts running away in waste and frustration. Three points are important here. First, the economic system must be organized with reasonable efficiency and honesty: lack of economic growth can sometimes be blamed on an inflexible and stupid administration, or on a prevalence of bribery and corruption. Second, the vigour of new ideas must not be suffocated by a dead weight of orthodoxy; and a problem here is that an orthodox community may not even realize that it is resisting new ideas. Third, the energy of the young must not be frustrated by the power of the old. A system which closely relates influence to seniority, and which regards it as a positive advantage to be ruled by old men, is no place to expect rapid economic growth.

(2) "Economic growth depends on the level of education."

This is one of those remarks whose apparently self-evident truth conceals the fact that it does not mean very much. There are several different ways in which lack of educational facilities may inhibit economic growth, and they call for different remedies, which are not accurately described by a general phrase about "raising the level of education". First of all, there may be specific shortages of technical skill—say, a lack of design engineers or of soil scientists. Such shortages, if they affect major sectors of the economy which in other respects are ready for vigorous growth, can properly be regarded as "key factors", and they call for specific efforts of training or re-training applied to limited groups of people. Second, the spread between efficient and backward producers may be too great. This calls for an educational effort of a complex kind. It must predominantly be adult education, if it is to take effect in a reasonable time. It must start by identifying *why* backward producers tolerate their own backwardness. Are they merely ignorant? Are they enjoying an easy protected life, without the trials of keeping in the front? Are the incentives to improve their ways too small? Are they held back by social pressures, or religious scruples, or faults of organization? To treat the disease by technical education assumes that ignorance is the main factor—that if the producer is told of a better way, he will follow it; and this is not necessarily true. Despite our elaborate and expensive system of agricultural education and advice, a considerable spread in farming efficiency remains.

Third, a generally higher level of education may contribute to economic growth by increasing adaptability to change. This idea involves, not instruction to meet a known need, but the development of ability and personality to meet unknown situations in the future. Instruction to meet a known need may in fact inhibit growth, if people become fixed in their habits of thought. We are, I think, in this country in danger of getting too much instruction in technology and too little education in creative technological thinking; and though this may help to relieve certain specific shortages of skill, it does not sufficiently assist our adaptation to changing conditions of trade.

Fourth, education may assist growth by altering the problem of communication. This is most obviously true of learning to read and write; the written instruction and message can replace the fallible memory of a verbal communication. Similarly an improvement in what is now called "numeracy" widens the range and precision of communication; a man who can interpret a graph, or read the message of a table of statistics, can acquire ideas more rapidly and accurately than he can from words alone. Again, if a country gives specialist scientific training to more people, it increases the number of those who are "tuned to the same wavelength" as scientists in other countries—it provides itself with listening or observation posts, so that it becomes more likely than before to pick up new ideas quickly and effectively. This factor we perhaps underrate, because we belong to a big country with large scientific resources, and we still half believe (what is, of course, far from the truth) that our own scientists and technologists are active in all the main areas of science and technology. In a small country—say, Ireland, with three million people—it is at once obvious that the majority of new ideas and new ways of doing things must flow from abroad, and that the central problem is to increase receptivity.

But more of the wrong kind of education may waste ability while doing nothing to promote economic growth; it may merely create a class of educated unemployables. More, even of the right kind of education, is achieved only at a cost—a shortening of working life, a diversion of ability into the teaching profession. The universities of this country, for instance, have a very large and increasing appetite for the services of their own most able graduates. First-rate ability is in desperately short supply, in industry, commerce, the professions and Government service. It is not entirely fanciful to suppose that in the short run our very necessary university expansion may be harmful to economic growth.

(3) My third proposition is that "Growth depends on a country's research and development effort". From what I have already said, you will see that this is a generalization which cannot stand; the economic growth of Andorra, Liechtenstein or San Marino cannot possibly depend on the research done within their frontiers. But there are three ways in which the active encouragement of research may be an important influence on growth, even in small and underdeveloped nations. First, the effectiveness of contact with new knowledge arising elsewhere in the world depends not just on having *trained* scientists but on having *active* scientists. You

cannot be an effective liaison for long in a subject which you are not actively following. Mere information officers will soon go stale. Second, the inflow of ideas often requires to be adapted to local conditions; thus, success with a country's agriculture may involve experiment in adapting breeds of livestock or strains of plants to local conditions of climate, soil and vegetation. Third, the mere existence of the research function creates within a community a pressure group in favour of change and of trying out new ideas. Economic growth creates change but is frequently slowed down by an unwillingness to change; such a pressure group is therefore of value. The great eighteenth-century agricultural improvers were, in a crude sense, research men, and they greatly altered the productivity of a conservative agricultural community by the pressure of their example.

(4) "Growth depends on having a social system which honours the innovator, and institutions which help, rather than frustrate, him." Every increase in the rate of economic growth tends to increase the rate of decline of old industries and of old skills. The human race has often been greatly concerned to protect what already exists, and this protection has sometimes taken the form of honouring tradition and regarding the man with new ideas as dangerous, a social outcast. We sometimes regard it as rather comic that the Americans go to the other extreme, of honouring quite worthless innovations, but the readiness to give status to the man who wants to change things may have been a great influence on their past record of growth. The conventional wisdom of the United States claims in addition, however, that great freedom of enterprise has been an important secret of growth, because it allows the man with a new idea to go ahead quickly on his own responsibility, while constantly exerting a pressure to remove the inefficient. In a free capital market the innovator can raise money; he is not subject to the decisions of some central government official, but only to the sensitive expression of the common will through the market.

Experience does not show, however, that free enterprise economies achieve economic growth more easily than centrally planned or mixed economies. This is partly because the reality of a free enterprise economy differs from the ideal; a society of speculators and market manipulators, grabbing for short-term profits, may create chaos rather than orderly growth. No doubt a rich man in Africa, if he were all-wise and eternal, ought in his own interests to invest in ports, roads, railways, factories; but in practice it is more attractive to speculate in stocks of goods. But I suspect that the contrast between the performance of free enterprise and planned economies illustrates my main thesis about the complexity of the influences which bear on growth. There is reason to fear that central planning will over-centralize decisions about innovation, and that a system of management of unwieldy size will tend to be resistant to change. It is perhaps significant that our own nationalized industries cannot claim to have outshone private enterprise in the success of their innovation, or in their readiness to allocate resources to research and development. But a planned or partially planned economy can do two things well. It can enforce the undertaking of long-term projects, which may be of the greatest value and importance and yet lie beyond the time-horizon of a sophisticated business man. (If the Duke of Bridgewater had been to the Harvard Business School, he would not have built his canal. By the standards which a modern company applies, it was an act of folly.) A planned economy can also enforce the transfer of resources from current consumption to capital investment. In a free enterprise economy, this transfer takes place in response to people's feeling about "jam today" and "more jam tomorrow", and is vitally affected by the (often irrational) feelings which people have about the uncertainties of the future. The motorway programme in the southern parts of this island is a contribution to economic efficiency and growth, of a kind which would probably never be undertaken by private enterprise, and is ultimately supported by the power of the State to restrict consumption so as to free resources for public capital investment.

(5) "Growth depends on a proper organization of international trade and payments." This view may appear to be supported by the British case, for we have repeatedly interrupted our economic growth because of our difficulty in selling enough overseas. There is a sense in which this difficulty has been made worse by the special position of the pound sterling in the system of international payments, but I am disposed to put the main blame on factors which are strictly our own concern—the weakness of British design and marketing methods, leading to a fall in our proportion

of world markets and to a great increase in our imports of goods which we ought to be able to produce better at home; and our systems of wage-bargaining and price determination, giving us a rise of prices which, with fixed exchange rates, further hampers our exports. The latter is a striking example of the influence on growth of a system of institutions and habits of thought which are not easily changed by Government action.

But in the under-developed primary producing countries, the relevance of the organization of international trade may be more immediate. Primary products (food and raw materials) show considerable variations both of price and of export proceeds. These variations make it extremely hard for the primary producers to diversify and strengthen their economies by planned industrial development, for they have an unreliable income and a correspondingly low credit rating. Although many experiments in the control of fluctuations by commodity agreements have been made, they have not been particularly successful; and this is in part because the developed countries have been anxious to exploit for their own benefit periods of low commodity prices. In the long run such an attitude may not be to their economic benefit, and it is certainly not to their political benefit. Commodity trade, in my view, suffers from an excess of free enterprise in exchanges between nations, and often from an excess of protection within nations.

Those of you who have contributed to the future of the race by having children will no doubt (being literate persons) have informed yourself about your task by buying some Baby Books. If you buy enough, you will find that their advice is contradictory, and this will have the valuable effect of reminding you not to take things too seriously; the human animal can grow quite healthily under a wide variety of systems of parental care. You will learn from the books, however, that if a baby cries it is either too hot or too cold, or hungry, or thirsty, or wet, or suffering from wind—or perhaps you have stuck a nappy pin into it, or perhaps it just wants to exercise its lungs. Neither the books nor the baby offer any guidance in how to distinguish between these conditions.

So it is with a failure of economic growth. In my reading of past history I do not find, and I do not expect to find, any one cause of stagnation, or any one system of remedies for it. The way to economic growth is to be found through a profound understanding, not only of the economic influences bearing on a community, but also of its social structure and ways of thought. For this reason I am very doubtful of the value of dispatching economic experts to help underdeveloped countries to achieve development—except that an expert may provide outside authority for doing something already seen to be desirable, but difficult to achieve. I do not believe that six months in India would qualify me to talk about Indian growth; to do that I should have to know how an Indian feels and thinks, and how the complex relationships of his society bear upon his actions.

But about British growth I am naturally prepared to speak. Indeed, since a doubling of our rate of growth would be worth about £500 million a year, I feel that it would be nice if the Government (on the precedent of the Great Post Office Robbery) would offer me £50 million to tell them how to do it. I can also offer from direct experience some comments about economic growth in the Republic of Ireland, a moderately under-developed country with a poor past record of growth. This record has recently greatly improved, and I would list the main causes as—

(*a*) A resolute attempt to attract enterprise and capital from abroad;

(*b*) A clear intention to have a plan of growth, creating confidence that growth will continue and be self-sustaining;

(*c*) A change in generations of those in power in Government and industry, with a setting-free of energy, and a new will to act instead of talking about the difficulties.

There are some lessons here for Britain. It is no good saying that we must have economic growth *provided that* we can also have increased welfare services, stable prices, a rising standard of consumption, fixed exchange rates, free wage bargaining, free enterprise or public ownership (as the case may be), and so on. These aims of Government action are probably contradictory, and it must be made clear which is to be sacrificed if sacrifice is needed. Neither of the main political parties has yet faced the consequences of giving growth an absolute priority. Consequently private individuals cannot sensibly plan for an expanding market, and we lose the cumulative effect of a nation-wide assurance that we are moving faster. I am impressed also by the extreme difficulty which we find in making resolute decisions on public issues. We are showing increasing signs of tiredness, not just in Government but in the civil service and in some parts of industry. We badly need the energy of a fresh generation.

We need, I think, in addition to our broad educational advance, some efforts of education specially directed to engineering design (perhaps to functional design generally), to marketing and to operational research. Our research effort is considerable, but needs greater support in selected areas of long-term national interest, including a readiness to use civil development contracts even if they yield a high proportion of failures. We no doubt need to divert more resources (by taxation) into capital investment, but this should be accompanied by a searching look at our methods of choosing investment projects and our intensity of use of capital. We need some hard thought and research on the efficiency of our use of the nation's scarce supplies of high human ability.

There is no technical or economic difficulty in achieving and maintaining for a considerable period a 4 per cent. or 5 per cent. rate of growth. The resistant difficulties will, I think, be found to lie in our social structure and habits of thought: in the sharp class distinctions between master and men: in the traditions of trade union bargaining and cost-plus pricing: in the pressures of democracy to get benefits now at the expense of the future. There is no simple formula to dissolve these difficulties.

15

THE PRICE OF GROWTH

T. WILSON

Aberdeen, September, 1963

TRADITION prescribes that a presidential address should give an account of some aspect of development in the subject with which the section is concerned. I have chosen economic growth as my topic because it is one that has come to receive increasing attention from professional economists and, indeed, from everyone who is interested in economic affairs. I shall try to put before you very briefly some of the reasons for this development. I shall then remind you that a rapid growth of output may involve sacrifices in other directions. Growth may be obtained only at a price. We shall ask how far economists can go with propriety in recommending that the price should be paid.

It is probably the case that in the discussion of public policy more attention is now being paid to growth than has ever been paid before. As countries have become richer, increasing emphasis has been placed on the means whereby they may become richer still. Naturally some protests have been made. One of the most widely read of recent works on economics has been *The Affluent Society*, by Professor J. K. Galbraith;[1] it would also appear, at least at first sight, to have been one of the least influential. For his protest that the affluence already achieved makes further growth less urgent has failed to stem the tide of modern opinion. The classical and neo-classical economists, for their part, have sometimes been criticized a little unfairly for their interest in growth. Not only did the greater poverty of their world do much to justify such an attitude, but they were usually at some pains to discuss the importance of other considerations, the more so because they were less inhibited

[1] *The Affluent Society* (London: Hamish Hamilton, 1958).

than their successors about the scope of their subject. Indeed, classical economists have sometimes been charged with the opposite fault of paying too much attention to distribution and the allocation of resources and too little to growth. At all events it is modern applied economics that seems to have accepted so wholeheartedly what Professor Galbraith denounces as "the conventional wisdom." Nor have economists been alone in placing this emphasis on growth. Its importance is now stressed by the political leaders of all parties, by journalists, scientists and businessmen, and even, with some hesitation, by the trade unions. This is so not only in the West. In Russia growth has long been the main concern of economic policy, and in the underdeveloped countries it has rapidly become so.

Yet it would be untrue to say that Professor Galbraith has failed entirely to influence opinion. For he has at least reminded us of the ancient truth that riches so eagerly sought may prove disappointing when acquired. Both "growth" and "affluence" are now emotive words, the one good and the other bad. If growth is really held to be so urgent even in the richer countries of the West while at the same time affluence is felt to be so unrewarding when achieved, then we may seem to be committed as never before to what can be described as "the rational pursuit of an irrational end."[1] Even in Russia there has been disillusionment which has found somewhat hazardous expression in some of the more critical works of Soviet literature. Mr. John Strachey describes some of these tendencies in his essay, *The Strangled Cry*, and goes on to observe that "Russian conditions have not become more nightmarish: they have become much better—and much more ordinary. The bastion in the process of being preserved has become, simply, another country in the process of industrialization. . . . The means have been terrible, the result commonplace."[2]

Some disenchantment with greater affluence must be anticipated, but the fact remains that it is easy to think of good uses to which additional production could be put even in the richer countries. Professor Galbraith, himself, has stressed the need for greater public expenditure and, even in the United States, the private ex-

[1] Cf. Max Weber, *The Protestant Ethic and the Spirit of Capitalism* (London: George Allen and Unwin, 1962), especially Chapter V.

[2] *The Strangled Cry* (Bodley Head, 1962), pp. 20–22.

penditure of a significant fraction of the population is still low. We must also guard against exaggerated views fostered by the spate of popular economic sociology about the distortions created by advertising and other forms of salesmanship especially in the U.S.A. No doubt the unremitting and sometimes outrageous campaigns of the advertisers may induce people to buy new cars, new refrigerators and the like, when, if left alone, they would have been quite content with their old ones. But an increase in the production of consumers' durable goods cannot be described as pointless simply because some fraction of it is designed to meet demands artificially created by "persuaders", hidden or open. Moreover, in Britain these durable goods account in total for only about one-fourteenth of consumers' outlay or for one-twentieth of gross domestic product.[1] Such facts must be kept in mind if the more rhetorical onslaughts on the follies of the affluent society are to be viewed in proper perspective.

What has still to be explained, however, is why the emphasis placed on the need for growth has been so much intensified since the end of the war. Several explanations suggest themselves. The first I shall mention may appear to be almost trivial, but it is in fact of some importance. This is the construction of international "league tables" that show the rates of expansion in different countries. To find one's country near the bottom of such a table is felt to be something of a disgrace even if the state of affluence already achieved is well in advance of that reached by its more rapidly growing neighbours. What these figures in fact reveal for the past decade or so—in so far, it must be added, as the figures can be trusted—is some narrowing of the gap between the rich countries and the international middle class. For it is an over-simplification to suppose that the gap between the "haves" and the "have-nots" is steadily widening. The rate of growth in the really underdeveloped world is admittedly slow for a variety of reasons which, if regrettable, are scarcely unexpected. But a middle group of countries has been outstripping both the rich and the poor. Thus, both Western Germany and France have

[1] The official definition of "durable goods" includes cars, motor cycles, furniture, floor coverings, radio, electrical and "other" goods. The fractions above are at factor cost and relate to 1961 (*Blue Book on National Income and Expenditure, 1962*).

achieved higher rates of growth over the past decade than have Britain or Sweden, but income a head in the former countries has only recently caught up with income a head in Britain, and may still be somewhat below income a head in Sweden. Japan has probably the highest rate of growth in the world, but her people are not yet well-off by British standards, still less by American. Italy has expanded very rapidly, but remains well behind Britain or Belgium. Output a head has grown much faster in Russia than in the United States, but is still far below the American level. While the slow progress of the really poor countries must, indeed, be deplored, it is less obvious that in the really rich countries the pace of advance must somehow be greatly accelerated. The fact remains that people in Britain have become increasingly disturbed by the country's low place on the league table, and similar concern has been expressed in the United States. Thus, the spirit of competition fostered by these league tables has in itself become a stimulus to the pursuit of growth. The economic statistician may be the most *subfusc* of agitators, but he is not for that reason the least powerful.

To turn to a more serious issue, anxiety about defence has made even so rich a country as the United States dissatisfied with her rate of growth. With Russian output rising so fast, the West may have to decide within the next decade or so whether to raise the proportion of output devoted to defence to something nearer the Russian figure, said to be between 15 and 20 per cent., especially as Russia appears to enjoy a comparative advantage in defence. For if Russia has done so much to establish her power while still a poor country, it is natural to ask what may she not do when she closes the gap in output. There is the further consideration that if technology helps growth, growth in turn helps technology, and on technology defence largely depends. It is true that in Britain the needs of defence have had less influence on public opinion than in the United States and have had virtually no effect at all on the opinions of British economists, who usually seem to regard expenditure for such a purpose as a tiresome extravagance that any sane Government should try to cut. (In this respect at least the economists' historical sympathy with "retrenchment" remains unimpaired.) In Britain, on the other hand, great stress has been laid on the country's precarious position in foreign trade. To stand still would be difficult even if it were thought to be desirable; to neglect the needs of growth might well lead to relapse.

Another reason for the increasing concern about growth has been the success achieved in dealing with the problem of unemployment, which naturally received so much attention between the wars. Admittedly the two problems are related. Unemployment and the threat of unemployment were in themselves serious hardships, but the loss of national output was also a reason for seeking appropriate remedies. With large numbers out of work, however, less attention was paid to what might be achieved by the long-term rise in productivity. Recovery from depression was then the primary objective. Since the war unemployment has not disappeared in the developed countries, but it has been relatively low. In Britain it has been very low, although some pools of regional unemployment have remained. With surplus man-power absorbed, the economy has thus been forced against the limits of scarcity, and attention has naturally shifted to the means whereby the growth of output a head might be stimulated.

A further reason why growth has come to receive more attention has been the wider recognition of the fact that the redistribution of income can at best do only a little to advance the standard of living of the bulk of the people. Admittedly this is no new fact. The low real wages of the early years of the nineteenth century reflected in the main low output a head rather than exploitation, and could not have been greatly raised even by a strongly egalitarian policy. In modern Britain further redistribution has little to offer, even if full account is taken of expenditure from expense accounts and the like. Thus, in 1962 the average male earnings of manual workers in manufacturing were already above total national consumption divided by the occupied population. Or, to take another example, if in 1962 all personal incomes from rent, interest and dividends had been somehow confiscated and handed over to the employed, without any consequential fall in output, wages and salaries would have gone up by only about 17 per cent.; in fact, average real income from employment had risen by nearly a quarter in the 1950s and will rise even faster in future if the N.E.D.C. target for growth is achieved.

Although there has been much reluctance, even among economists, to admit as much explicitly, there has been a growing realization of the fact that inequality in expenditure, while sometimes very unjust, is not of great *quantitative* importance. Elsewhere in the world the experience of post-revolutionary régimes or of those freed from imperialist rule has also had its effect on opinion. For with all the "bourgeoisie" liquidated or all the foreign "exploiters" expelled, it has become increasingly difficult to deny that higher output is the only really important cure for poverty. The panaceas have been exposed, and the new emphasis reflects a new realism. It also implies a less apocalyptic theory of social improvement, and one would wish to believe that this may bring with it greater tolerance.

This account of the reasons for the intensified interest in growth, incomplete as it is, may seem to have carried us some way beyond the normal boundaries of economic discussion. Thus, the mention of defence as a reason for desiring growth may be held to have introduced a "non-economic" consideration. If, however, we are really to draw pedantic boundaries of this kind we must be correspondingly pedantic about the use of terms. Economics is the art of making the best use of scarce resources, whether for defence or for private opulence or for any other purposes, and it is improper to describe some *ends* as "economic" and others as "non-economic." The implications of a strict use of the term "economic" are thus far-reaching. For on this strict basis economic analysis affords no more warrant for seeking greater opulence than for recommending heavier armaments or fewer armaments, or simply days of rest and idleness. How, then, can we justify the implicit assumption of much applied economics that a rising standard of living is so important an objective even in the richer countries that sacrifices in other directions should be made in order to achieve it? This is the next large question to which we shall now address ourselves.

II

If the applied economists have been incautious at times, the same cannot be said of the more specialized theorists. In formal welfare economics a significant feature has been the widening of scope that higher output permits. If a person consumes a larger amount of goods and services in year two than he could have consumed in year one, then he is said to be better off. Whereas in year one he was not in a position to consume as much as in year two, the first year's consumption is still within his reach, and he could rest content with it if he so wished. If, instead, he uses the greater abundance he can now obtain he is in a preferred position, and that is held to warrant the conclusion that he is better off. The basic choice is thus left to the individual; in formal theory the economist does not presume to take it for him. There is an implicit assumption of fact that each person is usually the best judge of his own satisfaction. Complementary assumptions are made about the desirability of freedom of choice between work and leisure and between saving and spending.

This approach has much to commend it, but it is clearly too limited to provide an adequate basis for policy. The technique is that of comparative statics: the same individuals with the same preferences are to make their choices, whereas in fact some individuals die or preferences change. It is one thing to maintain that wants should be taken as "given" in the sense that economics does not purport to assess their relative degrees of urgency, but quite a different matter to assume that wants are "given" in the sense of being constant. The change often comes from the side of supply with, in Marshall's words, "the development of new activities giving rise to new wants, rather than new wants giving rise to new activities."[1] This creation of new wants by suppliers is now sometimes described as improper and even vaguely sinister, but to Marshall the extension and refinement of wants was an admirable feature of economic progress. His reasoning thus amounts to an argument for growth, but it involves a further value judgement. There are other difficulties. The choice between work and leisure, or even between spending and saving, is not altogether free, and could not be made so without some sacrifice of the increased output by which consumers' choice is enlarged. Moreover, in any process of change there are likely to be losers as well as gainers, and economists have fought shy of interpersonal comparisons because it is so hard to devise any means of objective verification. The possibility of providing compensation for the losers and the principles by which it should be determined have been much debated. Although there may be some practical merit in the compensation principle in one or other of its guises, a fully satisfactory

[1] *Principles of Economics*, p. 89.

answer has not been forthcoming. The last complication I shall mention arises in the case of goods and services for communal use, to which the same individualistic test cannot be applied. Defence is a case in point. With communal goods it is the scales of preference of the Government rather than of consumers that are relevant, and in practice this largely means the preferences of officials. The choices made cannot be subjected to more than the most incomplete and spasmodic of democratic checks, and it follows therefore that in so far as increased communal consumption is the purpose to be served by growth, the decision as to how much should be sacrificed for this end must in part be authoritarian.

Formal welfare theory has tried to do both too much and too little. Within its prescribed field it has been over-refined, but this field has been unduly restricted. The trouble has arisen partly because some economists have been so anxious to demonstrate that even welfare economics, as distinct from strictly empirical studies, is a branch of science that has no particular link with moral philosophy. Indeed, we have reached a stage where mathematics is the only related discipline that the young economist need study at all seriously. Economists have long been afflicted with an inferiority complex *vis-à-vis* the natural scientists, and it may be worth observing to this audience that the British Association once contributed to this feeling of inferiority by attempting to divest itself of Section F on the ground that economics was scarcely a real science. With this event in mind, it is amusing to observe that the natural scientists themselves have now turned with uninhibited enthusiasm to social matters. It is true in doing so they have not always escaped the pitfalls that worried the economic purists—the hidden value judgements and the over-confident pronouncements on subjects not their own. But to admit as much is not to deny the value of these vigorous and stimulating excursions by our scientific colleagues.

The applied economists—and economists have become increasingly applied—have turned impatiently away from formal welfare analysis to what appear to be more practical and urgent matters. To this mood the study of growth makes a strong appeal. Apart from the other considerations I have already mentioned, higher output has the deceptive appearance of being objective and even physical. The choice of words is not without significance, for the reference nowadays is usually to "production" rather than "real income," notwithstanding Dr. Ian Little's sharp reminder that this distinction is meaningless.[1] There is undoubtedly much justification for this retreat to what is really a branch of applied welfare economics, but it entails certain dangers that ought now to be recognized. Dr. Little has observed that: "A serious economist hardly likes to be caught at the trivial occupation of discussing foundations."[2] The iconoclasts, of whom he himself is chief, have done a useful job, but I believe the reconstruction of welfare economics now needs to begin if we are to be saved from crude empiricism. We must decide how much can usefully be salvaged from the older theories and how the analysis can be extended to cover the gaps. If this task is to be performed in a useful way it will have to begin with the foundations. Not much will be achieved by simply erecting more elaborate structures of mathematical deduction on inadequate premises. Moreover, it must be recognized that social studies should not be unduly warped in imitation of the natural sciences. To speculate further about the ways in which the reconstruction of welfare analysis might finally be accomplished would take us beyond the limits of your patience and of my competence. I shall do no more than suggest the need for first-aid.

III

It is scarcely necessary nowadays to stress that applied welfare economics—and all statements that recommend are part of welfare economics—will involve value judgements. But it does not help much simply to carry the discussion to this point and then to stop. Nor does it help to accept explicitly the point about value judgements and then, in dealing with practical affairs, to bury these value judgements immediately like an anxious dog with a bone. A few examples will illustrate what I have in mind.

If offered a simple choice, most people in the developed countries —at all events most of those who are vocal—would probably prefer some measure of affluence to the pleasures of the simple life. Moreover, many would probably prefer continually rising consumption to stability, even at a tolerable level of affluence. It is not at

[1] *Critique of Welfare Economics* (Oxford University Press, 1950), pp. 88 *et seq.*
[2] Op. cit., p. 4.

these points that the question of choice becomes most acute, but rather in deciding *how much* should be sacrificed in other directions for the sake of *how much* more growth. Different compromises may commend themselves to different people, and there may be marked contrasts between countries which should be kept in mind in attempting to derive any lessons from international comparisons. For example, the high rate of growth in Russia has led very naturally to a discussion of the effects of more centralization in the control of economic affairs, but certain aspects of this centralization would be viewed without enthusiasm in the West. In his book, *The Political Economy of Communism*, Professor P. J. D. Wiles refers to "Stalin's emasculation of the trade unions," which he (Wiles) considers to be "a necessary condition of economic growth in any country." He goes on to say that "trade unions can have on growth nothing but a retarding influence."[1] Professor Wiles is not a man who pulls his punches! I shall not try to discuss this swinging generalization, for it will suffice to concede that British trade unions do sometimes hamper growth, for example, in printing, in shipbuilding and on the docks. The primary responsibility of the Russian trade unions is to raise production; if the British unions were to accept the same objective there would be a radical alteration in their attitudes to demarcation, apprenticeship and training, which might well have a marked effect on the rate of growth. We may accept that this would be so without going on to suggest that the trade unions should therefore be emasculated, as they would unquestionably be in a Communist Britain. Even if no third alternative could be found, it might be better to put up with slower growth than to overthrow one of the most effective forms of countervailing power confronting the State. But we would do well to be careful lest we accept too soon that an ultimate clash of value judgements has occurred. The factual assumptions need to be studied in detail, and we shall want to convince ourselves that no third alternative is in fact possible.

A similar issue is raised by wage-cost inflation, which has been one of the causes of the "stop–start" policies in Britain. In the United States, where cost-inflation has been still more clearly in evidence, growth has suffered from consequent anxiety about the effect of raising national expenditure. Let us now suppose—

[1] *The Political Economy of Communism* (Oxford: Blackwell, 1963), p. 257.

though this is not certain—that a national incomes policy would provide a solution to cost-inflation, but that this was rejected by the unions as a threat to their independence. We might then prefer to sacrifice growth rather than resort to compulsion. But we should recognize that such a sacrifice had been made, and allow for it in drawing the moral from international comparisons.

If the unions would thus be affected by the adoption of Communist policies aimed at growth, so would management, although to a lesser extent. To the more zealous managers in capitalist industry who are already much concerned with growth, the change might not, of course, seem so great. It is those who are content simply to jog along who would find themselves confronted with vigilant inspectors and threatened by severe penalties. Whether managerial efficiency would on balance be improved is, however, doubtful, for the able man might be hampered by too much centralization, while competition in a free economy weeds out the dullards in the end. Even if higher efficiency in the factory could be assumed, the inquisitions and the punishments—which imply, in the broader sense, a loss of social efficiency—might be thought too high a price.

The next proposition we shall consider is that more inequality is a price that should be paid for faster growth. The Russians have long since recognized that rapid growth is incompatible with a close approach to equality of incomes, and much emphasis has been placed on incentives. Moreover, the wide differences in gross incomes are not significantly reduced by progressive taxation. Unfortunately we have little quantitative knowledge of the effect of inequality on growth. Marshall may have been right in his contention that the degree of inequality in his day could not be justified by its effect on growth, and in the underdeveloped countries, inequality, although in some measure essential, may often be present to an excessive degree. But it is plausible to hold that any further attempt to reduce inequality in Britain by means of a steep rise in the progressive taxation of incomes would retard growth. On the contrary, growth might be stimulated by reducing the taxes that penalize marginal effort and saving and by substituting a tax on value added or on payrolls after the Continental pattern. Such a change would undoubtedly be opposed in Britain if it were feared that equality was being sacrificed even marginally.

We have already observed that formal welfare theory gets into difficulties when a change means losers as well as gainers; but there may also be objections, even if there are no losers, on the ground that inequality has not been reduced and may even be increased. To Marx, the overthrow of that somewhat mythical class, "the bourgeoisie," was at least as important as an improvement in the standard of living of that other somewhat mythical class, "the proletariat." A similar issue arises today in the discussion of relative rates of growth in the more-developed and the less-developed countries. Yet rapid growth in the more-developed countries will make them better able to help with loans and grants and—what is often more important—with increased trade. It is possible to imagine conditions in which the standard of living in the really poor countries would rise more rapidly if the gap between them and the richer countries was actually growing wider. Over the past decade output a head has grown more rapidly in Russia, Japan, Italy, Western Germany and France than it has in India, but it would be hard to show that the Indians have suffered as a consequence unless the widening of the gap is itself held to be an evil. The fact remains that progress all round is sometimes said to be insufficient in itself unless there is also some closing of this gap. This would seem to be a fairly clear example of a value judgement about which irreducible differences of opinion may be expected. I suspect, however, that these differences will be much reduced if the factual assumptions surrounding the value judgement are made explicitly and are carefully examined and debated. If economists do no more than elucidate the facts as far as may be, and thus prevent the adoption of somewhat extravagant attitudes based on non-quantitative assumptions, that in itself will be a very useful contribution.

The presentation of the facts will not, of course, help in this way unless the facts are related to all the important and relevant questions, not just to some of them. Unfortunately the facts about domestic inequality in Britain and the United States are usually presented as though the only relevant question was to consider how unjust is the distribution of income. (Justice is implicitly assumed to require equality, an inadequate assumption which we shall not, however, discuss.) Thus, the statistical divergence of the actual distribution of income from complete equality is indicated, or the percentages of income received by corresponding percentages of families is set out. The question that is rarely posed is what effect some specified measure of redistribution could have in raising the standard of living of, say, the wage-earners or those with less than so much a year. Yet this is the more relevant question if we are trying to choose between greater equality and faster growth.

It would be interesting to consider in what cases a possible conflict between growth and other objectives corresponded to a possible conflict between private and public interest. To do so adequately would require an extended investigation, but it can be said at once that no very close correspondence is to be expected. Sometimes the pursuit of private interest has been held to be socially harmful on the ground that growth was retarded; the most important instances are probably those where private interest is furthered by means of restrictive practices, whether on the part of management or labour. As far as management is concerned, however, the charge has usually been the opposite one that private interest fostered growth to the neglect of other social considerations. Much has been written, much of it admittedly by non-economists and much of it exaggerated, about the harshness of competition and the social disturbance it creates. But rapid growth is always likely to entail a price of this kind, whether the growth be publicly or privately inspired. The location of industry is a familiar example. It is not really sensible to suppose that a policy for rapid growth can be reconciled with a policy of taking industry to any small town, however unsuitable its location, that is losing some of its population or suffering from a little structural unemployment. An official policy for fast growth must recognize that in some areas output and employment will decline relatively and even absolutely, while in others they expand.

Growth requires a rapid transfer of some resources from less efficient to more efficient concerns, although this will not always, and may not even usually, imply large-scale movements between different geographical regions. A Government that is resolved to promote growth must not, therefore, be over-sensitive to the pleas of the less efficient managers or the less fortunate shareholders. It must expect a fair amount of redundancy, though not, of course, long-term unemployment, and must be ready, on the one hand, to face unpopularity and, on the other, to take practical measures to prevent hardship. Of course, it is not only private industry that will be affected: coal-mining is an outstanding example both of what can be done to raise efficiency by abandoning the inefficient units and of the opposition that is encountered, even when generous arrangements for redundancy have been made. We may note, incidentally, that the temptation to bargain may complicate the practical application of the compensation principle to a greater extent than its authors appear to have envisaged.

My next example is the manner in which the industrial structure may affect the rate of growth. Private enterprise has responded to market forces in such a way as to leave the United States with about half of her working population in the service industries. Now growth is believed to be slower in the service industries, although this may, admittedly, be partly a statistical hallucination. If the United States were to adopt Russian-style planning and place correspondingly strong emphasis on heavy industry her apparent rate of growth could be increased, although it may be doubted whether this would really be a sensible course for so affluent a nation.

It would be easy enough to find further examples of a possible conflict between growth and other social objectives. To mention only one, fast growth requires a well-educated "meritocracy." Privilege must not stand in the way. What may be less well recognized is that genuinely comprehensive schools may hamper expansion by holding back the clever child to a pace that suits the dullards. In various ways a "meritocracy" may seem unattractive, but it is favourable to growth.

IV

We have now illustrated several ways in which the needs of growth may conflict with other objectives. It is right that such conflicts should be brought into the open, but at the same time it is necessary to guard against a certain puritanical masochism that may lead to an exaggeration of the difficulties and to the posing of bitter choices that may not really be inevitable. After all, rapid growth will often help to solve many other problems as well as raising the standard of living. To take one of Professor Galbraith's own examples,[1] greater affluence has drawn much of the sting from inequality. It would be absurd to postulate an invariable conflict between growth and other social objectives as one between private and public interest.

Regional development is a case where a conflict of objectives may indeed occur, but must not simply be taken for granted. As we have seen, a policy of bringing industry to the worker, wherever he may be, would be inconsistent with a policy for rapid growth. But it should certainly be possible to foster the development of new industrial complexes at certain favourable locations within the less prosperous regions, and thus to serve both local needs and the national objective of expansion. Sometimes the evidence is too inconclusive to warrant the assumption of conflict. A case in point is the effect of demand-inflation on growth. The considerations are so conflicting in this case, and the evidence so difficult to interpret, that no clear presumption can be established either way even for a closed economy.

Moreover, it is by no means true that tighter discipline and more centralized control generally lead to faster growth. A good example of what is really an unnecessary choice of alternatives is provided by the proposal that for the sake of faster growth labour, or at all events certain types of trained labour, should be directed into particular employments. We need not worry much about this apparent conflict between freedom and growth for there is really no reason to suppose that direction by officials would usually be more efficient than free choice. Naturally advice and guidance are highly desirable, but compulsion would put far too many individuals into quite inappropriate jobs. Nor is it sensible to suppose that managers will on balance be more efficient if their activities are constantly inspected and their mistakes severely punished. The effect may rather be to discourage risk-bearing and initiative at the factory level, as is believed to have occurred in Russia.

In her book, *Economic Philosophy*, Mrs. Joan Robinson makes the challenging statement that: "The main advantage of wiping out unearned income is that it makes it easier, morally and politically, to prevent real wages from rising too fast."[2] What she means, presumably, is that if there are no private incomes from property

[1] Op. cit., Chapter XXIII.

[2] *Economic Philosophy* (London: The New Thinkers Library, Watts, 1962).

the workers will accept more submissively the austerity needed to release resources for investment. What may, in fact, be a lot more relevant is that their protests can be ignored or suppressed by a single-party Government. But it would, in any case, be unwise to assume that a flow of voluntary savings sufficient for rapid expansion is too much to hope for. Even in underdeveloped countries a shortage of savings is not always the most serious obstacle to growth, although it may, of course, be an important one. In the more developed countries of the West the propensity to save is not so low—unless forced down by penal taxation—as to make the more draconian remedies at all relevant. In Britain personal savings have quadrupled between 1953 and 1961, and this remarkable expansion has helped to establish one of the necessary conditions for growth, although it is not a sufficient one. What has been disappointing has been the low rate of return on the additional capital. It is the solution to this problem rather than greater austerity that should be sought, at least in the first instance.

In the West, although growth has its price, that price may not be so terribly high after all. Some mobility of man-power is obviously required, but a change of job, or even of home, may not be such a very terrible thing. The sacrifices of the losers can scarcely be accurately assessed from what is claimed by local politicians on their behalf! Nor need we take too seriously the stress and strain involved in growth. Admittedly, the accelerated production of cars or refrigerators or garbage-gobblers may seem to be obtained at an extravagant cost in terms of ulcers and thromboses. But the cost is exacted only from the executives, who are in any case temperamentally doomed to over-work; if denied this outlet they would find other ones, and these others might be more harmful. Keynes himself has advised us that

> "dangerous human proclivities can be canalized into comparatively harmless channels by the existence of opportunities for money-making and private wealth, which, if they cannot be satisfied in this way, may find their outlet in cruelty, the reckless pursuit of power and authority and other forms of self-aggrandizement. It is better that a man should tyrannize over his bank balance than over his fellow-citizens."[1]

[1] *General Theory of Employment, Interest and Money*, p. 374.

The truth in this statement may apply not only to the personal search for wealth but also to the more general pursuit of growth. Thus, one of the justifications for rapid growth may be that it affords a harmless and even beneficial outlet for human restlessness. In so far as this is so, the price of growth may really be negative.

Finally, let us examine the familiar proposition that Britain should reduce her oversea expenditure on both defence and aid in order to ease the pressure on the balance of payments and thus facilitate the purchase of the imports needed for growth. This suggestion is frequently made, and has even been given some improper support by the National Economic Development Council.[1] In this case the implicit value judgement would appear to be that the harm done both to the poorer nations and to our foreign policy and defence would matter less than the benefit to be derived from a more rapid expansion of output. I have a strong suspicion that when this value judgement is uncovered it would have fewer supporters than the initial proposition that expenditure on aid and defence should be cut. We may not unfairly suspect inconsistency and sheer thoughtlessness. Be this as it may, it would be rash to infer that the issue will finally turn upon personal value judgements which cannot usefully be discussed, for there are also assumptions of fact that call for critical examination. Clearly we should want to know how the underdeveloped countries would be affected by a cut in aid—a natural enough inquiry for economists. But we must also consider how defence would be affected. There is, for example, a well-informed school of thought which holds that the West should strengthen its conventional forces abroad in order to reduce its highly dangerous reliance upon tactical nuclear weapons. Of course, economists are not obliged simply to accept the validity of such arguments, but they have no right whatsoever to ignore them. Nor is it any excuse to say that growth is an "economic" objective while defence is not: to do so would be a gross misuse of the term "economic." We may now seem to be getting ourselves into deep waters, but there is a more elementary objection to the proposal that the Government's expenditure on aid and defence should be cut for the sake of faster growth. The orders of magnitude are simply wrong. Even if such expenditure

[1] *Conditions Favourable to Faster Growth* (H.M.S.O., 1963), paragraph 128.

were halved, the saving would finance the extra imports needed for a 4 per cent. rate of growth for little more than a year. Thus, there is no need, after all, for us to take our respective stands on value judgements. We can demolish this fashionable but muddle-headed proposal by referring to the statistics.

V

Let us now try to draw together some conclusions about the manner in which economists can approach the problems raised by policies for faster growth. The need for a fresh approach to the foundations of welfare economics has been emphasized above, and it is only to be expected that this will be a large undertaking. But the opening moves in dealing with these issues of policy seem clear enough.

The first point to be made may appear to be an obvious one, but it may not always be recognized. This is that most of the interesting propositions in practical welfare economics are highly complex: although they comprise value judgements, they are not simply value judgements. Consider even the proposition that more equality would be desirable. It would be quite mistaken to suppose that this is an ultimate issue where, like Luther, one must simply take one's stand. Indeed, it is most unwise to exaggerate the ultimate value judgement and thus arrive too soon as the position where further discussion is futile. For to do so increases the risk of intolerance. After all, even with regard to equality, differences of opinion may largely reflect different views about the facts and about the consequences of change, although modern anti-rationalism may be opposed to such an interpretation.

It follows, therefore, that in considering the price that may have to be paid under various headings for a faster growth of output, economists can perform an exceedingly useful function by unravelling complex and elliptical propositions and setting out as clearly as may be the issues involved. These issues may fall into the following categories:

(*a*) Technical issues about measurable factors that influence the growth of measurable output.

(*b*) Other factual issues that cannot be treated satisfactorily in quantitative terms, of which interpersonal comparisons of utility are only one example. Moreover, in a large number of critical cases, where quantitative treatment would seem to be possible in principle—such as the effect on growth of a change in progressive taxation—no exact relationship can in fact be established.

(*c*) Considerations of a kind not professionally studied by economists—e.g., strategy, public health, education, etc.

(*d*) Ultimate value judgements that may still divide two people who hold the same views about the facts and the causal relations.

One view is that economists, like good scientists, should confine themselves to (*a*). They would then be precluded in most cases from making final recommendations and would merely present alternatives. "If *X*, then *Y*. Is this what you want?" In fact, it will not be possible to go very far with the discussion of policy without bringing in (*b*), which are often highly important factual considerations if too elusive for strictly quantitative treatment. Furthermore, some of the examples we have considered show how soon and how often the discussion of policy will involve issues of the third type—that is to say issues not professionally studied by economists. The first rule to be observed here is that these issues should not be ignored or disposed of by means of hidden assumptions. (The treatment of Britain's oversea expenditure on defence is, as we have seen, a striking example of such impropriety.) The economists' recommendations must therefore at times be conditional and incomplete; at times co-operation with specialists in other disciplines may make it possible to proceed further. But it would be unwise, as Marshall warned us, to insist too much on specialization. Economists can often learn enough about a related problem to ensure that they do not talk too much nonsense or overlook too many of the complications. The possibility of more of them doing so would admittedly be greater were it not for the assumption that every economist, however unsuitable his bent of mind, must spend his time turning himself into a fourth-rate mathematician.

The value judgements—category (*d*)—remain. Admittedly the values of economists are no more important than those of other people, but it does not follow that economists should stop short at this point. Recommendations about policy are not simple value judgements: someone must synthesize the latter with interpretations of the facts and predictions as to the consequences of particular courses of action. Who is to do this if the economist draws back at the critical point and refuses to commit himself? Members of Parliament, civil servants, journalists—or Superman? Whatever arguments of principle may be advanced, however, I believe it to be merely unrealistic to suppose that economists will in fact refrain from making value judgements. What can be asked is that they should be explicit—at least in important cases, for common sense need not be sacrificed to pedantry. If the process of breaking down the complex propositions is followed this should reveal the value judgements in the more critical instances. In conclusion, however, I would reiterate what I have already suggested. I suspect that the value judgements will give rise to far less disagreement and uncertainty than is often feared, provided the factual part of the exercise has been carefully and thoroughly performed. I believe this to be true of economic policy generally, and I have little doubt that it will usually prove to be so in particular cases where we are considering whether the price of growth is excessive or should willingly be paid.

APPENDIX A

BIOGRAPHICAL NOTES

APPENDIX A

BIOGRAPHICAL NOTES

SIR HUBERT HENDERSON (1890–1952)

Fellow of Clare College and Lecturer in Economics, Cambridge 1919–23, Editor of *The Nation* 1923–34, Joint Secretary of the Economic Advisory Council, Fellow of All Souls from 1934. He worked in the Treasury during World War II and he served on the Royal Commission on Population 1944–49. He was elected to the Wardenship of All Souls in 1951 but because of ill health did not take up his office. His *Supply and Demand*, the first Cambridge Economic Handbook, was published in 1922. A Supplement of *Oxford Economic Papers* was devoted to his life and work in 1953.

SIR ALEXANDER GRAY (1882–1968).

He left the civil service to be Professor of Political Economy, University of Aberdeen in 1921, and he was Professor of Political Economy and Mercantile Law, University of Edinburgh from 1935 to 1956. His numerous publications include *The Development of Economic Doctrine*, 1931, the delightful *The Socialist Tradition*, 1946 and *Selected Poems*, 1948.

H. O. MEREDITH (1878–1964).

Described by R. F. Harrod in his *The Life of John Maynard Keynes* (Macmillan, 1951) as "A man of noble mien . . . beard, bright, flashing eye, he looked and was every inch a philosopher". He succeeded A. C. Pigou to the Girdler's Lectureship at Cambridge in 1908 and was Professor of Economics at Queen's University Belfast 1911–45. Meredith was President of Section F in 1939. His *Outlines of English Economic History* was published in 1908 and his *Four Dramas of Euripides* in 1937.

AUSTIN ROBINSON

An outstanding applied economist who played an active part in wartime planning after 1939. Professor of Economics, Cambridge University 1950–65 and Joint Editor of the *Economic Journal* since 1944. From

1959 to 1962 Professor Robinson was President of the International Economics Association.

SIR JOHN HICKS

Fellow of All Souls College and Drummond Professor of Political Economy, University of Oxford since 1952. Since *Value and Capital* appeared in 1939 he has been regarded as of the same company as Ricardo, Marshall, Walras and Keynes.

R. S. SAYERS

Sir Ernest Cassel Professor of Economics in the University of London since 1947. The Seventh Edition of his *Modern Banking* was published in 1967, it has been essential reading for all undergraduates in economics since 1938. Professor Sayers was a member of the Committee on the Working of the Monetary System (the Radcliffe Committee) 1959.

R. G. LIPSEY

A Canadian who rapidly became recognized as an outstandingly gifted economic theorist after being appointed to a lectureship at the London School of Economics in 1955. He is the Managing Editor of the *Review of Economic Studies* and he was appointed to be Professor of Economics at the University of Essex in 1964. Already Lipsey is a name almost as familiar to undergraduates as Samuelson or even Cairncross.

J. K. GALBRAITH

Paul M. Warburg Professor of Economics at Harvard. Author of *The Great Crash, 1929, The Affluent Society*, and the *New Industrial State.* He has served as the United States Ambassador to India.

C. F. CARTER

Vice-Chancellor, University of Lancaster and Joint Editor of the *Economic Journal.* He was Professor of Applied Economics, The Queen's University, Belfast, 1952–59 and Stanley Jevons Professor of Political Economy, University of Manchester 1959–63. Jointly with B. R. Williams he published *Industry and Technical Progress*, 1957, *Investment in Innovation*, 1958 and *Science in Industry*, 1959.

T. WILSON

Adam Smith Professor of Political Economy, University of Glasgow, since 1958. He edited *Oxford Economic Papers* for 10 years. A collection of Professor Wilson's essays was published in 1964 under the title *Planning and Growth.*

B. R. Williams

The first Professor of Economics at the University College of North Staffordshire. From 1959–67 he was a Professor of Economics at the University of Manchester. Before he left Manchester to be Vice-Chancellor and Principal of the University of Sydney he was a member of the National Board for Prices and Incomes, Economic Adviser to the Minister of Technology and a member of the Central Advisory Council on Science and Technology. He has been Editor of the *Sociological Review* and the *Manchester School of Economic and Social Studies*.

E. Victor Morgan

Professor of Economics at Swansea from 1945 until he was appointed to a chair of economics at the University of Manchester in 1966. Professor Morgan is a dedicated investigator of all aspects of financial institutions.

R. L. Ball

Professor of Economics at the London Graduate School of Business Studies. Professor Ball has taught at the University of Pennsylvania and Manchester and he was a Research Officer at the Institute of Statistics, University of Oxford. His *Inflation of the Theory of Money* was published in 1964.

G. L. S. Shackle

Brunner Professor of Economic Science in the University of Liverpool since 1951. His *The Years of High Theory* is the latest of a long series of significant books and articles on mathematics, philosophy and economic theory.

A. R. Prest

Author of *Public Finance in Theory and Practice* which was first published in 1960. In 1964 he left Cambridge to become Professor of Economics and Public Finance at the University of Manchester.

APPENDIX B

BIBLIOGRAPHY

Some 12 papers were presented to Section F of the British Association for the Advancement of Science each year from 1947 to 1967. In addition some of the evening discourses at the Annual Meeting were devoted to economic topics. Only selected papers which have been printed in full are included. The first paper listed each year is the Presidential Address to the Section. Bibliographies covering the periods 1860–1913 are included in Volume I, *Essays in Economic Method* and Volume II, *Essays in the Economics of Socialism and Capitalism*.

Abbreviations used: *A.S., The Advancement of Science*; *E.J., Economic Journal.*

* Indicates that the paper is included in this volume.

1947 D. H. ROBERTSON "The Economic Outlook" *A.S.* Vol. 4, Sept. 1947. *E.J.*, Vol. 57, Dec. 1947. *Utility and all that and other Essays*, George Allen & Unwin, Ltd., 1952

J. K. EASTHAM "Compensation Terms for Nationalized Industry" *Manchester School* Vol. 16, Jan. 1948

R. F. HENDERSON "The Significance of the New Issue Market for the Finance of Industry" *E.J.*, Vol. 58, March 1948.

1948 *SIR H. D. HENDERSON "The Price System" *A.S.* Vol. 5, Oct. 1948, *E.J.* Vol. 58, Dec. 1948. *The Inter-war years and other Papers; a Selection from the Writing of Hubert Douglas Henderson*, H. CLAY (Ed.) Oxford, 1955

IAN BOWEN "Building Materials Supply" *Yorkshire Bulletin of Economic and Social Research*, Vol. 1, Dec. 1948.

S. R. DENNISON "Industrial Productivity" *Lloyds Bank Review*, Jan. 1949

R. C. TRESS *The Diagrammatic Representation of National Income Flows, Economica* Vol. 15, Nov. 1948.

JOSEPH SYKES "Distribution of Industry Act and the Development Areas" *Manchester School of Economics and Social Studies*, Vol. 17, Jan. and May 1949.

A. J. BROWN "Inflation and the flight from cash" *Yorkshire Bulletin of Economic and Social Research*, Vol. 1, Sept. 1949.

A. M. Henderson "Prices and Profits in State Enterprise" *Review of Economic Studies*, Vol. 16, 1948–49

D. C. Hague "Economic Theory and Business Behaviour" *Review of Economic Studies*, Vol. 16, 1949–50

1949 *Sir Alexander Gray "Economics: Yesterday and Tomorrow" *A.S.*, Vol. 6, Oct. 1949, *E.J.*, Vol. 59, Dec. 1949

George Clayton "The Role of the British Life Assurance Companies in the Capital Market" *E.J.* Vol. 61, March 1951

Arthur Beacham "The Present Position of the Coal Industry in Great Britain" *E.J.*, Vol. 60, March 1950

1950 G. C. Allen "Economic Progress, Retrospect and Prospect" *A.S.* Vol. 7, Sept. 1950, *E.J.*, Vol. 60, Sept. 1950

Sheila Marriner "The Economic Functions of the Export Merchant" *Manchester School of Economic and Social Studies*, Vol. 20, Sept. 1952

1951 R. G. Hawtrey "The Nature of Profit" *A.S.*, Vol. 8, Sept. 1951, *E.J.*, Vol. 61, Sept. 1951

1952 D. T. Jack "Full Employment in Retrospect" *A.S.*, Vol. 9, Sept. 1952, *E.J.*, Vol. 62, Dec. 1952

*H. O. Meredith "Fifty Years of Economics" *A.S.*, Vol. 10, June 1953

G. L. S. Shackle "Economics and Sincerity" *Oxford Economic Papers*, Vol. 5, March 1953

James Lanner "The rediscovery of Bank Rate and the London Money Market" *Weltwirtschaftliches Archiv*, Vol. 71, 1953

1953 F. W. Paish "Open and Repressed Inflation" *A.S.*, Vol. 10, Sept. 1953, *E.J.* Vol. 63, Sept. 1953. *Studies in an Inflationary Economy, the United Kingdom 1948–61*, Macmillan & Co. Ltd., 1962.

Symposium on Uncertainty and Business Decisions

W. B. Gallie "Uncertainty as a Philosophical Problem: 1"

D. J. O'connor "Uncertainty as a Philosophical Problem: 2"

I. J. Good "Mathematical Tools"

G. R. Meredith "Methodological Considerations in the Study of Human Anticipation"

C. F. Carter "A Revised Theory of Expectations"

B. R. Williams "The Impact of Uncertainty on Economic Theory with Special Reference to the Theory of Profits"

A. D. Roy "The Empirical Testing of Alternative Theories of Uncertainty"

C. F. Carter, G. P. Meredith and G. L. S. Shackle (Editors) *Uncertainty and Business Decisions*, Liverpool University Press 1954, Second Edition, 1957

G. Clayton "The Provincial Stock Exchanges" *A.S.*. Vol. 11, June 1954

H. R. Parker "The Financial Aspects of Town and Country Planning Legislation" *E.J.*, Vol. 64, March 1954

S. B. Saul "Britain and World Trade" 1870–1914" *Economic History Review*, Series 2, Vol. 7, 1954

1954 *E. A. G. Robinson "The Changing Structure of the British Economy, *A.S.,* Vol. 11, Sept. 1954. *E.J.*, Vol. 64, Sept. 1954

Roy Harrod "Convertibility Problems" *Economia Internatzionale*, Vol. 8, 1955

C. F. Carter "The Work of the Science and Industry Committee, *A.S.*, Vol. 11, March 1955

P. Wiles "Growth Versus Choice" *E.J.*, Vol. 66, June 1956

1955 *J. R. Hicks "The Economic Foundation of Wage Policy" *A.S.*, Vol. 12, Sept. 1955, *E.J.*, Vol. 65, Sept. 1955. *Essays in World Economics*, Oxford, 1959

K. S. Lomax "Production and Productivity Movements in the United Kingdom since 1900". *Journal of the Royal Statistical Society*, Vol. 122, part 2, 1959

K. J. W. Alexander "Wages in Coal Mining since Nationalization, *Oxford Economic Papers*, Vol. 8, June 1956

F. R. Eels "The Economics of Shift Working" *Journal of Industrial Economics*, Vol. 5, Nov. 1956

I. F. Gibson "A Revision of the Jute Wages-Structure" *Scottish Journal of Political Economy*, Vol. 4, Feb. 1957

F. A. Cockfield "The Report of the Royal Commission on the Taxation of Profits and Income, *National Provincial Bank Quarterly Review*, Nov. 1955

1956 Gilbert Walker "Prices—and Competition—In Transport as an Instrument of Policy" *A.S.*, Vol. 13, Sept. 1956, *E.J.*, Vol. 66, Sept. 1956

B. R. Williams "Science and Industrial Innovation" *A.S.*, Vol. 13, Dec. 1956

Ian Bowen "Population and the Social Sciences" *A.S.*, Vol. 13, March 1957

H. D. Dickinson "The Economic Effects of Automation" *A.S.*, Vol. 13, June 1957

A. Hunter "The Control of Monopoly in Britain" *Lloyds Bank Review*, Oct. 1956

E. T. Sara "Progress in the United Kingdom Iron and Steel Industry" *Yorkshire Bulletin of Economic and Social Research*, Vol. 9, May 1957

1957 J. E. Meade "The Balance-of-Payments Problem of a European

Free-Trade Area" *A.S.*, Vol. 14, Sept. 1957, *E.J.*, Vol. 67, Sept. 1957

H. H. LIESNER "The European Common Market and British Industry" *A.S.*, Vol. 14, Dec. 1957, *E.J.*, Vol. 68, June 1958

A. D. KNOX "The Underdeveloped Countries: Some Aspects of their Problems" *A.S.*, Vol. 14, March 1958

URSULA K. HICKS "Obstacles to Development in South Asia, India, Pakistan and Ceylon" *Westminster Bank Review*, Nov. 1957

I. M. D. LITTLE "The Economist in Whitehall" *Lloyds Bank Review*, April 1957

1958 A. J. BROWN "Inflation and the British Economy" *A.S.*, Vol. 15, Sept. 1958. *E.J.*, Vol. 68, Sept. 1958

R. M. LODGE "Choice and Valuation in Industrial Research" *A.S.*, Vol. 15, Dec. 1958

JACK WISEMAN "The Economics of Education in Britain" *Scottish Journal of Political Economy*, Vol. 6, Feb. 1959. *Readings in the Economics of Education*, UNESCO, 1968

J. MAITLAND "Operational Research in Advertising" *A.S.*, Vol. 15, June 1959

RONALD BRECH "Economics in Business" *A.S.*, Vol. 15, June, 1959

1959 JOHN JEWKES "How Much Science?" *A.S.*, Vol. 16, Sept. 1959 *E.J.*, Vol. 70, March, 1960

ANDRÉ GABOR "The Economics of the Welfare State in Britain" *A.S.*, Vol. 16, Dec. 1959

R. W. DRINKWATER "Seebohm Rowntree's contribution to the Study of Poverty" *A.S.*, Vol. 16, Dec. 1959, *Yorkshire Bulletin of Economic and Social Research*, Vol. 11, Dec. 1959

WILLIAM WALLACE "A Tribute to the Life and Work of Seebohm Rowntree" *Yorkshire Bulletin of Economic and Social Research*, Vol. 11, Dec. 1959

B. R. WILLIAMS "Some Conditions of Useful Competition" *Yorkshire Bulletin of Economic and Social Research*, Vol. 11, Dec. 1959, *Technology, Investment and Growth*, Chapman and Hall, 1967

A. BEACHAM "The Restrictive Trade Practices Act" 1956, *Yorkshire Bulletin of Economic and Social Research*, Vol. 11, Dec. 1959

R. L. SICH "Progress Under the Restrictive Trade Practices Act" 1956, *Yorkshire Bulletin of Economic and Social Research*, Vol. 11, Dec. 1959

S. R. DENNISON "The Restrictive Trade Practices Court in

Action" *Yorkshire Bulletin of Economic and Social Research*, Vol. 11, Dec. 1959

G. MILLS "Public Expenditure on the Arts in Great Britain" *Yorkshire Bulletin of Economic and Social Research*, Vol. 11, Dec. 1959

SIR REGINALD WILSON "The Road and Rail Question" *A.S.*, Vol. 17, May 1960

1960 *R. S. SAYERS "Monetary Thought and Monetary Policy in England" *A.S.*, Vol. 17, Nov. 1960, *E.J.*, Vol. 70, Dec. 1960

A. HAZLEWOOD and P. VANDOME "Building a Model of the British Economy" *The Bankers' Magazine*, Oct. 1960

A. MAIZELS "The Effects of Industrialization on Exports of Primary Producing Countries, *Kyklos*, Vol. 14, 1961

BRINLEY THOMAS "International Factor Movements and Unequal Rates of Growth" *Manchester School of Economics and Social Studies*, Vol. 29, Jan. 1961

T. P. HILL "Wages in Coal Mining" *Bulletin of the Oxford University Institute of Statistics*, Vol. 23, 1961

L. A. DICKS-MIREAUX "The Interrelationship between Cost and Price Changes" 1946–59: A Study of Inflation in Post-War Britain" *Oxford Economic Papers*, Vol. 13, Oct. 1961

W. A. LEWIS "Economic Conditions for Greater Output" ch. 3 *Hunger: Can it be averted?* SIR E. JOHN RUSSELL and NORMAN C. WRIGHT (Eds.) British Association for the Advancement of Science, 1961

1961 C. F. CARTER "The Economic Use of Brains" *A.S.*, Vol. 18, Sept. 1961, *E.J.*, Vol. 72, March 1962

M. ZVEGINTZOV "The Unprogressive in Industry and some Remedies" *A.S.*, Vol. 18, March 1962

D. J. ROBERTSON "Economic Aspects of the Standard of Living" *A.S*, Vol. 18, March 1962

*R. G. LIPSEY "Can there be a Valid Theory of Wages?" (Lister Lecture) *A.S.*, Vol. 19, July 1962

W. G. MCCLELLAND "Economics of the Supermarket" *E.J.*, Vol. 72, March 1962. *Studies in Retailing*, Blackwell 1963

1962 W. B. REDDAWAY "Economics of Under-developed Countries" *A.S.*, Vol. 19, Nov. 1962, *E.J.*, Vol. 73, March 1963

ALLAN ORMEROD "The Prospects of the British Cotton Industry" *Yorkshire Bulletin of Economic and Social Research*, Vol. 15, May 1963

Symposium on W. S. JEVONS:

R. D. COLLISON BLACK, "W. S. Jevons and the Economists of His time"

W. MAYS "Jevon's Conception of Scientific Method"
ROSAMOND KÖNEKAMP "William Stanley Jevons, (1835–82) some Biographical Notes" *Manchester School of Economics and Social Studies*, Vol. 33, Sept. 1962
*J. K. GALBRAITH "The Language of Economics" (Granada Lecture), *A.S.*, Vol. 20, May 1963
J. BONNER "Planning and Wages Policy" *A.S.*, Vol. 20 May 1963
LAURENCE P. SCOTT "Can Competition Survive in the Newspaper Industry?" *A.S.*, Vol. 20, July 1963
1963 *T. WILSON "The Price of Growth" *A.S.*, Vol. 20, Sept. 1963 *E.J.*, Vol. 73, Dec. 1963, *Planning and Growth*, Macmillan & *Co.*, 1964
SIR JOHN BENN "Financing Technical Development" *A.S.*, Vol. 21, May 1964, *The Banker*, Oct. 1963
SHU-CHIN YANG "Foreign Trade Problems in Economic Development" *A.S.*, Vol. 21, May 1964, *Scottish Journal of Political Economy*, Vol. 11, June 1964
*C. F. CARTER "Problems of Economic Growth" (Evening Discourse) *A.S.*, Vol. 20, Nov. 1963
1964 *B. R. WILLIAMS "Economics in Unwonted Places" *A.S.*, Vol. 21 Jan. 1965, *E.J.*, Vol. 75, March 1965, *Technology, Investment and Growth*, Chapman and Hall, 1967
C. F. CARTER "Economics of Higher Education" *A.S.*, Vol. 22, May 1965
F. W. BACON "The Economic and Financial Impact of State and Private Pension Provision" *A.S.*, Vol. 22, June 1965
G. CLAYTON and W. T. OSBORN "The Economic Significance of Life Assurance" *A.S.*, Vol 22, June 1965
A. W. KNIGHT "Economics and Business Life" *A.S.*, Vol. 22, May 1965
1965 *E. VICTOR MORGAN "Is Inflation Inevitable?" *A.S.*, Vol. 22 Nov. 1965, *E.J.*, Vol. 76, March 1966
ELWYN O. JONES and J. MORRELL "Forecasting and Business Policy" *A.S.*, Vol. 22, March 1966
K. J. WIGLEY "The Cambridge Growth Project and the Fuel and Power Industries" *A.S.*, Vol. 23, June 1966
1966 *G. L. S. SHACKLE "Policy, Poetry and Success" *A.S.*, Vol. 23, Sept. 1966, *E.J.*, Vol. 76, Dec. 1966, *On the Nature of Business Success*, G. L. S. SHACKLE (Ed.) Liverpool University Press, 1968
*R. J. BALL "Economic Model Building for Control" *A.S.*, Vol. 23, April 1967, *On the Nature of Business Success*, G.L.S. SHACKLE (Ed.) Liverpool University Press, 1968

On the Nature of Business Success also contains the following 8 papers:

W. F. Cartwright	"Business Success as seen in the Boardroom"
G. H. Peters	"Farming as a Successful Business"
J. R. Perrin	"Business Success as Measured by an Accountant"
H. E. Wincott	"The Stock Exchange's Measurements of Business Success"
A. M. Bourn	"Dynamic Accounting and Business Success"
M. A. Aczel	"Mathematical Planning and Business Success"
R. J. Lawrence	"Market Forces and Business Success"
D. H. Allen	"Credibility Forecasts and their Application to Research and Development Projects"

A. H. COTTRELL "Science and Economic Growth in the United Kingdom" (Evening Discourse) *A.S.*, Vol. 23, Nov. 1966

1967 *A. R. PREST "Sense and Nonsense in Budgetary Policy" *A.S.*, Vol. 24 Dec. 1967, *E.J.* Vol. 78, March 1968, *Public Sector Economics*, A. R. PREST (Ed.) Manchester University Press, 1968

R. L. MEEK "Public Authority Pricing" *A.S.*, Vol. 24, March 1968, *Public Sector Economics*, A. R. PREST (Ed.) Manchester University Press, 1968

Public Sector Economics also contains the following papers:

F. A. Cockfield	"Central Government Taxation"
A. T. Peacock and J. Wiseman	"Measuring the Efficiency of Government Expenditure"
Sir Harry Page	"Local Authority Capital Finance—Practices and Problems"
M. H. Peston	"Reflections on Public Authority Investment"
M. P. Fogarty	"Incomes Policy—Fishing with a line or a net?"
A. D. Bain	"Monetary Policy"
J. R. Sargent	"Regional Economic Planning"

INDEX

INDEX